THE
SHAPE
OF
LOVE

ALSO BY GELSEY KIRKLAND
AND GREG LAWRENCE

Dancing on My Grave

DOUBLEDAY

New York   London   Toronto   Sydney   Auckland

THE

SHAPE

OF

LOVE

Gelsey Kirkland

and

Greg Lawrence

PUBLISHED BY DOUBLEDAY
a division of Bantam Doubleday Dell Publishing Group, Inc.
666 Fifth Avenue, New York, New York 10103

DOUBLEDAY *and the portrayal of an anchor*
with a dolphin are trademarks of Doubleday,
a division of Bantam Doubleday Dell
Publishing Group, Inc.

BOOK DESIGN BY CLAIRE M. NAYLON

Library of Congress Cataloging-in-Publication Data

Kirkland, Gelsey.
The shape of love / Gelsey Kirkland and Greg Lawrence. — 1st ed.
p. cm.
1. Kirkland, Gelsey. 2. Ballet dancers—United States—Biography.
I. Lawrence, Greg. II. Title.
GV1785.K49A3 1990
792.8'092—dc20
[B]   *89-28476*
                                                                      CIP

ISBN 0-385-24918-7

September 1990

First Edition

Acknowledgments

Without the support and encouragement of many generous friends, this book most certainly would not have been written. My husband and I wish to thank, first of all, Steve Rubin and his good offices at Doubleday. We owe a special debt of gratitude to our judicious editors, Jacqueline Onassis and Shaye Areheart, and to our lawyer, Lisa Filloramo. And for all of their help along the way, we are grateful to my mother, Nancy Salisbury, and to my sister-in-law, Paula Stricklin.

Our heartfelt thanks to the Royal Ballet, to the English National Ballet, and to the following individuals: Dame Margot Fonteyn, Anthony Dowell, Iris Law, Peter Schaufuss, Colin Sharp, Natalia Makarova, Dina Makarova, Ivan Nagy, Jane Hermann, David Howard, Merle Hubbard, Brooke Cadwallader, Peter Stelzer, Barry Laine, Stephen Greco, Julian Hall, Patrik

Moreton, Angela Vullo, Patrick McCormick, Peter and Judith Wyer, Judith Cruickshank and John Percival, Haila Stoddard, Christopher Kirkland, Trinidad Sevillano, Pilar Garcia Sussman, Patricia Bromley and Charles Grant, Stephanie Saland, Dreas Reyneke, Deane Rink, Carl Michel, Barna Ostertag, Demetri Papoutsis, Leslie Spatt, Donna Perlmutter, Bonnie Egan, David Fallon, Alex Gotfryd, Bruce Tracy, Deborah Artman, and Marysarah Quinn.

Precious inspiration was also provided by my two nieces, Chloe and Delta, and by my nephew, Tyler—who came into the world at just the right time.

In Memory of
Antony Tudor and Frederick Ashton

Introduction
by John Percival

As with all really great dancers, you need no special knowledge to realize, when watching Gelsey Kirkland perform, that something special is happening. Her performance appeals equally to the most devoted balletomane and to the uninformed spectator. To appreciate her range, it is necessary to see her in several roles, but the quality of her dancing is apparent at first sight. I have never seen her give a performance that was not beautifully danced, with a deep concern for the point and purpose of the choreography, and with a fresh individuality that enhanced the proper style. Every step looks right, looks natural, looks, for all the anxious care that went into her preparation, as if she just made it up.

Among the factors that give her dancing its unique flavor is her desire to find meaning in everything she dances. That is understandable, even if few dancers are prepared to put in the amount of effort she does. Indeed, some might argue that it is unnecessary, even undesirable. Learn the steps, get them right, listen to the music, and do what the choreographer wants. For many dancers, that is enough. Others stand out because they clearly think about their roles, try to find something new and personal in them. Kirkland's quest is slightly different: she is looking for the truth.

Much of this book is taken up with her own account of her methods and how she applied them to the roles she danced with the Royal Ballet in London during 1986. But she did not, could not see herself dance those ballets. So I must try to give you some idea (if you were not among the happy few able to be present) what her performances were like.

She had danced Juliet in this production before, in 1980, which makes it all the more remarkable that she wanted to start over, analyzing the character, the drama, and her response to them again from scratch. Those earlier performances had already been immensely rewarding and memorable. With her tiny physique, her big eyes, her capacity for amazingly quick, light movement, it was not surprising that she proved utterly convincing as the child Juliet who starts the ballet with her nurse. But she grew up very quickly on meeting Romeo and falling in love, and looking back at what I wrote at the time, I see that it was more tragic images that stayed most vividly in my mind.

There was the moment when she sat alone on the end of the bed, trying desperately to gather up her courage to seek help: she reminded me then of a twisted, tormented figure in a painting by Francis Bacon. And almost at the end, when she found Romeo's corpse, another painting came to mind: *The Shriek*, by Munch. Or, to take a different kind of image, there was the sequence when she was alone with the potion supplied by Friar Laurence. At first her movements were stealthy; then she became fascinated by the bottle like an animal at the mercy of a predator. Eventually, after bringing herself to swallow the contents, she looked as wretched as if she were physically ill. All of this was extraordinary in its insight and intensity, utterly convincing, and terrifying too.

When she came back to the role six years later, she again took every sequence apart, weighed it carefully, and put the pieces together once more with meticulous judgment. Sometimes you could point to a detail she had modified, a particular gesture she had introduced to clarify an incident or reveal a thought. But more often it was a question of emphasis in a sequence; for instance, making clear (in a way I had never seen so vivid before) that when compelled to dance with Paris in the last act, she was not so much straining away from him as reaching toward the window where she last saw Romeo.

Her performance had not only become richer and deeper, but had developed a stillness, an inwardness. Of course the speed was still there in her dances, and in that overwhelming moment when she picks up her cloak and simply runs across the stage toward Friar Laurence's cell. But she conveyed just as much emotion in the quieter moments; she has the ability, for example, to let you see the intensity of her yearning for Romeo without even reaching toward him. With a partner as sympathetic as Anthony Dowell, just their looking at each other could devour the distance between them.

In this Juliet, every detail became part of a living, moving whole. Never could there be any doubt that this was a real person, intense, passionate, and suffering, whom we saw fall in love, grow up, and die within three hours onstage and a few days of theatrical time.

The Sleeping Beauty also is about a girl growing up, but in this ballet the outcome is not tragic, rather a joyous resolution of all problems, and the way the drama is shown on stage is much more formal, stylized and reserved. It would be wrong to say this was not part of Kirkland's American heritage; in fact she had already danced the role of Princess Aurora with American Ballet Theatre. But the Royal Ballet has always concentrated far more on the historic repertoire, and she was dancing on a stage populated by memories of many dancers who had specialized in this and other nineteenth-century classic ballets. So one of the joys of her performance was that she found her own understanding of the ballet, and danced it in a way that was closer to the old Royal Ballet style in its balance and expansiveness, closer to the style of such remembered ballerinas as Margot Fonteyn,

Violetta Elvin, Svetlana Beriosova, than their own successors in the Royal Ballet of today achieve. Kirkland has absorbed a tradition, and made it entirely her own.

I wish I could show you the way she seemed positively to skip with joy at her first entrance to her birthday celebration, or how she brought a hushed enchantment to the moment when Aurora turns gently, raptly, among her four suitors. Somehow she caught up the other dancers onstage into the quiet magic of it. In her main solo of that scene, the way she carried and moved her arms became a metaphor for a young girl's shy excitement at being the center of all attention. Her next entry, as Tchaikovsky's music began to rush to a climax, was a light delirium of joy, destroyed by pain when she pricked her finger on the spindle, but turning again to an almost hysterical relief when she thought herself recovered—but only momentarily before the spell worked her collapse into a hundred-year sleep.

The scene when the Prince sees a vision of her, and falls in love, was marked on her part by such soft movement that the audience was drawn into extra alertness, as when an actor compels attention by whispering onstage. The adagio during which the Prince is drawn under her spell was done so delicately that the fabric of the dance seemed almost transparent; into this hushed atmosphere Kirkland's solo generated a warmth that became incandescent.

On the awakening, her gratitude to her rescuer came as a great rush of feeling; and afterward, the big set pieces of the wedding duet and solo, beautifully phrased, built gradually and inevitably to their climaxes. Right through the coda, she maintained a sweet, fresh delicacy, even where the briskness of the dancing can often cause a lapse. In the finale, her raised arm became a gesture of blessing and thanks, and her arabesque gathered into its long, slow sweep all the dynastic grandeur implied by Petipa's choreography and Tchaikovsky's music, and the promise of happiness-forever-after which the story demands.

What a pleasure it was to see so many young dancers, onstage and in the auditorium, with eyes out on stalks to take in every moment. One can hope Kirkland's example will now inspire others as Fonteyn's once did her.

John Percival is dance critic of *The Times* (London) and editor of *Dance and Dancers* magazine. His books include biographical and critical studies of John Cranko, Rudolf Nureyev, and Antony Tudor, and assessments of modern ballet, experimental dance, and the world of Diaghilev.

*I dare to hope for and prophesy a revival
of the more dramatic form of ballet . . .*

Ninette de Valois, 1926

1.

TRIAL
BY
FIRE
AND
FONTEYN

When I left for London early in 1986 to perform with the Royal Ballet, my husband and I were finishing my autobiography, *Dancing on My Grave*, which was due to be published in the coming fall. While I did expect my story to cause some controversy, my immediate concern was returning to the stage. I was coming back to a world that had once driven me to the brink of madness, and I was hoping to learn something more than whether or not I was still able to dance.

Having recovered from three years of drug addiction and gained a wealth of insights, I had decided to put myself and my art to the test. My husband encouraged me. Greg was the one who had persuaded me to stop dancing in the first place. By a simple act of love, the web that bound me to the stage had been rewoven between us. He had as much faith in me as I now had in myself; however, he also knew my fears and had heard enough about the ballet world to know the risks involved in my dancing again.

It had been almost two years since my last performance—a lifetime for any ballerina to have been away from the physical discipline. I was out of shape. I would have to face the mirror as well as the audience, knowing the inevitable strain on my body might turn out to be unbearable. The prospect of pain raised the harrowing possibility of defeat. To fail at this point would be to admit, once and for all, I was unable to overcome my past.

The pressures, the personalities, fame, the fashionable aesthetic, the flaws in my character, fate—each had played a part in my undoing. But at the age of thirty-three, I knew I was no longer the same person. Nor was I alone. After examining my life from womb to early grave and back, my story already seemed like old news to me—except for the part I was still living. If I were about to make another descent into hell, I had the advantage of a marriage made in heaven.

I carried that reassuring thought with me as we set out on our journey, boarding a night flight out of Kennedy Airport. It was February. We had given up the house we called home in the snow country of Vermont, and stored our belongings in the hayloft of a friend's barn, not knowing if we would ever return, prepared to abandon everything for a new start in London. We had come to believe this was the city of light and hope, the sanctuary for our dreams. However romantic our expectations may have been, our course was equally practical—I needed a theater in which I would be welcome and free to work in my own way.

I took a window seat and looked out for a moment over the wing, where mysterious clouds of smoke were rising, blown into ghostly shapes and driven by the wind. They seemed no more real than memories of my former lovers, phantoms conjured by the heart, yet too elusive for nostalgia. I let my head fall back against Greg's shoulder and heard him say, "Just close your eyes and make believe we're about to defect." It was a defection, though not the kind that would ever make the newspapers.

As I fastened my seat belt, elation and dread were gathering in the pit of my stomach. The decision to leave America had taken several months of soul searching and more sleepless nights than either of us could remember. Exhaustion had given rise to a giddy, conspiratorial air between us—the shared sense of humor that comes to those with burning eyelids and frayed nerves. My reactions were delayed. Turning again to the window, I saw only lights blinking in the distance, and slowly pulled down the plastic shade. I said, "I'm having some doubts. I mean . . . about defecting."

To the nearby passengers, we must have sounded like fugitives from some local asylum. When the pilot announced the flight would be delayed on the ground, Greg continued the melodrama, whispering that our escape plan had been discovered. He was cramped in the seat next to me, his legs folded up so that his kneecaps were almost level with his nose. Bundled in a dozen sweaters and wearing a wool cap pulled down over his ears, he looked like a huge balloon about to burst or float away. His face was full of mischief, but there were tears in his eyes as he pulled me into his arms, promising to protect me until the end.

When we finally took off, I was almost asleep, though still vaguely aware of our progress. Disquieted by the motion of the plane, I curled over and put my head on Greg's lap. I was awake enough to hear the pilot make one of those announcements meant to keep passengers like me in a state of cardiac terror, "Ladies and gentlemen, the weatherman says it's a grand night for a crossing; however, we may encounter some mild turbulence up ahead . . . so I'm going to ask you to stay in your seats for now . . . with seat belts fastened . . . until you see the lights go out." I experienced my own mild turbulence, drifting in and out of troubled dreams, unable to come to rest. I felt my heart racing each time I lifted my head, wondering how many hours had passed.

There was one dream I remembered and later wrote in my journal. I was onstage at the Met for a dress rehearsal of *Swan Lake.* The director was yelling corrections at me over a loudspeaker, talking too fast for me to understand anything he was saying. When I bent down to tie the ribbons on my toe shoes, I suddenly realized I had forgotten my costume, and started to panic. One of the swans in the corps offered to lend me her tutu, but the director shouted at me to get off the stage. When I tried to go into the wings, the scenery moved in front of me, blocking my way.

I found myself wading across the lake. In my dream, this was a real lake, with real swans. Their white feathers floated on the surface of the water, like giant flakes of snow shimmering in the glare of stage lights. I heard the orchestra tuning behind me, far away, as if I had already walked a great distance. I was desperate because my shoes and tights were wet, and that meant I would have to change. When I tried to move, my legs were held by the current. I felt the water rushing between my thighs and lost my balance.

Pulling up my arms to catch myself, I was startled to see that my hands were covered with wet feathers. Then I felt a touch on my shoulder and spun around. I saw a man I knew was Nijinsky. A platform appeared in front of us, and he mounted it with a single leap. He was dressed all in gray, cradling a swan under one of his arms. I heard a voice say, "Watch him, Gelsey! Watch him!" He was executing a slow pirouette when his hand suddenly shot out with a knife.

I knew what he was going to do before I saw the blade flashing over his head. I tried to turn away, but someone was holding the back of my neck, forcing me to look. My back arched so violently it felt like it snapped. I screamed at whoever was holding me, "I won't watch! You can't make me watch!" At that moment I jerked my head up from Greg's lap, stifling a cry in my throat. I could still see the swan and the blade of the knife dancing in the air—the image fading away without a climax as I realized it was only a dream.

I came to my senses, trembling in a cold draft. The dream left me dumbfounded. What was I trying to tell myself? I had to make an effort to recall the details and relate them to Greg, whose reaction took me by surprise. "So, by waking up when you did, you saved the life of that swan. Isn't that right?" He was trying, as always, to find the humor in my nightmare. It was his nature to search for irony, to turn every cloud inside out in the hope of revealing a lining of unexpected color, not silver or gray, but some unimagined hue.

Shifting my legs beneath a blanket, still shivering, I said I felt like my unconscious had just sent me a message I missed. "Well, who do you think was forcing you to watch?" Greg asked, reaching for something more to say. But that was where the conversation died, because I had no idea who that demon had been. At least, I told myself, I was not going to be dancing *Swan Lake*.

A little boy popped up over the seat in front of me, his head appearing and disappearing as if he were playing a flirtatious game of hide and seek. A smile was enough to win him over, and for a short while, this adorable stranger became my reason for dancing. How did it happen that such enthusiasm was lost to us by the time we became adults? To create such a picture on the stage would mean reaching inside for something irretrievable. This boy had more energy and raw talent than I would ever have again, and more freckles than I had ever seen. I supposed his freckles would outlast his talent, but hoped I was wrong.

Greg, who had dozed through most of this encounter, opened one eye long enough to read my mind and make a quick appraisal. "If you wait about twenty years, maybe you'll have a partner." To push me around in my wheelchair, I was about to say, but my husband was already winging his way back to sleep.

The child's attention eventually turned to the movie screen at the front of the cabin. Hollywood always had been difficult for me to compete with. I went back to counting the minutes and missed the movie. Somewhere along the line I found myself staring at Greg's hands, which were folded and resting on his knee. His long fingers were ringless—neither of us ever felt the need to exchange rings. I took one of his hands into mine as if to read his palm, but I saw only the change in my own fortune and wondered, not for the first time, if there were a child in our uncertain future.

My thoughts turned to the work ahead, and I asked myself if I still had it in me. I came up with the same answer I had given Anthony Dowell, one of my former partners who was now the newly appointed director of the Royal Ballet. I remembered the telephone call from London and his soft voice on the other end of the line, exclaiming, "I knew you'd do it, Gelsey! I knew you'd come back!"

That was months ago, when I was still casting about to see if I had any options. I had contacted the directors of several American and European companies, but Anthony was the only one whose attitude put me at ease. All he wanted to know was when I might come and what ballets I wanted to dance. No explanation was necessary. No accounting for lost time. No audition. I told him I wanted to do dramatic roles. We settled on *Romeo and Juliet, Giselle,* and *The Dream.*

Those choices were not made lightly. I realized how fortunate I was to be in a position to choose and opted only for ballets that promised to challenge me as an actress. Even though I had danced the roles of Juliet and Giselle in the past, I wanted a chance to measure myself against them again, to alter my portrayals in light of the present. My thinking had changed in so many ways, and yet I was still drawn to the same source of inspiration. Each of the three ballets had something to say about love. I was counting on that old theme to see me through each variation, each phrase, each moment.

As far as the company itself, I would be going in somewhat blind. I had performed with the Royal Ballet as recently as 1980 and seen the company intermittently over the years, but except for Anthony Dowell, who would be partnering me, I was really unfamiliar with many of the dancers. It had been a full six years since I had seen Anthony. He told me over the phone the company was in a period of rebuilding. The critics were asking difficult questions about the theatre and its future direction, sharpening their knives by reminding everyone of past glories.

Anthony had grown up in the midst of those glories and become a celebrated artist in his own right. Not only was he a great dancer, he possessed the intelligence and drive that might one day make him a great director. Surely he was the perfect choice for the position at a time when the Royal Ballet would be moving into a new era and struggling to maintain its tradition. He was a child of the theatre and Royal Ballet School. His experiences might light the torch for the next generation of dancers, if he were lucky enough to put across his vision.

Both vision and luck were needed in this world as far as I could tell. The oldest tradition of dance as a form of drama was being cast aside, more and more, in favor of a modern trend that had little to do with the art as I knew it. That was why in the end I had chosen to leave America, where the overall direction of ballet seemed to limit my horizons, and where the very idea of the ballerina as an actress was on the way out, at least for a while. Maybe I was dead wrong, but that was how it looked to me as I pulled up the window shade and tried to put the world of ballet out of my mind.

Reality came pouring in. We had flown all night. The sun had now risen and seemed to be everywhere in the sky. My ears were popping, but I was able to hear the loud, abrasive voice of a stewardess offering coffee and hot towels. Greg's face was weary and swollen. I figured I was probably in the same condition. After the stewardess and her trolley passed us, the pilot announced the sights we might take in as the plane made its final descent. He also reported the weather in London: rain and fog. No surprise there, but how in the world were we going to see any sights? Greg leaned into me and kissed my ear, saying only, "Well, it could be worse. We could be landing in Moscow."

When the other passengers stood up to leave the cabin, we stood up as well and fell into line, following like a pair of sleep-walkers. My mind was in such a state of fatigue only my body seemed capable of acting, but with all of my joints creaking as if they needed oil, it was all I could do to put one foot in front of the other. I was wearing what had become a characteristic out-fit: a blue knit sweater and some old sweat pants. My winter coat was slung over one arm and the straps of a canvas bag over the other. I was a sight. "A suspicious-looking character," said Greg.

We moved arm in arm off the plane and staggered, after an endless wait, from the baggage claim area to customs, with nothing to declare. I was praying for a cab to take me to the nearest bathtub when a customs official pulled us aside, our luggage rolling in front of us in what looked like a fancy super-market cart, wobbling almost out of control under the weight of suitcases.

The customs agent was intrigued by a small leather case Greg was gripping a bit too protectively. It turned out not to contain the terrorist's time bomb that might have been suspected, but merely the uncompleted manuscript of my autobiography. Af-ter placing the pages on a metal countertop, the official turned the case on its side and out came the small hammer I used to soften the pointes of my toe shoes. Not exactly a concealed weapon, but enough of a find to elicit a raised eyebrow.

My canvas bag was next. The customs agent removed the contents, giving each item meticulous scrutiny before putting it down on the counter: a dozen pairs of pink toe shoes, a can of Fabulon floor wax (used to harden the shoes), a pair of false eyelashes, several containers of stage makeup, and a hard-cover copy of *Romeo and Juliet*. From a hidden side compartment, he slowly pulled out a coil of ribbon, unraveling it the length of his arm like a magician pulling a scarf out of his hat.

The search ended with a shopping bag, out of which emerged two bicycle tires, each about two feet in diameter. Seeing the puzzled expression on the agent's face, I tried to find the words to explain what they were doing in my bag. Greg stepped in and offered a free demonstration, spinning one of the tires around his forearm. This was an unorthodox exercise that I used to develop the upper body. With a crisp British accent and a tone I thought was probably reserved for Americans, the customs man advised us to repack and enjoy our stay. After we loaded our luggage back on the cart and started moving toward the exit, he called after us to say he would be coming to my performance. He wished me luck.

Someone from the Royal Ballet was supposed to meet us at the airport, but our flight had arrived late, and we were the last passengers out. The arrivals area at Heathrow was crowded at this hour of the morning. While Greg sat on the baggage cart, I stood looking into each passing face for a sign of recognition. A man in a trench coat caught my eye, and then came the warm flash of his smile. He hesitated for a moment, and cocked his head, "Gelsey? Is that you?" We broke into laughter that carried us through a long embrace. It was Anthony, looking fit and younger than ever.

He was quick to offer me an apology, admitting with an innocent blush that he had already approached a woman whom he had mistakenly identified. "Well, there was a resemblance from behind, you see. Same hair . . . and she was with a man. But when I approached her from the front my heart stopped, dear. I said to myself, *Oh my God, she's had her face done!* I realize this must sound frightful, but she did have me in a bit of a panic, and

as it turned out, she weighed, well, more than I'd have expected. But then it's been such a long time, I thought it might be
possible you'd put on a few—" He held up his hands as if to ward
off the image of the ballerina gone the way of the flesh, his gaze
now moving back and forth between me and Greg, whom I
hastened to introduce.

Anthony was relieved to see me more or less in the shape that
he remembered—a hundred pounds at most. But his mouth
dropped open when I confessed, as casually as possible, how
long it was since I had been inside a ballet studio. There was an
old saying that lately crossed my mind: when a ballerina misses a
day of class, nobody notices; when she misses two days of class,
she notices; when she misses three days, everybody notices.
Anthony would certainly notice a partner without stamina or
muscle tone.

"You mean you haven't been taking class at all?"

"Well, I've been giving myself class in my kitchen."

"Oh, I see. Grand jetés between the pots and pans?"

The laughter released the tension. Anthony then took the
lead guiding the three of us to a huge black taxi and loading us
inside. I asked him how he managed to keep his youth. For a
man who had just celebrated his forty-third birthday, he was
amazing, his boyish face apparently untouched by time. Depending on the angle and light, he could appear to be the curly-
haired urchin out of Dickens, or the most gallant prince from
Shakespeare. He had what is known on the stage as range. "But
it's all done with mirrors," he quipped, evading the compliment
with his puckish grin.

The drive into London lasted over an hour in the heavy traffic. Having gained a second wind, I managed to blurt out, almost
nonstop, a summary of recent events, sparing Anthony none of
the more lurid details. I gave him a blow-by-blow account of my
departure from American Ballet Theatre, where the two of us
had first danced together eight years before. "You wouldn't
recognize the place, Anthony. Tudor is all that is left, and he
sounds more fragile each time I talk with him."

Over the years both of us had worked with Antony Tudor, the
venerable British choreographer who was a mainstay for ABT.
His roots traced back to "the beginning of time," as he once put

it. They certainly went back to London and to that tradition of ballet to which I was most devoted. It was Tudor who taught me the purpose of dance was not merely to explore movement for its own sake, but to master the passions, to shape every character inwardly as well as outwardly. In a way, coming to the city where he had first started to choreograph, I was following his footsteps to their point of origin. That pleased me no end.

The windows of the taxi were fogging over. Anthony pointed out the Royal Ballet School in Baron's Court, where the company took class and rehearsed a good part of the time. As we passed by, I wiped a little hole on the surface of the window and saw what appeared to be an old factory building, two stories of dark brick, like a picture postcard from the nineteenth century.

"Do you remember it?" Anthony asked.

"No. Not really. Not the outside anyway."

Greg had his nose pressed against the glass. He had been quiet most of the ride, facing me on a seat that pulled down behind the driver. "It does look ominous in this weather, doesn't it?"

"It's what goes on inside that's ominous," I said, making light of the obvious.

By the time we arrived in the district of Kensington, where we were to stay, I had prepared Anthony for my memoirs, and promised to give him an advance copy. I wanted him to know I would understand if he had any last minute misgivings about my being a guest with the company. He was unconcerned. He listened attentively, but the scenes I described seemed like happenings on some other planet. He was most curious about the way that Greg and I had overcome cocaine addiction by going into seclusion and immersing ourselves in classical music and poetry. It did seem like a miracle. Who would ever believe it?

I had one more confession to make. "You know, Anthony, now that I'm healthy, I'm likely to be more difficult than ever. I hope you weren't expecting an angel in the studio."

"I should hope not."

Greg used the opening to satisfy his curiosity. "Did you ever have any trouble working with Gelsey? I know how stubborn and demanding she can be when it comes to—"

"Well, yes, she was insistent, and the work in the studio was quite intense. She never missed any details. But, you see, the two of us always did seem to manage rather well . . . and I had only to see the results. I never doubted Gelsey's artistry."

"That's more than I would ever have said of myself back then. It was Anthony's wit that always kept me going."

The taxi came to a stop in Ennismore Gardens, an oblong block of stately Victorian houses surrounding a central garden. The Royal Ballet had arranged for us to rent a flat here. After we had deposited our luggage on the sidewalk and settled with the driver, the three of us were greeted by a landlady who led us in the front door and up more flights of stairs than I was able to count. The flat was as tiny as a dollhouse. Its three rooms, as charming as they were, had apparently been furnished with that scale in mind. Everything seemed to be miniature and decorated in powder blue.

"Welcome to the land of Lilliput," said Greg, flopping onto the bed with his feet dangling over the end. The feeling of confinement was dispelled as soon as I drew open the curtains and saw the windows overlooked the gardens. Anthony went out to buy us groceries, an errand of mercy from which he refused to be dissuaded. Meanwhile, Greg hurried down again to retrieve the remaining bags, and I started unpacking. The place would do nicely for the time being, even with only one tiny closet.

The thought came to me while I was alone that Greg and I had never been apart for more than an hour during the entire two years we had been together. The writing had been an ongoing act of collaboration, but the reason we were so inseparable had more to do with ballet. His passion for drama happened to match my disposition toward dance. Between that shared obsession and the simple joy of being together, we had shaped a marriage of wondrous convenience. Why should we ever part?

When he walked through the door, I was seated at a small desk in the corner of the living room. I asked him, point-blank, "Did I ever tell you what Mr. Tudor said to me before we left New York? Back when we first met?"

With bags in both hands and obviously out of breath, Greg shook his head, exasperated and amused that I should choose this moment to reminisce. Hooking one leg behind, he closed the door.

"We'd just finished rehearsing *Lilac Garden,* and Tudor came over and whispered, 'I hear you've found your other half.' I told him I thought I had, and he looked away, you know, like he was meditating on the fate of the universe. Then he turned back and said, 'Scary, isn't it?' That was all he said. He walked away as if he had passed final judgment. What do you think he meant by that?"

Greg, still holding the bags, walked by me without saying a word and stopped in front of the window, where he dropped the load onto the floor. Then he gestured toward the gardens and said, "Well, do you think there are any lilacs out there?" Taking him literally, I rose and crossed to the place he was standing. I thought of Anthony out in that gloomy fog and felt a twinge of guilt. Greg continued, "What I mean is this. You were dancing the role of Caroline in Tudor's ballet, *Lilac Garden,* right? He was probably trying to tell you about her character. She's the one who chooses between true love and a loveless marriage, right?"

"Right. She marries the man she doesn't love. It's a Victorian nightmare in one act," I replied, slowly seeing what he was getting at.

"So maybe Tudor was telling you why she was trapped into marrying the wrong guy . . . because she was scared to give herself to her other half, to her real lover."

"Of course. But why on earth didn't he just say so?" There was a knock I hurried to answer, adding over my shoulder, "If only I had known. All he ever told me was she and the lover were best friends."

Anthony walked through the door and handed me a plastic bag that contained the essentials: eggs, cheese, butter, milk, and orange juice. Before leaving us to recover from our jet lag, he promised to call on the following day, even though he abhorred telephone calls and claimed he never answered the phone himself. He reminded me that class would start on Monday, the day after tomorrow. Rehearsals for *Romeo and Juliet* would begin later in the week. He accepted our thanks with his usual grace, embracing both of us at the door, and then he was gone.

I was famished, having avoided all food on the airplane. After Greg and I made a short order of the groceries, I turned to my dietary staple of the moment, which happened to be popcorn. I had brought along an electric popping machine from America and a converter for the three-prong British outlets. Unfortunately, upon plugging the contraption into the wall in the kitchenette, the circuits blew, creating a small mushroom cloud of smoke. Greg came charging to the rescue, yanking the cord out of the socket while I cautioned him against electrocution.

Holding the blackened machine out between his hands, its insides still spewing forth a stream of smoke, he said, "Scary, isn't it?" and with a wry smile playing across his lips, "Why don't we try to get some sleep now, darling!"

It was early afternoon by the time I had bathed and joined him in our tiny bed. He had already passed out, and I was not far behind. We slept through the entire day. I got up once in the middle of the night dying of thirst. Stumbling around in the dark, I grabbed a door frame and looked back at Greg. There was an eerie light shining in from the window, covering the bedspread. He looked as if he were under a blanket of moonlight. But there was no moon, only the stray beam of a streetlamp.

I climbed back into bed and wrapped my legs around his legs, burying my forehead between his shoulder and the nape of his neck. I told myself, "No, it isn't scary, not really." Then I lifted my head and said those same words softly into his ear. After that neither of us stirred.

I was awake before dawn. I threw on a robe and then marched straight to the window as if to confirm that we were still in the same place we arrived the day before. The garden was floating in a sea of mist. I put my hand on the windowpane and felt the chill creep along my fingers. There was no clock in the flat and neither of us had a watch, so I went into the living room and turned on the television set, but the screen was blank. Whatever the hour, I resigned myself to starting the morning routine—a cup of tea, a tub of hot water, and then down to business.

The rest of the day was going to be mind over matter, if I could just escape the feeling of there being no escape. Careful not to make any noise, I lugged some of the furniture to the side of the living room, leaving enough space to stretch out on the floor, and started a series of therapeutic exercises, slowly warming the muscles, first opening those around the spine and inside the shoulder blades—those needed to support every gesture on the stage. Then I found the center of gravity deep within my pelvis, the point of balance needed to sustain a body in motion. Even lying flat on my back, I was already reaching for an ideal shape—that timeless form out of which a character might eventually be brought to life.

These exercises were as gentle as they were methodical. I measured each breath from the diaphragm, like a singer, and extended that simple inspiration into the entire body, from the torso out through the limbs. I concentrated only on that world within—not some mystical nirvana, but those sensations that would guide my skeleton into alignment. The isometric rigor was about as far from aerobics as one could imagine, but still I was breaking into a sweat.

I heard bells chime somewhere just on the edge of my awareness. It was Sunday. There had to be a church nearby. I folded my hands and stretched my arms away from me, turning the palms out with fingers locked, lifting inch by inch toward the ceiling, until my hands had completed an arc over my head. I had come to the point where I was able to turn out my body from the heart. This was more than a mere figure of speech, it was the figure that might enable me to speak through the dance.

Whatever I felt—whatever mysteries might be locked inside those ribs, whatever beauty, whatever truth—none of it would ever be revealed, or read to an audience, unless I were able to turn out the upper body with the same facility that I was able to turn out my legs. This was where emotion was supposed to enter the picture. How ironic it was that I had not yet done a single ballet position or step. It had taken me more than an hour just to prepare myself for class, just to feel like a human being.

When Greg came out of the bedroom, I was turning in a slow circle, the bicycle tires spinning around my arms. With hair in a tangle and sleep still in his eyes, he raised his arms and imitated me, like a clown in the mirror, exaggerating every movement until I was almost drawn into imitating him. Then he broke away with an enormous smile on his face, heading into the bathroom, calling out to wish me good morning.

I completed a few more circles, increasing the intensity of my effort, arms almost motionless inside the revolving tires, keeping them in orbit with an impulse from my back, and finally letting out a short gasp as they went flying into the air, the magic slipping away. Fortunately, there was nothing broken except my concentration.

I heard Greg in the shower, doing his own rendition of Beethoven's Ninth, disregarding the notes as well as the neighbors, his voice rising and echoing as if he were conducting an orchestra in the bath. I picked up my notebook and moved to the couch, doing my best to ignore his boisterous ode to joy. The habit of writing down my ideas to prepare for a role was still new to me and did not come easily. I had to force the pen into motion.

I opened a book of da Vinci reproductions to a place I had marked. I had become fascinated by the strange figure of the angel Gabriel in *The Annunciation,* an unlikely place to start my search for Juliet, but there was a certain quality in the painting that captivated me. The way the angel seemed to be reaching out with both heart and mind, and yet resisting, kneeling without allowing his knee to touch the ground or shoulders to fall forward—without losing his dignity.

I wrote in my journal:

How is it possible for a figure that is perfectly still to look like it is moving? If I can accomplish only that much on the stage, I will have succeeded. Leonardo must have been devilishly clever for his angel to move the way it does . . . the curve of the back and the outstretched arm blurring the distinction between heaven and earth. I have to find a place for this wonderful creature. Sneak him into the theatre if I can . . . disguised as me.

Anthony called. He arranged for me and Greg to go to the studio at the Royal Opera House in Covent Garden. We had only to ring the stage door for a fireman to let us in. Anthony would give me a wake-up call tomorrow morning for company class, but today I might get a head start on my own. Greg walked out of the bathroom, fully dressed. An umbrella was hooked over his arm. I thought I detected a sour note of impatience when he said, "I'm ready to go—shall we?"

"I'll be right with you." Those words came out more harshly than I intended, and I could see the hurt cloud his eyes. But the moment passed as quickly as it had come, replaced by a sudden tenderness as he helped me gather my things together and then packed them into my canvas bag.

I stuffed a worn pair of toe shoes inside, saying, "Well, now you know what ballet does to your loving wife."

Pulling the straps over his shoulder, he said, "Turns us both into bag ladies, doesn't it?" Then, seeing me bury my journal in the desk drawer, he asked, "Aren't you going to bring your pen?"

"Not today. I can always borrow yours."

With collars turned up against the weather, we started out for a nearby tea shop. The landlady had given us directions for a shortcut through a stone gate and across an ancient churchyard. After feeling like we had walked back centuries in time, we came to a thoroughly modern thoroughfare, across from Harrods, the gigantic department store where you might buy anything from anywhere.

Everything was closed on Sunday except our little tea shop, where we ordered brunch. I had fish, Dover sole to be exact, broiled without butter, a dish that would be my main source of protein during the months ahead. Greg suggested we go to Dover Beach, and went so far as to quote from the poem by that title, the famous lines about being true to one another because the world was such a nightmare. My mind was somewhere else, though I did like that part about being true. I knew he had no intention of going to the beach. He was only trying to get a rise out of me, but I was already in the theater.

We chased down one of those black taxis, forgetting for a moment this was not New York City. The cab sped into a maze of side streets, squeezing through impossibly tight holes in the traffic, the driver chatting away amiably the entire time, pointing out the palace as we passed. After a last hairpin turn, we pulled over at the back of the opera house. The place was deserted. We rang the bell and knocked on the glass door until a little elf of a man let us inside. The lobby desk was closed off behind a metal gate, but we could see a photograph of Dame Margot Fonteyn through its metal bars.

She was without any question the greatest ballerina I had ever seen, and even the reminder provided by a dated, faded photograph was enough to make me pause for a moment in astonishment. It was more than a memory. To see the glow in her matchless face was to know, once again, the sublime shape I was seeking, the playful innocence, the purity, the noble carriage of the woman all of us must sometime long to be.

The fireman interrupted with a gruff voice, deeper than I expected from someone not much taller than me. The mention of her name was his cue: "They do not make them like her anymore. One of a kind she was." Without elaborating, he led us to an elevator and told us to go up to the fourth floor. As soon as we stepped inside and the doors closed, Greg asked, "You seem intimidated by her, or is it just my imagination?"

"Margot is the ballerina by whom everyone who dances for this company is going to be judged, maybe forever . . . and she cannot be imitated. It's not intimidation, it's more like terror." The elevator came to rest and the doors opened with a hiss, like the sound of a vacuum seal being broken. We walked along a short hallway and then through a pair of glass doors, both of us silent except for the echoing of our footsteps.

As we came to the entrance of the studio, Greg juggled the bag and put a hand on my shoulder, halting me in my tracks. Then he moved behind me and gently squeezed the back of my neck, a shudder running down my spine as he massaged the muscles. He said, "The weather is already taking its toll on you. You've got a knot the size of my fist." He was waiting for me to deliver a punch line.

I stepped away and gave my neck a quick turn, hearing it crack and loosen. Then I said, catching his eyes, "Years ago Margot heard I was unhappy and sent me a message, advising me to take heart by remembering that I could do something that nobody else could do. Those were actually her words, but you see, I couldn't find consolation in them at the time. I can now, but only when I feel that I can teach someone else to do the same thing. Do you know what I mean?"

He nodded without conviction, as if asking for an explanation, so I went on. "It's not enough just to act the role. It's not enough to come up with an interpretation. The audience actually has to be able to see me think, and I have to think the purest thoughts and link them together, step by step. It's like what you said to me one time, what you called 'the shape of love.' Well, that's what beauty is to me."

"I don't remember ever saying that."

"You say a lot of things."

He laughed as he opened the door for me. The shock of the mirrors was almost more than I could take. The studio was empty, sterile, and large enough to hold a small horse show. My hopes went skidding to the bottom as fast as they had streaked to the top during our little talk outside. Between the reflections, the memories, and the familiar smell of rosin on wood, my brain was too stunned for any more words. Greg took a seat on the floor in a corner, spreading out my handwritten notes and draft for the last chapter of memoirs. I emptied out my canvas bag.

Avoiding tights and leotards and the line of my body, I slipped into a bulky sweater, a pair of baggy sweat pants, leg warmers, and black leather slippers. The cold wind in the room actually called for my wool coat and mittens. The damp air would twist the muscles like so many rubber bands unless I went to work straightaway. What I had won in the morning had been lost, though less time would be needed for recovery. I was on my back again searching for warmth and first position.

Thank God there was no mirror on the ceiling, pinned to the floor as I was like a specimen. Not a butterfly. I had no wings. I did have fitted iron weights strapped on to both ankles and wrists, a burden that might help me more than prayers by the time I actually had to find the last breath for the last act of the ballet. I was getting too old for this kind of thing. It did occur to me I was almost ten years younger than Margot at the point she began her partnership with Rudolf Nureyev, but she had not abused her body either with drugs or with the contortions of a modern repertory. She had not burned herself out.

Finding the level I needed, moving forward in a way like the angel in the painting, I started the exercises at the barre, now riveted on an inward focus that began with the simplest plié. I worked to the cassette tape of a class given by my teacher in New York, David Howard. The Royal Ballet had kindly agreed to bring him to London to teach, but he was not to arrive for several weeks. His class was flexible enough for me to adapt to my needs as far as conditioning and a fluid sense of form. But the logic of positions and steps would ultimately have to be motivated by the drama.

I was groaning as if experiencing death agonies. An hour or so of slow torture at the barre was enough at times to require some sort of release. Greg called out to tell me not to worry, the building was sound. He had heard it all before. Stepping away from the barre, I was suddenly devastated. The work in the center of the studio was beyond me. I was unable to cover space, unable to put together the combinations of steps that had been second nature for me in the past. A grand jeté traveling off one leg was now like trying to fly to the moon. Sensing my frustration, Greg started circling around me, watching from every angle, trying to get a fix on the problem. Another hour or century must have gone by. Hell froze over.

At last he said, "Dear, you've been in the kitchen too long." The mixture of truth and absurdity brought me to my knees. There are moments when a situation can seem so hopeless that the spirit rebels, not with tears, but with the kind of laughter that might be dangerous if heard in public. So it was that we left the studio, abandoned to mirth and resigned to my early retirement, the spirit carrying us back to where we started, shaken but not defeated.

Underneath, of course, I was utterly discouraged. But underneath my discouragement, I was resolved to continue until I dropped. That evening, after a meal and a brief reading of the book-in-progress, I devoted several hours to sewing my toe shoes, none of which fit. The floor of the living room was covered by a pale blue braided rug, which in turn was covered with shoes, ribbon, thread, needles, razor blades, tiny pieces of silk, scraping tools, and a hammer. I had created this sort of disaster area wherever I went for years. I managed to salvage one pair of shoes for the first day of company class. That seemed a major triumph.

I soon retired to the refuge of the bathtub. Stretching into the luxurious warmth, I watched the water pour over my legs, contemplating nothing more than my pink knees, like two islands in the middle of a soapy lake. I let my head fall back against the edge of the tub and closed my eyes. Then I lifted one foot and twisted the little handle on the tap until there was silence. I heard Greg yell out, "Gelsey, wherefore art thou?" I made no reply, thinking only of Juliet's line, "Take him and cut him out in little stars." How was I going to dance that poetry?

The flat was not without its amenities, and the best was a rack for warming towels. I took to sitting on it just to start the day with heat. Tonight I had placed my terrycloth robe there, prepared to rush from the bath, still dripping, with robe in hand, to bed and waiting husband. But exhaustion cooled my heels if not my desire. I pulled up the plug in the bathtub and watched as the water escaped, a whirlpool forming over the drain. Then I stepped out and slowly dried myself, wrapping the towel around my head, leaving the robe on the rack for morning.

Moving out of the bathroom, I had to hopscotch my way through the mess I left behind me to get to the bedroom. The door was open. Still naked except for the towel, I stopped in the doorway and peered into the darkness. Greg was already in bed and fast asleep. I could hear him breathing as I crept to the window and opened the curtains. Then I slipped into bed and laid across his outstretched arm, sensing him wake with a start. I said, "You're only dreaming." The next thing I knew, morning was all around us.

The weather had broken. There was a sun in the sky, a cold smear, its bright glow offering little in the way of solace: it was Monday. Anthony called as if to tell me that my pardon had been denied. Greg helped me pack up for class and tried to console me with a flurry of kisses. We were parting at last. He was unable to come with me today because he had to track down a computer compatible with the one we left in America, so that we might finish the work on the memoirs. We had a deadline to meet.

He escorted me downstairs and helped me find a taxi, loading my canvas bag onto the floor and telling the driver where I was going. I was caught up in a whirlwind. I could actually hear the pulse pounding in my ears as Greg closed the door behind me and slowly backed away, still facing me from the sidewalk. I was in a moving cell, the taxi jolting forward. I gave a last wave, my farewell hand on the glass. Then the tears started streaming down my face, as he looked away.

2.

TO
MAKE
A
JULIET

I was feeling quite brave by the time the cab dropped me at
the Royal Ballet School. I had composed myself between tears,
catching my breath as I might have done in a performance. I
thought of my former self, the old Gelsey who would have asked
the driver to turn around and take her home—I watched her go,
and with that simple fantasy broke again with my past. I had to
laugh as I made my entrance, seeing my face reflected in a
window at the front door. I told myself that I was ready for
anything, even my image in the glass.

There were familiar faces and looks of recognition in the halls
—dancers I remembered and teenage students scurrying duti-
fully by me. I paused in the lobby and stood with my nose in the
air, as if trying to pick out an elusive scent. I was actually trying
to read the signs on the doors; my eyesight was not what it was

when I was a child. The dark paneling and cloistered atmosphere gave me the impression of going back in time; then came
a moment like déjà vu. I really had been here before, but my
memory was a blur. I looked around trying to figure out which
way to go, not wanting to give myself away by asking anyone for
help.

The caretaker approached me, appearing so suddenly I
thought he had come out of the woodwork. He was a sweet,
gnome-like man, whose neck and shoulders seemed permanently awry. I was touched when he remembered me. He shuffled up the stairs ahead and led me to the door of a dressing
room on the second floor. I knocked and listened, and turned to
thank him again, but he was already retreating back down the
stairs, his deference almost painful.

Poking my head through the doorway, I found the new director of the school, Dame Merle Park, who offered a warm greeting. She was one of the first Juliets I ever saw—and still carried
herself with that dignified bearing I associated with the great
ballerinas of the Royal Ballet's past. I asked her if there were
something in the water around here that kept everyone in a
state of eternal youth. She was less reserved than I expected, her
high-pitched laugh and broad smile making me feel instantly
welcome, as if I had come home.

The dressing room was the size of a large closet, with nothing
more elaborate than a wash basin and mirror. I congratulated
Merle on being appointed to head the school and asked about
her plans. She was revising a syllabus for the school's training
program, as well as trying to stay in shape herself. Echoing what
I had heard from Anthony, she explained how the company and
school were experimenting, bringing in teachers of various
backgrounds. It was a time of change for everyone in the theatre.

I launched into a long-winded back-to-the-classics lecture,
bending Merle's ear for an hour with talk of Plato and poetry
and a lot of very heady ideas indeed. She seemed more than
enthusiastic, even suggesting I think about teaching for the
school. I was thrilled with that idea. Changing into another
version of the practice clothes I was already wearing, I said,
"This might sound like madness, but the truth is I'm really more

interested in teaching now than in performing. I don't know what I'll wind up doing in the end—if I ever get through this. . . ."

"But you must do everything!" She made it sound so simple.

With Merle's promise to give me a grand tour of the school later in the week, I said good-bye, then slipped out the door, bag in hand, hoping to make a quick getaway after class. An hour or so later I found myself in the middle of an exercise, facing the mirror again, and doing everything I could not to lose my wits. A fear flashed into mind as I felt my joints straining, the fear of injury, like an old enemy who had come back to haunt me.

"We know you are actress. But now, must work on other things! . . ." It was a voice out of my nightmare. The accent was Russian. I had died and not gone to heaven, but to Moscow. The teacher was now smiling tentatively, a wisp of a woman, elderly and pale, formerly a Bolshoi ballerina. I knew she meant well, but I was unable to answer her. I stood at the barre, holding on to the wood with one hand and wiping my brow with the other. I forced a pleasant smile in her direction, feeling all the muscles in my face tighten like a mask.

I had arrived early and worked on my own prior to class. I had prepared. The pride with which I had entered the studio this morning was still evident as I checked my placement in the mirror, seeing the teacher move away behind my reflection. Perhaps that was why she had singled me out, determined as I was to remain aloof and avoid distraction. Pride was a tragic flaw as old as the world, but mine was neither arrogance nor conceit. I was simply pleased with myself for having come this far, trying to concentrate on what I had to accomplish.

I was considering those "other things" she had in mind, the technical aspects of ballet. However, I made no separation between those aspects and the necessity to act on the stage—they were all one to my way of thinking. I had chosen to take class with the men, supposing it would be slower than the one given to women in the company—slow enough, I hoped, to work through these positions and steps instead of trying to keep up with pages out of a Russian picture book. No such luck.

The studio contained a few dozen men and several women, lined at the barre all the way around the room, struggling gamely just to keep the limbs moving apace. Russian classes required that each movement of the legs be accompanied by an appropriate movement of the arms and head. Unless you had grown up in the system, there was rarely enough time to phrase the steps and follow through with the entire body, which moved from one pose to the next—endlessly. To an outsider, it must have seemed like some marvelous drill for marionettes.

I heard Anthony groan nearby, and then whisper something I was unable to catch. He was doing well even under the strain, pushing himself and keeping a watchful eye on me. As we moved from the barre to the center of the floor, he flung an arm over my shoulder and said, "You look fabulous!"

"It's all done with mirrors," I asserted, recalling they were his words. Then I said, "The Russians never seem to give enough pliés. I'm still rigor mortis from neck down." His grimace was a warning I might be overheard. Bending over to fix my shoes, which no longer seemed to fit, I sensed the teacher's footsteps coming from behind me. And then came the voice.

"You are warm enough?" she wanted to know.

"Give me about three days," I replied. That brought a knowing smile to her face as I looked up. Anthony emitted a laugh and mentioned something about the cold weather and the floor freezing over under our feet. *Soles of lead,* I mused, trying to lift my legs and remember that line of Romeo's from the play. I was looking forward to the work in the center, if only to see whether I could move at all.

I needed the challenge of coordinating steps other than those I had been giving myself during the past months in the kitchen. The eyes of the teacher might at least help me put a few turns and combinations together. Juliet did know how to dance, how to use space as well as words to her advantage. The ballroom where she was to meet Romeo for the first time would exist only so far as it existed in my imagination—only so far as I was able to define her world with my own body. That meant covering enough space on the stage for such a world to become visible to the audience, to be felt by every person in the theatre. My muscles were barely able to carry me across the studio without loss of grace, let alone transport an audience to that distant, moonswept balcony.

Her voice found me again in the middle of an attitude turn, a slow spiral with one leg raised and curving behind me. "Must go round like doll!" This sort of correction carried no insight, except to tell me that my balance had been thrown off by the tension left over from the high-speed exercises at the barre. "Show me more beautiful leg!" I was becoming more disconcerted and less coordinated by the minute.

She was close to me now. I spun around in a pirouette and waited for the inevitable. "Hands dead! Must hold strong like ballerina!" I had to pursue this one with her. I stopped the pianist and asked the teacher what she meant, though I had a vague idea that I had failed to extend the movement all the way through my fingers. To question a correction was a disruptive event in any class. A hush fell over the room, surrounding the two of us like we were inside of a bubble.

Seconds ticked by while she thought, apparently pleased that I had thought enough to ask. She seemed somewhat puzzled, but I could see kindness in her face as well as effort. At last she drew her arms into a low circle in front of her, the fingers of her two hands almost touching. She said, "Like electricity," gazing as if there were sparks leaping between her fingertips.

I promised to try again, fascinated by the image she chose, but realizing what she saw from the outside had little to do with what I needed to feel from the inside, to make my own hands speak as fluently as the rest of my body through that pirouette. This was more than a problem of translation for me; it seemed like an instant replay of my entire career.

I felt almost faint as I prepared to repeat the movement, sensing the muscles along my spine, imagining that wicked little circle through which I was about to turn myself. Anthony watched from the side, quietly amused. The sudden intensity of my effort sent me flying across the floor as if I had somehow put my toe into an electric socket. I recovered quickly, relieved that the loss of control did not bring disaster, only embarrassment—a fleeting moment of paralysis in the midst of laughter.

It was Anthony who brought me to my senses—"A bit too much voltage, I think, dear." When class broke up, he followed me to the side where I left my bag. Trying to match his play on words, I said, "Well, I guess I'm as shocking as ever." He was quick to agree, wholeheartedly, as if struck by some memory that proved the point.

He pulled the bag from my hands and suddenly became aware of its weight. Hoisting the straps over his shoulder, he quipped, "And your sewing machine as well?" Still bantering, the two of us headed out the door, deciding to share a ride as far as Harrods. I suggested that an hour and fifteen minutes for a class was not really long enough, that I was going to have to remedy the situation this afternoon in my living room. Then I prodded him outside the studio, "Don't you think a couple of hours might be better? I mean just to give the body a fighting chance. . . ."

"Well, yes, that was rather brief today. But you see, it's the unions." He filled in enough details, using words like "bureau-cracy," "budget," and "headache," for me to get the picture. I was still naive enough to think that London would be more civilized. Anthony offered hope that David Howard's class might run a bit longer, if something could be worked out next week with the pianist. We would just have to wait and see.

As an afterthought, I asked him why he was going to Harrods. He beamed. "To buy you an alarm clock!"—which was exactly what he did.

That night I went over everything from the sweet sorrow in the taxi to the fiasco in class. The two of us were eating dinner at an Italian café not far from the flat; Greg was leaning back in a chair built for someone half his size. The waiter placed a cup of espresso on the table in front of him and another in front of me. The dishes had been cleared, if not the air.

I raised my arms in a sweeping gesture that could have been an entreaty or even a threat. We might have been lovers having a quarrel, but we weren't quarreling. I was only giving a demon-stration of the arm positions known as port de bras, still recount-ing my day, the serious tones of our conversation blending into the romantic atmosphere. We had chosen to eat Italian on a whim, hoping to find shades of Renaissance Verona; instead, we found mood lighting and a mural of modern Venice. There was a statue of a gondolier on a shelf over Greg's head, along with countless bottles of wine.

The waiter, a silver-haired man with the natural gift of talking with his hands, had raised them in despair when I first gave him my order, refusing sauce or pasta. Now that I had passed on the desserts, he was gesticulating almost tragically.

Coming forward in his chair, Greg tried to explain in a word, "Ballerina," with a nod in my direction.

The waiter's eyes softened, and his hands froze, perfectly framing his face. "Ah, ballereeeena! *Belleeesima* ballereeeena! I seeee. She not eat . . . she dance!" After that outburst he left us in peace; and I went on, talking a blue streak, cup in hand.

Greg was keenly attentive, not allowing me to skip over any details; only when I had run out of breath did he make a comment. "You always did have a problem speaking Russian. The question is . . . can you still walk?" He was ever tongue-in-cheek about my difficulty with Russian training. A flush came into my cheeks that must have been obvious from across the room.

I had been telling him about the encounter with Madame Sulamith Michailovna Messerer, the seventy-eight-year-old former Bolshoi ballerina who had given class this morning. I was quite fond of her and that made the frustration all the more frustrating. Madame Messerer was the aunt of Bolshoi legend Maya Plisetskaya and the sister of one of the Bolshoi's leading teachers. So her eye could not be casually dismissed.

"Yes, I can walk . . . but I can't jump! No better than yesterday. The coordination just isn't there, and I'm never going to get it back with a Russian teacher. Not even Vaganova herself could help me!" The vehemence surprised my husband, and drew the attention of our friendly waiter, who was still fussing over us. I drained the cup and paused, staring into the bottom, as if reading the future from the grinds. There were only six weeks until my opening night in *Romeo and Juliet*—not long enough for me to get into condition and rehearse the ballet.

Without looking up, I said, "I'm afraid I'm going to disappoint you."

With his elbows on the table and his chin resting between his hands, he waited until he had my eyes. "I'm afraid I'm going to disappoint you. So I guess we're even."

The waiter intruded with a check. He thanked us with a gracious gesture and told us to take our time, but we were the last customers. Greg left some money on the table and the two of us went quietly, promising to return soon. Once outside we wondered aloud what the fellow must have thought. I snuck my hand into Greg's coat pocket as we hurried away, but before going more than a few steps, the man suddenly reappeared behind us—my husband had forgotten his umbrella.

After saying good night all over again, we started back to the flat, hunting for the shortcut through the churchyard. There was no rain, only a cold mist that came swirling into our faces, forcing us to turn around and walk backward, arms linked as we turned. The streets were empty. Harrods was lit up like a surreal Christmas tree. It soon became clear that neither of us knew where we were going. We had arrived in daylight by cab, and now that darkness had fallen, we were lost.

We walked as far as the Victoria and Albert Museum, which was too huge to be missed, and then we turned around again. The problem was there were two churches on opposite sides of the road. Which was which? One was gothic, and the other baroque; both were stone, but neither was recognizable. Greg led us to a storefront out of the wind where he unfolded a map against the window. I looked past him, taken aback by several manikins showing off the latest bridal gowns. They were so lifelike, one of them poised to toss her plastic bouquet into my arms.

I nudged Greg's elbow and said, "She looks more human than some dancers I know. Maybe she could dance Juliet for me! Do you think?"

He crumpled the map and then glanced up at the window. "Maybe she could just point the way for us." As we headed out onto the sidewalk, he added, "I wish my old pal, Tom Jones, were here. He'd point us in the right direction." His voice trailed off as I tried to keep up with his quickening strides, putting my hand back into his pocket to slow him down. I had heard him mention the name before, someone from the past.

"Which Tom Jones? Who do you mean?" I could never be

really sure with Greg whether he was talking about one of his old friends, or a fictional character, or someone from history. He spoke about them all the same way, with the same passionate tone. It was always a rose by any other name for him, until I made him say which rose and which garden he had in mind. While we waited at a crosswalk, he set me straight.

"This Tom Jones was an architect I went to school with. He knew London and Manhattan like the palm of his hand, and he could tell you the history of any building you passed. Tom was always talking about preservation of daylight. He was trying to import some British laws going all the way back to Shakespeare's time . . . to New York, you see, so the skyscrapers wouldn't block out the sun. . . . It used to be that people owned the sky over their heads."

"Wait a minute, you've lost me."

The light changed. As we crossed, Greg went on distractedly, ignoring my complaint as if he were dreaming. "Darkness at noon, that's what Tom predicted for America, though only after he had a long night. . . . He was really a dear man, another defector, you could say—" He stopped short, cutting himself off.

"What happened to him?" I persisted, tugging his coat.

"He left," he said flatly.

"Like us?"

"In a way . . . in a way. Why does anyone leave?"

I pried out of curiosity whenever Greg's past came up between us. The writing of my story put me at a disadvantage: he knew more about me than I knew about him. I wanted to press him further, but I felt like I might be straying into a foreign territory, over my head, and there was something in his voice that said not tonight. The cold was getting to both of us.

We decided to try our luck with Holy Trinity, an eerie stone building almost lost in shadows off the road. A far cry from any gothic cathedral, it turned out to be the local parish and the right choice. We made our way through the gate and into the cobblestone courtyard. The place was pitch black except for a light in one of the upstairs windows—"Shakespeare's Friar burning the midnight oil," according to my guide. From here we raced home, not wishing to disturb anyone.

The phone was ringing as we came into the flat. Greg an-

Romeo and Juliet, Act I, Nursery Scene, with Gerd Larsen as the Nurse.

Ballroom Scene, with Julian Hosking as Paris.

Ballroom Scene, with Anthony
Dowell as Romeo.

Balcony Scene, with Anthony Dowell as Romeo.

Balcony Scene, with Anthony Dowell
as Romeo.

PHOTO BY DINA MAKAROVA

PHOTO BY LESLIE E. SPATT

Romeo and Juliet, Act II, Wedding Scene, with Anthony Dowell as
Romeo and Christopher Newton as Friar Laurence.

swered while I turned on the lights and opened the pull-out couch in the living room, thinking the couch might have a larger mattress than the bed. I heard the excitement in his voice as he hung up and turned to me, crying, "We're moving!" The caller was Dina Makarova, an assistant to one of my earliest idols, Natalia Makarova—it seemed Natasha had heard I was in London to dance and was offering to lend one of her two flats to the cause.

I was overwhelmed by the generosity. Natasha had been encouraging us with the book, sending secret messages through Dina, a mutual friend for many years—and now this. We whirled around in a jubilant little dance that landed us on the couch where nature took its course, helped along by the good news and my foresight with the mattress. It seemed all our days and hours had tumbled down to one dizzying, mischievous moment. I rested my head against a cushion and heard my husband say, "There must be a catch somewhere," as if he were reading my mind again. "It sounds too good to be true."

He kissed my forehead and scrambled to the television, playing with the channels until finding the news. The outside world seemed out of place now, but Greg settled back and needled me to stay awake with him. The newscaster's soothing voice acted like a sedative; my eyelids were hanging by threads. A picture of Mikhail Gorbachev appeared, followed by a funeral scene from Northern Ireland. There was nothing from America tonight, not even some ghastly murder or drug scandal to hold my interest.

I was roused temporarily by the image of President Marcos and his wife fleeing the Philippines, and blurted out, "She gave me a ring one time. Ivan Nagy, you know, my partner, took me to some party she threw in New York and she gave me this gigantic ring. I figured it was probably glass."

"Mrs. Marcos?" he screeched, as if she had just walked into the room.

"Yes, but I barely knew who she was back then."

Greg's curiosity was piqued. "So what happened to the ring? Do you still have it?"

"No. I was moving out of my apartment and on the day of the move, it went down the drain, in the sink. I didn't even realize how valuable it might have been, didn't have a clue. I just forgot all about it. . . . It was gaudy anyway."

"Maybe you could tell that story on '60 Minutes,' not saying where you were, of course. Half of Manhattan will be on the phone to the plumber to come over and check the pipes. What a marvelous thing—like the time Orson Welles told the world the Martians had landed in New Jersey . . . and now, the search for the missing Marcos ring!"

I pulled him into my arms and told him to pipe down. It was still early for him, not even midnight according to the new clock I waved under his nose. In no time, he was at the desk, sitting shirtless in front of the glowing computer. I heard him fuming at the machine as I opened my notebook and tried to think of something that might help me tomorrow when I returned to Moscow. I picked up a paperback of Agrippina Vaganova's *Principles of Classical Dancing*, not exactly the wisest choice for bedtime reading.

Vaganova had been the fountainhead of the Russian school in the twentieth century, and her system was being used almost everywhere. I had been studying her book, but there were no principles as far as I could tell, only recipes for classroom exercises, not really any help in my situation. When I found myself drawing mustaches on the figures meant to illustrate what she called "Poses of the Body," I knew it was time to turn attention elsewhere.

Greg finally hit the ceiling. "We may never finish the last chapter unless I can get this damned thing to work!" He leaned his forehead against the glass screen as if trying to communicate directly with the computer. I moved behind him and rubbed his shoulders, kneading the muscles between my fingers, and reminding myself to make an appointment for a massage. I knew how sore I was going to be in the morning.

"I thought you loved these machines."

He craned his neck way around and squinted up at me, saying in a soft voice, "You can't love a machine. I guess I'll have to take it back to the shop tomorrow while you're in class," then added quickly, "but I'll try to meet you later . . . at rehearsal. I promise."

He waited to see how I would take the disappointment. I

went back to the couch, now our bed, and slowly curled up with pen and journal. There was nothing else to be done for the moment. Unsettled as I was, I scribbled onto the page: "There are curves more precious than a lover's body, and beauties unknown to night . . . In the balcony scene, Juliet must command a vow from Romeo, establishing their trust, not allowing him to swear by the inconstant moon." Then I gave up—setting the clock for an ungodly hour.

What did I really know about him? Greg was a mystery, but I supposed most husbands and wives were mysteries to each other. That was the way it worked. I did know he was romantic and hopelessly so. Morning brought fresh evidence. I had left my journal open to the last barely legible entry. He must have stolen his way into it during the wee hours. There was a note in his graceful scrawl under my hieroglyphics; it went to the quick even before I was able to focus my bleary eyes.

> Once in our lives it is given to us to know a timeless love. I have locked you in my heart and given you the only key.

He was only saying something we said on the day we were married, yet he must have known I needed to hear the sentiment repeated. Torn from the notebook, it became something tangible for me to take to rehearsal, something to carry along should he fail to show. I grasped the scrap of paper in my hand the way some people might hold a charm for luck, then stuffed it into the pocket of my favorite sweater.

I was going to need a skeleton key today. My feet had swollen over night so none of my pointe shoes fit; my joints and ligaments were frozen solid from head to toe. I was moving around like I was in a body cast, or a body bag, trying to punch my way out—gently, methodically, going through the old routine without a break, pushing myself out the door without waking up my slumbering husband, not even the pressure of my lips on his cheek being enough to bring him out of his coma. As soon as I stepped into the outside world, I was greeted with a blast of snow that stung my eyes like so many tiny needles. A taxi was not to be found. With the strap of my bag strangling me, I set off for the tube station near Harrods, trudging forward, the slush sneaking into my boots and up my pant legs, thinking with each step: *Here we go again, Gelsey!*

I was in desperate disarray by the time I went down into the subway, my ribs meeting along the way with several well-placed elbows delivered by my fellow commuters, none of whom said a word, or even took notice. They all seemed to be accustomed to bumping into each other, and I quickly adopted their style. It struck me there should have been some sign about abandoning my bag as well as hope on entering here, as both were destined to be buffeted by the crowd.

While I figured how many stops there were to the school, it came to me, again and suddenly, how far I was from New York City—the London subway was actually clean and relatively un-threatening. I could even read the map of the system, posted behind glass and free of graffiti. I was still pondering the wonder of it all as I boarded behind a group of teenagers, creatures really, with hair teased into outrageous spikes, dyed pink and purple, set off against their otherwise shaved scalps. Unlike simi-lar types I had seen in Manhattan, these kids did not seem to be high on drugs, as if they had actually chosen to look this way for some reason. It was the safety pins pierced through the ears that got to me. What would my sweet Juliet make of them?

The block from Baron's Court station to the school ran adja-cent to a four-lane highway, which was filled with cars and puddles and trucks. One splash the size of a tidal wave was enough to finish me off. The snow had abated but my temper had been whipped up to murderous proportions. I could have slayed Romeo with a single glance, and banished all the feuding families and even love itself from the whole world. I stormed into the building, stamping my wet boots in the hallway, making echoes like thunderclaps.

I had the good sense to skip class, or rather, to give myself class alone. Afterward, while waiting for Anthony to rehearse, I sprang my tale of woe on Iris Law, his tireless assistant, the Artistic Administrator, a gracious woman with boundless cheer and a laugh that could have been bottled to meet any world shortage. Iris had an office on the first floor. Outside her door hung bulletin boards with the rehearsal schedule, casting lists, and official notices—a daily magnet for the dancers in the company as well as infrequent guests like me. Anthony's connecting office made the area a constant hub of activity.

When he joined us, I was lamenting the loss of my toe-shoe maker, who had retired; Iris briefed Anthony on this latest crisis —no shoes meant no Gelsey, as absurd as that seemed to all three of us. He took everything in stride and managed to allay concerns for the time being, dulling the edge of my panic long enough to pull me into a small studio, along with a pianist. I complained of writer's cramp, as I stooped down to force the square peg of my foot into the round hole of my toe shoe.

Anthony hobbled over, announcing his back was ready for "a museum devoted to the spines of those male dancers who had lifted too many ballerinas in their time." He had both of us in stitches as we made ready to run through the balcony pas de deux—by hook or crook, or crutch.

There was a story behind the ballet when it premiered in 1965, the first full-length work by Sir Kenneth MacMillan. He was commissioned to choreograph *Romeo and Juliet* after the company was unable to acquire the Bolshoi production by Leonid Lavrovsky. MacMillan used Sergei Prokofiev's famous score from that Russian production and set the ballet for Lynn Seymour and Christopher Gable, who were certainly more than superb talents. However, the honor of dancing on opening night went to Fonteyn and Nureyev. Those two established stars received the greatest ovation ever given at the Royal Opera House—forty-three curtain calls lasting more than forty minutes—not the easiest act to follow. But Seymour and Gable made the parts their own, as did two couples who followed them —Merle Park and Donald MacLeary, Antoinette Sibley and Anthony Dowell—all names entered somewhere in ballet's glittering firmament.

Romeo had been Anthony's first full-length role. If I were not exactly a starry-eyed Juliet-come-lately, I was sensitive to being an outsider. Before we started to rehearse, I mentioned in passing that I always sympathized with Lynn. She had deserved the opening and been burned. Still, her own performance had been unforgettable. In my mind, her Juliet was more sensual, Margot's more sublime—two poles of interpretation between which a great deal of freedom existed for each succeeding ballerina. One of the amazing things about this ballet was how it lent itself to so many approaches, and yet for me here and now, there could be but one portrayal—one of absolute necessity.

I told Anthony, "Don't expect Lynn's curves from me. She had an instep that was instant drama—her arch alone told a story. Whatever curves we bring into this ballet . . . we're going to have to create between us, from scratch, hopefully, with the circular patterns and the meaning that we build into the steps."

"Or, with plastic surgery," he suggested, innocent as a child in arms. I winced, holding back laughter.

"Very funny, but I'm not budging on this one! I can't move any other way. Besides, you know we've always had more luck trying to solve these mysteries. You're not going to be satisfied until I am, and I'm not until you are." He widened his eyes, enjoying every moment, as he always had in the past, though now, perhaps, with the satisfaction that came with age. He also must have known I was asking for his help. "Let's just see how much I remember," I offered, easing up.

The pianist was no doubt mystified by our exchange and relieved to turn to the familiar melodies of Prokofiev. Anthony and I swept through the scene from Romeo's entrance, and did surprisingly well until we came to two rather awkward lifts at the end. The action here was really straightforward: Romeo tried to kiss her, and Juliet backed away, but then she came back to him, running and leaping backward into his arms, finally coming around for a kiss. It seemed we were being overly cautious with each other.

"Anthony, why don't we just forget the steps for a minute. If Juliet's going to let Romeo kiss her, she's taking an awfully big chance, right? I'm going to have to trust you here, to make this more exciting. Why don't I jump . . . from a bit farther away. When you feel my weight, go with the momentum and swing me back and around . . . so we can find the natural curve of the lift. We don't have anything to lose!"

When he saw the distance I intended to jump, he raised his

eyebrows to his hairline, as if he wanted me to assure him that I would pay our hospital bill. In the language of ballet, I was going to fouetté into an attitude croisé front, as he caught me (if he caught me), and swing my front leg through to low arabesque, then rond de jambe around to the original position, as he turned supporting my back. It was a kamikaze lift, but if we managed to carry it off, the acrobatic risk might throw a light on the drama. Juliet was asking a lot for a kiss.

Before we began, I added, "Now really swing me, as if you might really drop me!" I was tempting fate. Even the pianist, who normally hunched over the keyboard, poised on the edge of his stool. The music was beside the point now. I measured the breath I would need to carry me as far as Anthony's arms, seeing only the fuzzy silhouette of a dark sweat suit. I raced toward him . . . feet moving quicker than thoughts, a sound like wind in my ears.

There was a split second of free fall, and then the sensation of his hands as he took me from behind, just above the waist, his fingers closing as if I had ten new ribs. I felt him sway under me as he shifted his footing and swung me around, while I kept my ribs down and turned out from the heart for all I was worth, the mirrored room revolving around me in a full circle—my back, neck, and head taut, curved like a bow.

I broke away as soon as my feet touched the floor, and ran until he caught the back of my hand. Then I turned to him, ready for the kiss, slow and tender, our lips already threatening to smile with the knowledge we had come to this moment without any loss of limb. Though we had exaggerated the steps, the motivation of the two characters had come to the surface, and hopefully, would be retained as we refined the movement. It entered my mind that we had not actually changed any of the choreography, though that would be for Kenneth MacMillan to decide when he came to rehearsal. We could worry about that later.

Anthony was ecstatic. "That was much better for me! How was it for you?"

"Great! Really great!"

I was amazed by his willingness to explore the material, still nagged as I was by vivid recollections of more than one former partner of mine who lacked the patience to work this way. Here was Anthony who had been dancing the role for more than twenty years, now enthusiastically adapting himself to a new set of demands and a new Juliet, meeting her daring with strength and grace, allowing her to take the initiative exactly as Shakespeare wrote the part. How the words rang true, "Women may fall, when there's no strength in men." I could have kissed him again.

After rehearsal, Anthony accompanied me by tube to a store near the Royal Opera House—a show room for Freed of London, where we received the happy news that my toe-shoe maker had agreed to come out of retirement, at least temporarily. This mysterious craftsman, whom I had never even seen during all of the years he had been making my shoes, was something of a legend. He was known only as "Y-maker," and he was said to be deaf and dumb. The retail sales people had passed on messages of urgent appeal, along with my latest measurements, and he was now suddenly answering the call. I wondered if Anthony's presence had somehow helped bring about this fortunate turn of events.

In the subway again, both of us aiming toward Harrods and home, I told Anthony about the upcoming move to Natasha's flat. He raised his voice over the loud, rumbling noise of the train to inquire, "And how is Mother Russia?"—his affectionate reference to my absent benefactress, whom he had partnered any number of times over the years. As far as I knew, Natasha was in America at the moment with her husband and child. Greg and I would be staying in the flat that had been her first home in the West after her defection in 1970. I remarked how curious I was to see the place, having heard it was gorgeous.

Anthony assured me, "You won't be disappointed."

The train abruptly shrugged to a halt before coming into Knightsbridge station. With the afternoon rush hour already in full force, the two of us had been lucky to find a pair of seats. We were surrounded by a mob of straphangers, their waistlines at my eye level. Several young women struggled heroically not to fall into our laps when the train lurched forward once again. Anthony asked, "Where's Greg today?"

"He's nursing a sick computer."

"What?"

"It's a long story."

Anthony tucked in his chin to loosen the collar of his shirt, saying, "I missed him. I thought he was going to come to rehearsal."

"So did I," I said, feeling a pang of something that made my voice sound shaky. "We've been printing our book on a computer, you see, and he had to take the machine to be fixed. I guess he must have run late."

"Is the book actually finished?"

"Pretty much. Natasha's reading it, or rather, Dina's reading it to her, translating into Russian."

"You mean, you're letting some people read it early?"

"Well, yes. I told you I hoped you'd give me your opinion. You should have a look at it soon, before our editors and lawyers get hold of it. We're still worried it might not be published."

"It's that bad?"

"I'm afraid so."

The train groaned, as if it were another sick machine grinding to a stop. The doors opened, and we knifed through toward daylight. After I picked up a set of ankle weights in the sports department at Harrods, the two of us were ready to part ways. Released from his embrace, I thought he appeared a bit haggard, his face disfigured by shadows invading the road in front of the store. I watched to see if he were going to look back, his figure receding without the usual bounce in his stride. His day had been no easier than mine.

The twilight was magical, even with my cold feet. The ache in my shoulders and neck was like an invisible companion, squeezing me as I ambled along the cobblestone path through the churchyard. If only there were a shortcut through the shortcut, I said to myself, hearing the scuffing sounds of my bag dragging behind me. I stopped to rest when I came to the gardens. From here I could see lights in the flat—he was home. I filled my lungs with the cold air and looked straight up, into the ice blue. The sky was alive. There were a million quiet stars, and a moon frozen like the purest white wing.

The silliest of rhymes from my childhood came into mind: *Star light, star bright . . . first star I see tonight . . .* But my eyes took in the whole sky at once, too vast for picking out any first star tonight. Still, I hoped—enough to count as a wish—that my husband had the foresight to open the couch, where I intended to collapse, just as soon as I climbed the stairs.

In the days that followed I made slow progress, still without shoes that fit, frustrated by my growing collection of blisters and bruises. March was by far the cruelest month, with no thaw in sight for muscles locked in deep freeze. I adapted to the Russian classes by doing the exercises at half tempo, or by changing them altogether, or by simply not doing them at all. The teacher was wise to allow me to work on my own. Her arm positions were lost on me. I would attend to the arms in each ballet only as I created the dramatic shape of the character—from the heart—which would have to come first.

But Juliet's heart was proving more elusive than I had ever imagined possible. There was one question turning over and over in my mind—why on earth did she kill herself? Without an answer to that one, I would never even have a character. Unable to convince myself of a motive, how was I going to convince an audience? I read the play and racked my brain, as the hands of the clock in our living room spun, relentlessly, toward my own anticlimactic ruin. I had seen one famous ballerina who appeared to have a string of orgasms from the balcony pas de deux to the very moment of Juliet's death. That seemed a rather easy way out, not really in keeping with the Shakespeare, though perhaps not quite so far from the choreography.

One night I dozed off, moving mentally between the steps and the story, drifting toward bewilderment. "Take your hands off me!" I shrieked and then bolted upright on the mattress. I was dreaming again. Greg came flying from across the room where he had been working at the computer. He curled his arm around my shoulders and brushed the hair away from my eyes, trying to see if I were able to recognize him. The concern in his face slowly registered. I said, "I won't play dead. . . . Kenneth wanted her dead!"

"What are you saying? Darling, are you awake?"

I let out a laugh, like a funny stutter that came from the back of my throat. "All I remember is that last scene. Kenneth was there, in the tomb. We were rehearsing and he was telling me to play dead. Anthony was sticking up for me, saying, 'Well, maybe she doesn't really have to die until the performance.' But Kenneth said, 'No. That will never do.' Then he tried to push me down. That's when I woke up. I remember him grabbing me by the ear."

"Let me get this straight. You were rehearsing Juliet's death scene with Anthony and Kenneth?"

"Yes. It was a full call . . . a dress rehearsal."

"And you were refusing to play the death? Or were they really trying to make you go through with the suicide?"

"Not me—Juliet!" I stared at him as if he were the one making no sense. "All they wanted me to do was finish the scene so everybody could go home. I think I had the knife in my hand. I had something in my hand. But I couldn't figure out the end, you know, where she stabs herself and falls. It didn't make any sense. So Kenneth was saying just pretend, play dead, don't make such a big deal out of it—do you see?"

"You cause as much trouble when you're asleep as you do when you're awake. I can see that." He bent both knees under him and crouched before me like a sphinx, tossing his head back. His interest was waning, "What about Anthony?"

"He was on my side," I explained.

"Good for him." Greg yawned and let himself drop.

It was evening, but the clock was turned away from me on the end table. I must have been napping for more than an hour. My arm was still asleep from being wedged under me, the skin tingling like prickly heat. I was not about to go back to the dream or that limbo of pounding the walls. I rolled on top of Greg, who was now lying face down, groaning under my weight, his voice muffled by the mattress. My hair, falling forward, became a tent around our two heads. He said, "Shall we go out for a walk and have dinner . . . or try the play again?"

"I just want to go over the tomb scene. Okay?"

"You may not find the answer there," he warned, lifting himself with some effort while I reached for the play. We sat on the open couch, the two of us tangled in sheets and blankets, trying to keep warm. The heat in the flat was never dependable. We went through most of the play by taking turns reading aloud, stopping only to make ourselves coffee and a small meal that burned on the electric stove, neither of us being able to cook.

Shakespeare was not going to yield his secrets easily, especially with me tripping over my tongue, mangling so many of Juliet's beautiful lines. Still, I began to get a feel for her ability to think on her feet. There was more than a simple sweetness to this character. Each word out of her mouth seemed to have a triple meaning, and she always knew exactly what she was saying. When I came to her line, "O, happy dagger!", I turned to Greg, "Now what could be happy about a dagger?"

"What could be happy about her death?" The bluntness of his question startled me, but suddenly I knew what she had to be thinking at the exact moment she plunged that blade into her breast. Not in so many words. My thoughts were a twisted ribbon running back through the whole story. If only I could get the audience to think with her, to feel all that outrage and love —to know what she had come to know, to see the happiness as well as the horror in her resolve.

I just looked up at Greg and said, almost mournfully, "How will I ever get it across to anybody? How will I ever get it across? The families don't even come together at the end of the ballet. Kenneth cut that part of the story . . . the goddamned key to the tragedy! The meaning has been robbed right out of Juliet's grave!"

"Well, you'll have to be a lot smarter than she was, won't you?" His voice was calm, and what he said seemed so right, but somehow I had been thoroughly crushed. I vaulted to my feet and made for the door, which I closed softly behind me, without a word. I went into the stairwell just outside the flat and sat on the steps, with a sinking feeling, as I thought of the ballet and all the despair in the choreography. It was beyond me how I was going to make that ending into what I had in mind now. I wanted her death to have more meaning than a million tears. I wanted the whole world to cry itself out. I wanted to seize that tiny, indestructible grain of joy that she held in her hand as she went falling forever.

When I came back inside, I found Greg where I left him, with a comforter pulled all the way up over his head. The lights, except one on the end table, had been turned off. There were signs of life coming from the television, which we sometimes left on without sound as a night light. The picture flickered up and down with a game of billiards called snooker. Players knocking balls into holes with a stick—endlessly. Soothing for insomniacs, I guessed, turning out the light and then slipping under the covers next to my husband.

He was wide awake, his voice coming out of the dark as my head hit the pillow. "You're all right?"

"I'm fine," I assured him. He found my hands and warmed them between his. I knew something was coming.

"I was thinking about this old parable I heard. Suppose, just suppose you discovered some truth that could work a miracle of peace . . . that could wipe the violence out of people's hearts. Imagine a truth like that. Not magical words but something you could say that would heal the wounds for all the generations to come. Something wondrous! But, there's a catch, you see—as soon as you say the words, as soon as the truth passes your lips, you're doomed . . . condemned to die. That's the only way you can prove those words are true, the only way you can get across —by giving up your life. Do you follow me?"

"You think that Juliet wants to be a martyr?"

"No. I think she learns the truth about love, from all the characters around her who make affection so trivial and deadly," he said with a sharp edge in his voice.

"I think she learns to love the truth," I came back, going him one better, "and she buys the Friar's idea of the marriage as a way to end the feud, and she leads Romeo right along that same path. And that's how I intend to play her—if I ever get the chance." He gave himself up to silence and I followed him, stretching out along the length of his body, circling him with my arms, not sensing any disproportions between us as I laid my head across his chest, and let myself be lulled on by the rhythm of his breathing, knowing he was still awake.

It seemed as if I held the secret of all secrets in my arms—the simplest of all truths, not to be lost between us in the dark.

At three-thirty in the morning I was already pouring myself black coffee in the kitchenette, pulling leftover sole and salad from the fridge, then fumbling with the plug of a new popcorn machine Greg had recently bestowed. By three-forty I was in the bath, aware of the danger of my falling back to sleep and drowning. I could hear the last kernels bursting like plastic bullets from the magic popper. My skin was turning red, and tiny beads of sweat were trickling down my forehead into my eyes. After another ten minutes I was well done.

I made my exit from the tub, grabbed my robe from the towel rack, and left a set of wet tracks from the bath to the living room and back to the kitchen. How was I going to connect Juliet's will to this body? That was the question of the hour. I downed another course of breakfast and tiptoed around collecting my scattered thoughts and clothing, which had been strewn from here to there. I put myself into sweat pants and leaned across the back of an armchair, where I was able to rest my chin on a windowsill and peek out at the dark houses on the other side of the garden, imagining the sleepers inside, still warm in their beds.

At five I perched precariously on the towel rack, with journal in hand and several books piled on the sink. I made some notes for the end of my memoirs and then jotted whatever came into my head as I tried to summon that flash of conviction from last night: "Resist despair with courage and nobility of spirit. Make the families come together over her grave—the audience should be able to see them if I can see them, even though they're not on the stage. Juliet can see into the future—use that ill-divining soul of hers to set up the tragedy."

An hour later I nearly fell from the throne as Greg came stumbling into my chamber. He took one look at me and the sink, and muttered in a sleepy voice, "Oh, is this the lending library? I must have gotten off on the wrong floor . . . I'm sorry!" It would have been hard to say which was more stark—the picture I made, scooping books into my arms like a madwoman, or his nakedness as he tried to help, bumping his head as he went down to retrieve my pen on its way out to the English Channel.

The hilarity this morning verged on hysteria. We were still

laughing as I prepared for class and he returned to the computer, which we were now calling "that dreaded box" because it
had "swallowed" the only copy of our rough draft of the last
chapter. He would have to type over everything, a chore I
would gladly have done but for the fact I was no better at typing
than I was at cooking—worse, in fact. I had never typed a word
in my life. While he carried on about the box "spitting out those
pages," I tried to close my ears, bracing on the floor with my feet
tucked under the couch for leverage, opening myself up into a
kind of bodily prayer.

The sun had splashed the walls of the flat by the time I left
him, at half past seven, with his promise to meet after rehearsal.
I lucked out with a taxi before going to the subway. My spirits
were as high as ever. Today was David Howard's first day of
teaching and I was relieved—if only to think my thigh muscles
might unlock long enough for me to really get into the air. I
needed a class that would bring the disjointed parts of me into
some semblance of harmony.

Arriving early, I found the dressing room empty and went to
work sewing my shoes. Nothing I was wearing seemed to match:
a pink sweater. A lavender head band. Sweat pants and leg
warmers washed too many times for any colors to survive. Giving up the idea of changing, I made another little foray into
Juliet's psyche, writing again in my notebook: "Why does she
fall for Romeo? She sees beneath the surface, into that heart of
his. Paris may be better looking—a real knockout according to
her mother and nurse. But Romeo offers something that's far
more valuable, something that may even last forever. It is the
quality of her movement that must reveal the quality of her love
—exposing those around her!"

Class was scheduled for ten-fifteen. At ten I entered the studio. I chose a spot where sunlight came streaming down from
one of the windows above, glancing off the mirror, making a
bright puddle at my feet. Catching sight of my double, I thought
for a second I might walk away without her, leaving her behind
to work in my place. Why was it such things never really happened? Turning away, I put her out of my mind. There was no
wavering as I started moving, my purpose suddenly clear—

Something wondrous, I said to myself, recalling my husband's words.

Other dancers took places around me. Mostly men. Most of them younger than me. Anthony introduced David as somebody who had danced for the Royal Ballet in the past and since become "a major teaching force in New York." I thought of the forces in New York, and thanked God for the Atlantic Ocean. David appeared slightly nervous as he moved to the barre with all eyes following him, a touch of the Harlequin in his pastel sweat suit as well as his gestures. "We'll start in second and take three grands pliés releasing the arms to the fifth . . . demi-plié and then change into the first." He demonstrated in somewhat exaggerated fashion, emphasizing transitions rather than poses, allowing dancers and pianist to pick up a tempo from the singsong cadence of his voice. The accent was British.

"Left hand . . . on the barre. Arm one . . . and two."

And so it went for a full hour and a half. At one point, as I tried a particularly fiendish pirouette, David noticed the tension in my hands, which turned into a pair of claws each time I went around. I was holding myself rigid, unable to release any of those muscles down through the elbow, wrist, and fingers; the more I tried, the more frazzled I became, until the floor seemed to give way under me. My focus was in the wrong place entirely.

"Think of your sides, dear, and when you turn to the left, resist to the right," he advised me. "Let all of the joints contribute to the energy of the turn—rotate around the spine, and resist in the opposite direction. Use your sides—replace one with the other."

It worked like magic. Suddenly I had control of the movement and the mirror; that impossible turn now appeared completely effortless. An almost perfect illusion. Like I was spinning off an invisible string, at the same time resisting its pull. What looked to be a clever trick was actually closer to a science. Technical insights such as these were bringing about a revolution in ballet; the form had already changed dramatically as dancers became better athletes—if not necessarily better artists. I could now whip through that pirouette with hands freed. But it was only a pirouette—and certainly not Juliet's pirouette. At least, not yet.

Class broke up with a polite round of applause for David. Merle Park hurried by me, saying with high-pitched enthusiasm, "He certainly gets you going, doesn't he?" David and I went to the cafeteria, a cheerful dungeon in the basement. I let him know how grateful I was that he was here. To have a teacher who worked this way, even for a week, could mean a world of difference. David knew what I was up against—he knew my body about as well as anyone.

As we sat with our trays in the dining room, catching up and finishing a light lunch, he asked me, "So you don't miss New York then? Not at all?" I could almost see question marks dancing in the air.

"It really comes down to tradition. Europe is where I belong, at least for now. There's support in the theatre for what I do. It's not like I'm speaking a foreign language, I mean, in the studio. I don't know how you manage back there!"

"Well, of course, it's quite different. Dancers in America are more physical. They work harder—more energy in the body."

"Sure, but directed where? The schools are turning out more and more perfect acrobats. How many great Giselles have you seen lately? How many dancers do you know who can hold the stage for more than thirty seconds? There are so many promising talents who go nowhere, who turn into mediocrities. They're used up, then thrown away. You've seen it a thousand times. It's just so tragic!"

I could see David's eyes batting away jet lag. He was momentarily flustered. His brow creased, adding wrinkles to a face that was surprisingly smooth for a man now in his forties. My words were almost a taunt, coming so close to home. I loved playing devil's advocate with David. By challenging him, I was really challenging myself, trusting his talent to deal with my extremes. He had been a staunch ally for years, even putting his reputation on the line during those times when being my friend had carried a real stigma.

"At least American dancers," he came back at me, measuring his words, "have enough quality in their movement, so if they find the emotion, they can put it into the steps."

"But there is no quality without emotion . . . and not just any old emotion any which way. Nobody is teaching them how

to act, how to create a character . . . how to shape that emotion with the body to really say something. They're getting by
with looks and agility, and maybe a dash of personality thrown
in. Dramatic flair, the critics call it. Look at Cynthia Harvey.
She's here. I can see how she's benefited from your teaching—
more fluid, more graceful. She was a good dancer even when
she was with ABT, but she needs to go the next step to be—"

"Oh, but that must come from her wanting to be that good,"
he got in edgewise. "She must want it!"

"I can want the moon, but unless somebody teaches me how
to get there, I'm gonna be stuck right here. None of the great
teachers from the past—name whomever you want—none of
them left behind anything but calisthenics. There's nothing but
that hollow form. How do you fill it? Where's the poetry? It
takes a hell of a lot more than a pretty face . . . or triple joints
. . . or wishing it were so. How do you teach someone to be an
artist? Tell me that."

"That takes time," he conceded, as unflappable as ever.

"Speaking of which"—I waved the little pitchfork with which
I had been spearing a salad, and got up abruptly to leave—"I'd
better get going. I'll see you in rehearsal, one o'clock in the
Garden Studio. Right?" He repeated the time and rose to hug
me. The next thing I knew I was rushing off to the dressing
room, thinking I never gave David a moment of peace. No
sooner had he arrived than I had besieged him and pulled him
into my routine. The work was like quicksand, a bottomless pit
for anyone who shared it with me.

On my way upstairs, I ran into Anthony coming out of his
office. He was with an older man in a sport jacket and turtleneck
sweater. Distinguished. A mane of silver hair and slightly darker
mustache. His eyes glistened as they appraised me. It was Kenneth MacMillan. He seemed different somehow than I remembered—softer, calmer, more composed. His exclamations of surprise suggested he might be thinking the same thing about me.
He put a finger under my chin as if to turn my face into the light,
while Anthony offered glowing testimony about my condition
and our work on the ballet. All very pleasant.

"You look so . . . well," Kenneth remarked.

He had been Artistic Director for the Royal Ballet from 1970

to 1977 and was still Principal Choreographer. In 1984 he became Associate Director at American Ballet Theatre, dividing
his time between New York and London. With the management
of ABT disclaiming my existence, I was cautious around Kenneth and more than mildly astonished he was being as cordial as
he was.

While the three of us huddled, a brief exchange passed between Anthony and Kenneth. It seemed they were expecting
me to dance Juliet for the opening in the spring season—April
11, which was five days earlier than I had anticipated. I had
mistaken the date and would be losing five rehearsals. There
was no one to blame but myself, and the distress coiled in my
stomach as we continued trading pleasantries.

Ready to break away, I turned to Kenneth. "Time's running
out. I hope you'll be coming in to rehearse soon, so we can get
back to old times. You remember all the fun we used to
have. . . ." I said lightly, referring to our first meeting in the
studio six years ago. My Juliet was not the same willful child she
had been back then; the sooner Kenneth saw what I was doing,
the sooner I would know if the new interpretation was accept-
able to him.

He always had the final word.

"Yes, I'll be in soon . . . to catch up," he intoned wearily. His
face hinted he had seen all the *Romeo and Juliet* rehearsals he
really needed in this lifetime, though he was not putting me off,
not entirely. I headed toward the dressing rooms, sensing a mild
rush of anxiety, though actually rather pleased with the prospect of Kenneth's aid. On the one hand, there were so many
questions I had about that choreography that he could answer;
but on the other, what a nightmare if he should tear apart my
Juliet—I might be the one needing the tomb.

That last thought brought a smile as I walked into the dressing
room for another go at those shoes. I found the répétiteur,
Monica Mason, who would be handling the rehearsal today, and
greeted her with apologies for my clutter on the floor. She
seemed unperturbed, standing royally upright by the basin,
wearing gray sweat pants and a short-sleeved, black leotard.
The outfit accentuated a powerfully compact figure she had
used to great advantage on the stage. Monica was from South

Africa. A strong, patrician face set off by waves of salt and pepper hair. Sensitive, almond-shaped eyes. I had first seen her perform in the late sixties when the company, unsurpassed at that time, had toured New York.

"You're looking so well, Gelsey!" she exclaimed.

"Must be the weather," I said, beginning to wonder if there were not a conspiracy behind all the compliments coming my way.

Monica came across as being highly proper and initially somewhat remote, radiating a distant warmth that I had trouble reconciling with my memories of characters I had seen her create. I reminded her of the performance she gave as one of the harlots who cavort with Romeo and his pals in the marketplace. Whatever the rationale for such an unlikely character in the ballet, her portrayal had been spectacular. With the power from her torso and some extraordinary footwork, she had whirled Nureyev's Romeo all over the stage.

I said, "I'll never forget. You made her into a real hussy—a wench! Dancers who do that role today usually look like they've just stepped off Forty-second Street and wandered into the theatre by mistake. So many ballerinas are now trying to cultivate that sort of look for every role. Saves them from having to worry about any other characterization, doesn't it?"

"Oh, yes," she concurred, the mood lifting.

We laughed and traded stories about Nureyev and Tudor. When Monica noticed the time I was having with my feet, she suggested I talk with Jennifer Penney, one of the veteran principals in the company. "You might get some New Skin from Jenny for those blisters. I'm not sure what it is exactly, but it works." Jenny was the expert in the foot department. She had been threatening to retire from the stage because of problems she had getting toe shoes to fit. Like me, she had to take each new shoe apart and then sew it back together, just to make the shoes stay on our feet for the one or two days they could be worn. It seemed the craft of making shoes, passed down through the years, was in trouble—and so were we.

Just before one, Monica headed for the door, saying she would see me in the studio. I was still trying to get myself organized with needle and thread. No sooner had she gone than she came

back, saying she had forgotten something. She hurriedly re-
trieved a notebook tucked among the personal belongings she
had stored away. "The book of secrets," she announced mysteri-
ously, seeing that I had watched her, and then she vanished out
the door again. I was intrigued by that book. As répétiteur,
Monica was the guardian of Kenneth's choreography—were
those his secrets?

Whatever may have been in her book, she certainly did know
Kenneth's production, and a great deal was going to depend on
our rapport in the studio. That exchange would either encourage or undermine the exchanges with the rest of the cast. I
had a few misgivings, but I was grateful this was not a staging for
which I would learn the steps from a notator or choreologist,
even the best of whom often mistake their little symbols and
stick figures for dancers. The fabric of a ballet is utterly fragile,
and the methods used for recording its production are far from
perfect on paper, or even on film. With Monica, I might focus on
that fragility of things behind and beyond the steps, if all went
well.

Two hours of traffic onstage and four days in the life of Juliet
had to be covered in approximately thirty rehearsals. Scenes
were scheduled out of order depending on the availability of the
dancers, who usually rehearsed several ballets each season. Today Anthony and I would be returning to the balcony for a half
hour, and then he would leave and I would go through my first
pas de deux with Paris. The challenge was to keep my eye on
character. Unlike the rehearsal for a play, where actors have
already learned their lines and look to the director for guidance
with dialogue and motivation, a dancer in a ballet is constantly
occupied with steps, and only rarely these days does a choreographer or répétiteur guide the acting process. Rather than a
breakdown of the plot, the dancer is more likely to hear an
ongoing string of physical cues.

Coming into the studio and seeing Monica, I was suddenly
reminded of a rehearsal I had called to a halt back in 1980. She
had been showing me how Juliet handled a cape, which had to
be picked up from the floor, then flung around the shoulders
with a sweeping flourish as Juliet began her desperate flight to
the Friar in the last act. I had been trying for an effect attributed

to Galina Ulanova, the heroic Russian Juliet who once inspired Fonteyn. But I had become paralyzed by my own frustration that day. Unable to master the moment, I had taken flight myself, expressing regrets for not being able to continue and leaving Monica in dismay. Was that why she had seemed so distant at first in the dressing room?

I nodded hello and pulled on a practice skirt.

David took a seat to observe; and Anthony made a wisecrack about another frolic in the garden, referring to the pas de deux under Juliet's balcony. It actually was a frolic. With all the high-minded ideals I had borrowed from the play, I could not afford to forget that exhilarating speed with which she was swept away, the heedless wings of her youth. Coaching myself while the pianist found his place in the score, I made up my mind to stay ahead of the music here, to work against Prokofiev in a certain sense and sustain tension. If I were to fall behind, I would lose a crucial element of surprise. There had to be a more volatile side to Juliet's passion, as well as buoyancy and playfulness. I was not about to succumb to Prokofiev's heavy hand—or my own.

First came the pirouette. After watching Romeo's solo, I was to rush toward him and stop on a dime, whirling through a double or triple turn, going another half to end up supported from the back and opening out my upper body. Then rond de jambe en l'air, as it were, swinging my right leg forward, to the side, and back, almost like a pendulum, with him lifting me from behind suddenly as that same leg swept around again. During our first rehearsal, I had only gone through the motions. Now I would have to make the whole thing into one continuous gesture. A single beautiful thought passing between us.

But what brutally painstaking efforts were required for us mortals to create such a thought! Juliet used words like "boundless" and "infinite" to describe her love. How was the body to describe anything so vast? What shape was infinite? My hands were free as I spun again and again into the pirouette, as if I might simply reach out for the answers. Feeling Anthony take hold from behind, I stopped short. I looked up at him and said, "If you can push me down harder at the hips, I can get a curve going in my upper body. I'm telling you how my love is boundless. It encompasses the whole world. But you have to push down for me to lift and turn out the heart. I need that leverage . . . otherwise I'm stuck when the leg goes round on the rond de jambe."

"Like this?" he asked, still somewhat tentative with his hands, thinking perhaps he might hurt me if he actually put all his strength into it.

"Harder and lower," I urged him.

"You're kidding!"

"Push me right into the floor!"

He raised those eyebrows as if to say, "There's an idea." As he increased pressure below my waist, I had something to work against, resisting with all the muscles in my back, so I was able to lift my torso as high as Juliet might ever imagine. With both palms upturned, I was holding on for dear life, robbing time in a way as I waited now for the music to catch up with me. It really made a difference like day and night—that open heart would be visible to the last row in the balcony. The mirror proved the point for us, and Monica approved. There was a shared sense of excitement as we prepared to piece it all together.

"Great! Let's try it," I said, relieved for all of us. I launched myself again, spinning into Anthony's waiting hands. That one moment seemed to give us the whole scene. This time as I came down from the lift with his arm curled around the front of my waist, he quickly turned me into him and I lunged from side to side—each time allowing my hand to sweep across my brow, and fall, going with his momentum almost to the floor—back and forth, right and left, like a terrific, never-ending swoon.

The feeling was euphoric, but the arms were wrong.

"Perhaps a trembling quality," Monica suggested from her chair at the side. Then she uncurled one of her arms to show me what she meant. I had some doubts, but when I repeated the step, my arms and hands fell into place, and so did Juliet's vulnerability. Suddenly there was another layer, another aspect of her personality—perfectly balancing those other qualities I had been reaching for. It was as if her strength gave rise to a more fragile nature—she was barely able to endure the burden of this love.

Anthony, who was really the one who made it work with his

partnering, seemed thoroughly delighted. I was even more so, knowing I could count on Monica for the help I needed here.

The clock had run out on my Romeo. He collected his things quickly and brushed my cheek with a kiss on his way out. Waiting to start the scene with Paris, I caught myself staring down at my hands, which were covered with white dust from the rosin used for shoes. Rubbing the palms together as if to keep warm, I glanced over and saw David, still sitting quietly near the piano. *She must want it,* I heard his voice say again, somewhere in the back of my mind, where our conversations always continued. How much did anyone really want it?

Paris was being danced by a young principal, Julian Hosking, who certainly cut the handsome figure appropriate for the part: high cheekbones; a square jaw; long, blond hair. A believable match for any Juliet to judge by his looks alone. He also possessed considerable talent and a great desire to learn from this experience. His willingness was obvious from the outset, but I was going to need him to go beyond himself and his previous renderings of the role. As the spurned suitor, he would provide another measure of Juliet's mettle, testing her resolve to honor the secret marriage with Romeo against her family's wishes. As with many younger dancers, Julian's partnering was going to require special attention.

We started with a pas de deux set in Juliet's bedroom. Almost before we were even underway, I interrupted the music, saying for all to hear, "You don't mind if I think out loud for a minute, do you? There seems to be a lot going on here. Romeo has just gone out my window. . . . We've already been married and he's been exiled for killing my cousin . . . and my mother and father are bringing Paris right into my bedroom to tell me I'm supposed to marry him. . . . It's all been arranged. So what am I doing? The Friar has me and Romeo hoping to go public with the marriage and put an end to the fighting, right? But it's too early to say anything to anybody so I have to play along. I'm pretending I'm in mourning, aren't I?"

Cutting off the soliloquy, I turned to Monica and shot my question to her. "This moment with Paris seems pretty limp to me. What exactly are we supposed to be saying?"

Having just come out of a spiraling promenade, I was to lean forward at an angle with him supporting me from the waist, as if I were suddenly overcome, almost fainting away. I seemed to drop down like the most ludicrous shrinking violet—at the mercy of Paris and fate, and all the forces swirling around me. The character would lose integrity with such a haphazard flop of arms and head. How could there be anything so arbitrary in Juliet's movement?

"Well, she might go into a mental haze," said Monica, speculating. "As you say, there is so much going on at once."

"No," I said without hesitation, "she's thinking too hard to go into a haze. Juliet knows her own mind—she's not some spoiled child. The Friar has given her that sleeping potion so she already has a plan to get out of this nightmare." Turning my gaze to Julian, I said pointedly, "We're not married yet! So don't come so close on the promenade. I need enough room to—"

"You know," Monica jumped in, "I think . . . it must be the touch! His touch makes you . . . cringe!"

"Oh, that's good," I agreed, wheeling back toward her. "It really is as if he's making me sick. If I bring the arms in just a little, I'll be nauseous instead of limp. I'm trying to control my feelings and manipulate the scene without looking at him or my family, without dropping my head. I'd rather die than be stained marrying this guy!" Julian himself seemed to cringe slightly, as if he might be taking some of this too personally. Gripping his arm, I put him at ease, saying to Monica, "That is in the play. She actually says as much to the Friar."

"I'll have to read it again. It's been such a long time," she confessed.

We were moving along briskly. Monica was very practical, offering suggestions that helped unsnarl bits and pieces of the action. Between the two of us, Julian was lured into the story. As I continued to promenade, he hesitated, as if sensing he was not getting through, saying, "I'm trying to reach you here."

"You mean you're really trying to speak to me?"

"Yes, I'm trying to speak to you," he asserted.

"Then all I have to do is avert my eyes and incline my head—as if Juliet were trying to shut out your voice."

Another moment quickly fell into place, but we had some difficulty with three lifts traveling toward the window. Each time Paris put her down, Juliet reached gingerly for that place where Romeo had departed. Here Julian lacked the smoothness and weight in his partnering for me to fulfill the shape. He was too brittle and timid, as if playing an attitude rather than creating any real depth. David came in from the sidelines to demonstrate, saying, "Always when we go down, we're working the level of the body up. And when we go up, we're pushing down, out and away, through the body and away from the floor. You have to give Gelsey all the resistance she needs to move against you."

Julian made some progress, but I still felt like I was moving against the air. I stopped in the middle of a lift and faced him. Then I asked him to place his hands on my chest just below the collarbone. He complied, looking somewhat bewildered. I said, "Now push me, as hard as you can. Don't be afraid. Just push!" Overcoming his reluctance, he exerted himself, warily at first, and then with all his might. As he pushed with his arms against my chest, I pressed forward, slowly, forcing him back across the floor. We may have looked like contestants in a martial arts duel, but the intention was quite different.

"Now that's how hard you're going to have to work to get at the quality the scene needs," I said. "There's no other way. Believe me. You have to want it that badly, as much as you might want to throw me across the room!" That seemed to get a reaction, so I continued, "It's not brawn or brute strength. I'm using an energy pattern that keeps me moving under you. Imagine one of da Vinci's horses pulling a load up a hill—all of the muscles in your back have to be working, not just those arms. Let's try again. I promise, Julian, I'll shut up as soon as we get it right."

As we pushed back and forth taking turns, he began to see what I was going for. Then we took pains to phrase the lifts in such a way as to seem unnaturally quiet, as if we were generating an eerie sort of silence with our motion, like an evil spell that now held Juliet under its power. The mirrored walls moved up and down around me, continuously, and my feet found the wood beneath me without a sound. I heard Julian whisper, "It's never been like this before!"

After the third lift and a struggle downstage, I was to break away from Paris and rush to the window upstage, where my dilemma would be illuminated by my stillness: Romeo was outside that window in front of me, and my family was behind me. I would cradle a perfect world between my forehead and breast, and try to hold it there for an eternity, while waiting again for the music to find its moment. Resigned, I would walk, trancelike, arms glued to my sides, back downstage, where my dance with Paris would resume, ready to consent to marry him—inwardly seething, and yet prepared to play along once again.

As there was no set, everything had to be manufactured by imagination. The curtained window was the back of a metal folding chair. The other characters who were absent—Father, Mother, and Nurse—would also have to be imagined, standing near an imaginary bed at the center of the studio. The light in the room seemed hazy. It had to be early afternoon, but I had lost track of time. The scene in my mind took place in the evening; there were long shadows, like the bars of a cell, everywhere.

No sooner had I arrived at the window than I heard Julian coming from behind, too fast. I turned on him just as he was bending over to take hold of the hem of my skirt, preparing to gather it in for a kiss.

"What's my back telling you?" I asked him.

"Your back?" His expression was a curious blank.

"You should be getting a pretty strong whiff of something that says 'stay away'!" I explained.

Monica added, "What Gelsey means is you need to take more time and approach her more . . . carefully."

"There has to be something between us besides space," I told him. "What are you doing here?"

"I'm trying to be kind to you at this point," he replied.

"What kind of a person is Paris?" I asked, trying another tack.

"Well, I think he has his way with women," he said with a sheepish grin. "He likes to chase them."

"But you don't quite have your way with me, do you? Look, you've done nothing wrong other than treat me as your possession. I'm like another little ornament for you, aren't I? That sort of love is awfully childish, and even corrupt, but my anger is going to force you to respond differently—so there has to be some sign of that response in your movement. Otherwise, we have nothing to shape between us but the goddamned air!"

"You mean, you make me feel something for the first time?"

"Exactly," I said, breathing a sigh of relief. "Paris must be capable of love, like everyone else in the world, and Juliet is going to bring out the best in him—even if it kills her."

He seemed almost shocked. "Oh, that's fantastic, Gelsey! I love that idea."

"Well, don't take it too literally," I told him.

Our time was up, but we ran through the scene again, even with dancers wandering in for the next rehearsal. Julian was on the mark this time. Monica added a final touch, helping with the placement of my head, and the three of us were ready to call it a day. We thanked David, and the pianist, and each other. Julian planted kisses on both my cheeks, and Monica said, "Today went quite well, I thought."

"Not a moment wasted," I agreed.

Packing my bag on the floor, I looked up and found my husband standing over me, smiling at my surprise.

"How long have you been here?" I asked. His coat was unbuttoned, and his scarf came swinging down between us as he stooped to lend a hand.

"I watched most of it from outside the door," he said, offering no opinion.

He took the bag, and I arranged to have the pianist make a tape of the score for me. Until the performance, I was going to listen to the music every night, visualizing my movements and making a million alterations. Greg followed me as I hurried back to the dressing room to change my shoes and get my coat, and then I followed him out of the building, the two of us exiting like a pair of Keystone Cops. I was relieved to be outside, even with an assault of noise and exhaust from the roadway. The air was raw, and the sky had turned into a chalky overcast.

Walking to the tube station, Greg grabbed my arm and said, "What I love is the way you ask everyone so many questions. It makes it seem . . . as if you're the only one who doesn't know what you're doing."

"I swear to you . . . it's my only gift."

The rest of the afternoon was taken up with costume fittings in the wardrobe department near the opera house in Covent Garden. Greg waited patiently, reading our manuscript while I was measured and pinned, and transformed into a Juliet manikin. Afterward, we picked up a new batch of toe shoes and caught a cab to a steak house in Kensington, where we met David for dinner. That was six o'clock. By eight I was back in the flat for a massage. A young Scotsman set up his table in the living room, and I gave myself up to his soothing hands for two hours, allowing my mind to wander between alternating sensations of anguish and bliss, the latter winning out.

When the masseur departed, I took an inventory of my body. There was some swelling in the ankles and the area of the metatarsals. My right foot looked like something out of a science fiction movie. That was normal. Nothing to worry about yet. The massage had given me back some of the flexibility in my right hip, where chronic bursitis constantly threatened to put an end to my turnout, if not my career. Soon I would be ready for my wheelchair; but tomorrow I would spend an hour or two with the company's physical therapist, bathing the trouble spots with laser rays and ultrasound—everything that modern medicine could throw at me.

An old-fashioned ice pack would do for the moment. Greg came out of the bedroom, where he had been hiding out during my massage, and found me going at the freezer with my hammer—the trays were frozen solid and stuck inside the icebox, which looked like it had not been defrosted since the days of Pavlova. There were now pieces of chipped ice all over the floor of the kitchen, melting into treacherous puddles. One slip was all I needed—a thought I could see pass across my husband's face as he stood looking down at my feet.

"Have you been to the zoo today?" he asked.

"What?"

"It looks like an elephant stepped on your foot—either that, or it's going wonky on you."

"Funny," I said, not terribly amused. "It's just a little circulation problem. Nothing serious."

He scooted around me and took over with my hammer. Before I knew what hit me, he had me lying on the open couch, where he wrapped a towel full of ice around my ankle. Then he sank down onto the mattress beside me and asked, "You really think you're going to hold up?"

He looked tired, his blue eyes rimmed with a pinkness that came from staring into the computer too many hours.

"I have so far," I replied, feeling it was my place to reassure him. "Why?"

"Well, you don't have to go through with this, you know." His voice sounded strange, and he was avoiding my eyes.

"What are you talking about? Of course I have to go through with this! Why the hell have we been doing all this work for the past two years?"

"I'm only saying you mustn't feel like you have no choice. You don't have to dance again . . . and you might keep that in mind. I can see how you're driving yourself. You've got a book coming out that's going to make the health of dancers into a real issue. So how do you think it's going to look if you drop dead before it gets published?"

"I've been dead for several years!" I caught myself, lowering the decibel level of my voice as I saw his point and the concern in his face. "How will it look if I'm not dancing? Who do you think will believe me?"

He slowly turned his head away and said nothing.

"Listen, this is the best work I've ever done in my life. It's the first time I've walked into the studio and really felt like I might be in control. Do you know what that means to me? Do you know what a joy that is? All of these ideas we talk about are coming to life. I love this character. I'm putting the best of myself into her . . . the best of us, I hope."

I was down to a whisper. I saw a faint smile flicker across his lips as I finished off, "When I can't go on, you'll be the first to know. I promise you."

"It's a deal," he said. Suddenly on his feet, he added, "I really do know how much you love this work, but don't expect me to sit by quietly if I see either of us going over the edge."

He retreated to the bedroom while I sat on the living-room floor and treated my shoes with floor wax, dabbing it on the soles with a toothbrush. The flat soon filled with noxious fumes from the wax so I had to open up all of the windows and put on my coat. This was another ritual performed many times over the years. Greg stuck his head into the room long enough to gag and make a face, asking me, "Was it something I said?"

Later, just before midnight, he ventured out to make some long-distance phone calls from a table in the living room. We stayed in touch with our families and a few friends in the States. I usually let Greg do most of the talking, not wanting homesickness to distract me, and not really knowing how to answer the question "how are you?" without running up the bill outrageously. Tonight, however, I had to make a call I had been putting off. I had given Antony Tudor most of my book, and I wanted to hear his reaction. This was an occasion I had been delaying, not so much because I feared his review, but because his voice always called up such bittersweet memories for me.

It was the faraway voice of an old man, who answered that first question, "I'm tired, Gelsey. How are you?"

There were long silences during which I imagined his bald head and chiseled profile. The mind behind that brow still possessed a savage wit. He was enthusiastic about the memoirs, bestowing his compliments and offering a wry comment, "I was enthralled. I knew you'd tell the whole story, but they won't make it into a movie. They'll never be able to cast it!" The thought of a film seemed a great amusement, and he repeated his contention that it would never be made. I was happy to agree.

Then he surprised me with a strange request. For some time, we had been talking about the possibility of my staging *The Leaves Are Fading*, a ballet he had choreographed for me in 1975. He asked me if I would mind if he were to suggest the idea of my "taking care of his ballet," as he put it, to the management of ABT. I was dumbstruck at first. We had previously considered several other companies—the very idea of American Ballet Theatre seemed outlandish, even with his position there.

"But, Mr. Tudor, they'd never let me do it. . . ."

"I know," was all he said.

Suddenly, I felt that familiar twinkle of his, and found myself overcome by laughter. It was all I could do to put two words together. "Good luck," I said, encouraging him to make whatever mischief he pleased.

I called him "Mr. Tudor" out of habit and longstanding respect. He was one person I knew attached the same meaning to the word "quality" as I did. Why was the quality of dance now in jeopardy? That was the question we always seemed to come back to. He had created his first ballet in 1931, and seen the better part of this century. I went on about the disregard of mime and drama by my generation; and he made an observation that would trouble me for the rest of the night and many nights to come.

"Why do you think," I asked him again, "so few dancers are bringing quality into the dance?"

"Because they are no longer trying to become human beings," was the reply.

I was stung by the resignation in his tone and wanted to make him take back those words. Though I accepted the truth of what he said, I recoiled from the insinuation there was nothing to be done. That was simply old age talking. The phone seemed to go dead for a second. All I could hear was the sound of my breath in the receiver while I tried to think of something more to say.

"Hello? Are you still there?" I asked.

"Yes. I'm here," he said, his voice fading.

"Someday we're going to have a talk about teaching."

"You never say die, do you, Gelsey?"

"Never. . . . My Juliet is a real gadfly, and I'm becoming a little Mr. Tudor in the studio by terrorizing everybody with a lot of the Shakespeare. But I am getting them to think with me."

"Good for you! They'll get used to it."

"The problems start in the classroom. Everyone seems to believe the Russians have the answers, even here—"

"Shame on them," he cut in, "for putting the Russians first! You set them straight, do you hear me?"

There was a wave of static on the line that made me pause. "I know Merle Park would love to have you come over to work with the kids, but she seems to think you'd never come."

"That's true," he laughed, "I never would. I like a life of no responsibility, and you will too, in fifty years. . . . When do you open?"

I told him the date, adding, "Too soon."

"Plenty of time. . . . You're going to lay golden eggs—aren't you, Gelsey?"

"Once you know there are golden eggs to be laid, it's so hard to settle for silver or bronze. It's an act of conscience. I know that you know what I mean. I'm just afraid—"

"Don't be," he cut in again, sounding almost fierce, the way I remembered him. I motioned to Greg, who had listened to my side of the conversation, staring at me intently from across the room.

"Do you want a word with my husband before we say good-bye?"

"No. I'm afraid . . . he'll chew my ear off," he quipped.

"I think of you all the time, Mr. Tudor."

"And I think of you."

"I'll call when it's over."

"Good," was the last thing he said.

The days seemed to be getting closer together, blurring into one marathon rehearsal. March was drawing to a close, but there was not yet any hint of spring in London. My impression of the city was limited for the most part to what I could see from a taxi; and more often than not, my mind was traveling on ahead of me. The outside world was reduced to mental snapshots and occasional headlines. I was only vaguely aware of the hostilities between America and Libya being reported in the press. With both the ballet and final editing of the book hanging over me, I had little time to ask myself if I were going over the edge.

When David Howard returned to New York, I was left to fend for myself in class, with several Royal Ballet teachers and a German guest, Jurgen Schneider, who was on loan from ABT. To escape this rotation, I took a number of private classes with Oliver Symons, an unassuming teacher who offered the flexibility and focus I needed. Rehearsals continued with Monica Mason and with another répétiteur, Donald MacLeary, one of the great dancers from the company's past. He took over on some of my solo rehearsals and helped me and Anthony refine each pas de deux.

There were everyday miseries like fatigue and anxiety, sometimes overwhelming with as little sleep as I was getting. But they were always offset by the sense of purpose I found in the studio. My joy seemed to return, full force, during those moments of intensity that gave rise to the simplest gestures; and in the end that simplicity would enable me to tell the story, which was by far the greatest challenge.

"I want Juliet's death to be a protest," I told Julian before rehearsal, "against all of the corruption and violence going on around her." We were waiting in a studio at the back of the opera house, preparing to go over the first family scene in the last act. I was lecturing again. "The Friar is the one who encourages her to shape this love into something beautiful, in this world . . . not the next! He guides her, and she guides Romeo, and their marriage is supposed to strike a balance between passion and reason, so the families—"

"But the Friar is a villain, isn't he?" Julian asked, his brows furrowing.

"Is he?"

"Well, it's his fault—he's the one who gives her the potion," he argued.

"How can you blame him? What about those families that are slaughtering each other? Who really causes the tragedy?"

"I never really thought about it," he said. "You see, we don't usually have time to work like this."

"I know," I told him.

The rehearsal started promptly under Monica's guidance. She had been consulting with Kenneth MacMillan on the outside to get approval for the initiative I had taken previously, but since he had not yet attended any of the rehearsals in person, I still felt like I was proceeding with a dark cloud overhead. Looking up at the clock high on the wall, I thought of that odd expression Greg used, *Darkness at noon.* The title of a book, he told me.

It was twelve o'clock.

I made a quick dash to the rosin box, like Groucho Marx on the run with his cigar, and then sped to the center to start my scene with Juliet's Nurse, played by Gerd Larsen, a British-Norwegian dancer who, in 1938, had originated the role of the French Ballerina in Tudor's *Gala Performance,* with his short-

lived company, The London Ballet. As principal mime and senior teacher at the Royal, she did a number of character roles.
She had been doing this scene as the Nurse ever since the ballet
first opened in 1965, and her performance had not changed in
any drastic way since the days she enacted the part opposite
Fonteyn.

Gerd and several of us "older girls" often shared a dressing
room and daily gossip. The others were Monica, Merle, and the
renowned ballerina Antoinette Sibley (who once entertained us
with some amusing ideas on the design of a bed where she
planned to spend her retirement). Gerd was stately in manner,
with a wonderfully expressive mouth and hint of the Scandina-
vian background in her features. Her Nurse was a full-figured,
earthy creature, who bustled and fussed about such that my
Juliet sometimes had to grab her shoulders to get her undivided
attention.

"Watcha like me to do then?" Gerd asked me when I first
proposed a few changes. "Just tell me, Gelsey. I don't mind."

"When I'm on the bed here pretending to be asleep and you
enter to tell me that my parents are coming in with Paris, you
don't actually have to wake me up, do you? After all, Juliet
would recognize the Nurse's footsteps, wouldn't she?"

"Yes, I see," she said, sounding uncertain.

"So you don't need to shake me. I'm actually wide awake, and
the pace of your footsteps tells me that trouble is on the way."
She was blinking as if to punctuate my sentences. "You know
Romeo and I spent our wedding night in this bed, and you are
my ally, after all, so I don't have to pretend with you."

"Yes, yes, all right," she chirped.

Monica added from her seat at the side, "There should be a
closeness between the two of you here."

The bed was another folding chair, with which we did our
best to make do. Gerd had difficulties adjusting her approach,
though she made a magnificent effort. As we repeated the
scene, over and over, she grew more and more flustered, unable
to alter the habitual way she carried out the action. Trying to
remember the new directions I was giving her, she went into a
panic, her cheeks turning red as a pair of apples.

She stammered, "Oh, Gelsey! Gelsey! You'll soon have me getting out of my car this way."

It was as if I had broken some crucial link in the chain of her logic. She tried to get me out of bed, put a shawl over my shoulders, and tell me that my parents were coming—all at the same time. But it came across in pieces, without the clarity an audience would need to know what was going on. I would not let her off the hook. To slow her down, I had her verbalize the mime, saying in words what she was trying to say with her gestures—until she became so cross with herself, and me, she got it wonderfully right.

We had a good laugh and continued with the scene.

The Father, Lord Capulet, was performed by Derek Rencher, an experienced principal who had danced the part of Paris during my visit six years ago. Derek was a tall, strapping fellow, soft-spoken and ruggedly handsome, losing some of his hair since I saw him last. He had an engaging smile; but he would not be smiling in the scene as he tried to coerce my Juliet into marrying Paris against her will. The Mother entered first. Lady Capulet was Sandra Conley, an attractive, dark-haired ballerina, who was well-suited for the role, with a wide, aristocratic face.

The action progressed in fits and starts as I attempted to pin down each moment. I soon realized I would go nowhere unless I were able to bring to light each of Juliet's relationships with the other characters; this meant somehow drawing the rest of the cast into the story. As I moved from one side of the room to the other, the focus shifted with me—from the Nurse, to Mother, to Father, and then to Paris as he tried to kiss my hand. I turned away from him abruptly, saying, "This doesn't feel right at all. Can anyone help me?"

No one said a word. There was a terrible, awkward silence, like a curtain had suddenly come down around me. I was supposed to pull my hand away from Paris, avoiding his kiss. But the gesture seemed petulant, completely out of character. It was the act of a spoiled child—not Juliet. I persisted, asking, "Why do I pull my hand away from him like this?"

Derek came to the rescue. "You must react to being touched

by any man other than Romeo. You've been with him all night, so you really can't stand being kissed by Paris, can you?"

"It's the touch," Monica agreed.

"Oh, I'm sure that's part of it," I said, turning to Derek, "but I'm also enraged that you're bringing Paris into my bedroom. When do I find out you've already decided I'm going to marry him? We haven't even established that yet, have we?"

"Thursday!" Derek exclaimed. "Doesn't one of the characters in the play say, you shall marry on Thursday?"

"Great! Maybe Paris can say that when he goes for the kiss, and that's why I pull my hand away. Then I can turn and direct all my anger at my father. I'll give you the evil eye, Derek. I know you're the one behind this. You're the real tyrant!"

Suddenly everyone came alive, and the scene moved along until Juliet's confrontation with the Father. Here we ran into another snag. The exchange started with an exaggerated shake of the head by Juliet. This refusal provoked him into pushing her to the floor. Once again her gesture seemed overly peevish and inappropriate. As Derek came at me, I asked him, "What are you actually saying to Juliet at this point?"

"You shall marry," he said confidently.

"Okay, try the line, and remember all the vile names you've been calling me. I'm just a piece of baggage or raw meat as far as you're concerned. You're giving an ultimatum."

"You shall marry!" he bellowed this time as he came at me, threatening me simply by heaving his chest.

"Noooooooooooooooo!" I screamed back at him, loud enough to shake down the moon, creating a more natural gesture of defiance.

"Now knock me to the floor, Derek. With a backhand." I was not actually calling for him to hit me, merely to deliver a stage punch. From the angle we were now facing each other, one vicious swing with the back of his hand coming near my face would create the illusion of a blow to my head.

As we tried to get the timing with his swing and my fall, we ran into more trouble. Monica stepped in to demonstrate for me, but when I tried it again myself, the movement somehow seemed phony.

"Go ahead and slug me," I told Derek.

"No!" he said, "I might kill you, Gelsey."

"Oh, go ahead. I guarantee you I'll survive."

"No. Really! I couldn't afford those bills!"

As the others roared with laughter, I said, "It's wonderful to be so loved! Let's give it a whirl anyhow. What do you say?"

The Fates must have decided to tickle me here. As I shifted my weight and prepared to hit the deck, his hand flew by under my nose, coming so close I could feel the wind. There wasn't even time to flinch. I landed on my rear, looking up into Derek's startled face.

"Are you all right, Gelsey?" he asked.

"I think I've got it," I said. He missed, but had he come any closer, I would have had a beauty of a fat lip.

After rehearsal, everyone had something to say.

"Are we still friends?" I asked Derek.

Smiling broadly, he told me this kind of work fascinated him. "You know, I never analyzed what I did until you asked me. It was always instinctive."

"Breaking it down and putting it back together," I told him, "is the only way we can pass on knowledge to the next generation. How else will dancers who may not have your instincts ever figure out how to fill your shoes?"

Monica chimed in, "Yes, it's so hard to get them to ask the right questions, isn't it?"

Sandra, looking younger than her Lady Capulet, came over as I was packing, and asked, as if she had overheard, "Gelsey, why do you have to think about it all so much? You do everything right instinctively."

"That's because I've thought about it before, and before that, and before that. Believe me, I'd be awfully boring any other way."

I doubt if my reply satisfied her, but my feet hurt, and I was anxious to leave.

On my way out I thanked Gerd for her effort. She went up on her toes suddenly, turning like the youngest ballerina of all. I said, teasing her, "You'd make a great Juliet!"

She came back with a bit of delightful mischief, saying, "Why don't we just switch parts then!"

"Next time," I said. "It's a promise!"

The next rehearsal confronted me with the most vexing scene in the whole ballet. Monica and I worked together on this one with the pianist. The action seemed to be nothing more than a simple transition from the family's departure to the point when Juliet decides to seek help from the Friar. I was to start from the floor where my father had knocked me down. It was the same scene that had frustrated me in the past—the one leading to the cape.

I watched as Monica got up from the floor and showed me how to cross the stage. The choreography called for Juliet to move as if the blood had been drained out of her, picking up the cape and breaking down in despair, letting it fall from her hands as she retreated to the bed. This was where most ballerinas died in the role—sitting on the bed and facing the audience, trying to remain completely still for what seemed like an eternity, the longest sixty seconds any dancer was ever likely to experience onstage. No wonder Margot had chosen not to play this scene seated upright; instead, she stayed on the floor, draping herself across the foot of the bed to great effect.

I imagined myself sitting there and felt a jolt of fear. The audience would be asleep before I was able to retrieve the cape, get it over my shoulders, and make my exit—unless I were to lure that audience inside Juliet's mind. But how could a body that was motionless do such a thing? How could I put them on the edge of their seats if I were frozen on the foot of that bed like some pathetic little girl? After watching Monica go through the scene again, I said, "It's really a killer. Why don't I tell you what I have in mind."

By the look on her face, I could see I was going to have to persuade her to reconsider the way Juliet should move on her approach to the bed. Monica was standing directly over the cape, which lay in a soft pile at her feet. I went around her so I was looking over her shoulder. "Let's just talk it through, from the beginning," I said. "I'm on the floor. My family has gone. But I can still hear the echo of my father's voice. I reach out and scream, 'Why can't you understand?' It's the rage that gets me to my feet. Are you with me so far?"

"Yes. Of course. She's quite upset. . . ."

"Because she realizes the family is hopeless, and she's controlling her anger, turning it in on herself. Yet she knows she has everything and they have nothing. None of them are even capable of love at this point. They're destroying her and Romeo, and they don't even know it!" Sensing that my tongue was about to outrace my brain, I caught myself. Then I continued where I left off, "So I get up—"

"And cross toward the door where they've exited," Monica interjected pointedly.

"I don't even know where I'm going. I see the cape out of the corner of my eye . . . and stop . . . and pick it up. It reminds me of something. I gather it close to my breast, and then it comes to me, like you say—this is the same cloak I was wearing when I married Romeo! So there's a glimmer of hope entering here."

"This is where she breaks down," Monica instructed me.

"I can't break down! I haven't given up, have I?"

"No," she replied, "but we do need to see your vulnerability."

"I don't have to break for you to see I'm vulnerable!"

"Well . . ." She hesitated, brushing her fingers across her cheek, perplexed.

There was no stopping me now. "The cape reminds me of him, but it also makes me think of my family. It's the same shawl the Nurse has wrapped around me since I was a child. . . . Oh, but she's turned against me, like the others, and Paris was the last person who touched it! I can feel despair coming up in my throat, but I'm not going to let go of the hope—it's all I have left! That's what carries me to the bed."

"I like what you're doing, but I think it may be getting too complicated, Gelsey," she objected.

"The scene has to move from rage to hope," I said, trying to control my voice, "and we have to see her make a choice when she sits on that bed. Otherwise, we may as well give the audience a refund and go home!"

Monica looked terribly troubled.

"She realizes," I said quietly, "she's willing to face death in order not to betray love. It's that simple."

Monica bent over and gathered the cape into her hands. Then she straightened up, appearing utterly desperate. She had become Juliet and was struggling to find the transition, turning slowly, dropping the wrap behind and walking toward the bed. There were tears in her eyes when she looked at me and said, "You're right. I was thinking of Monica—of what I would have done—not Juliet."

I was at a loss for words. Her beauty at that moment touched me as much as what she said, which seemed true enough. I felt my own eyes welling up, and wished I could have seen her perform the role, though she had never been given the opportunity as far as I knew. Some time later she told me, "Kenneth says you can keep the rage going . . . all the way through." It was a victory of sorts, but I was still going to have to figure out how to get beyond the ordeal on the bed, and that was going to take more than rage, or raw emotion, or that convenient cape.

With Monica's blessing, I was able to refine the sequence of action and emotional tone of the scene in keeping with my own reading of the character and play. The minute of stillness would now appear within a frame slightly at odds with the weight of the music, which usually swept over the ballerina in great, bombastic waves, washing out any performance which seemed to be moving in a similar direction. If I were to pit my body, and especially the rhythm of my breath, against that surging backdrop provided by the orchestra, there would be a subtle tension created that might work to my advantage.

After all, Juliet was fighting just to breathe.

The score at this point, as I listened again in my bathtub that evening, seemed to correspond to her oppressive environment rather than to her emotional state. I was not dancing to provide some sort of accompaniment for the music; the music was going to accompany me as I interpreted the story—that was a given. The orchestra would be conducted by a Russian guest from the Bolshoi Opera, Mark Ermler, who brought with him some of Prokofiev's original score sheets.

We would have a faithful rendering of the composer's intentions—an outpouring of the Russian soul, note by note—or would we? A conflict as old as ballet itself was already shaping up. The relationship between musicians and dancers was like a marriage in which neither side ever talked. In the hope of instigating a dialogue, I had arranged with Monica to attend one of the orchestra rehearsals. Settling again into the bath water, I smiled, remembering her joke, "Sometimes we have to go to bed with the conductor just to get the right tempo! It's awful, isn't it?"

It was awful: there was rarely anything like a shared vision running between the pit and the stage. Ulanova told the story of one of the early rehearsals in Russia, when the dancers had not even been able to hear the score during one of the scenes. Prokofiev himself mounted the stage and sat with the dancers, and was forced to admit they were right. Fortunately, for Ulanova in 1940, the composer was still alive to make a few changes.

Greg poked his head through the door, and said, "Jesus! It's like a steam room in here. That tape recorder is going to short circuit on you."

Ignoring him, I turned on more hot water. The splashing drowned out the score and forced my husband to raise his voice. He shouted, "I just wanted to tell you . . . your stepfather called to say we forgot your mother's birthday. It was two weeks ago! How could we have missed it? The Ides of March."

"Oh no!" I groaned.

"I'll send her some flowers tomorrow, from both of us," he volunteered. "She'll be here next week."

"What?" I asked, even though I heard him, his words slowly making sense in my ear.

"I'm melting. I'll tell you later," he yelled before withdrawing his head and closing the door.

I felt a sharp twinge of guilt. I had been thinking so much about Juliet's family, I had forgotten my own. My mother had already gone through several years of anguish thanks to her fallen daughter. I still shuddered to imagine how embarrassing it must have been for her to explain me to her friends in those dark times. Her birthday was not the only occasion to slip by unnoticed. An early Easter came and went without so much as a painted egg or a call home. Still, she would be coming for the performance, forewarned that I would probably not have any time to spend with her until afterward.

I shut off the water and let my thoughts drift back to the music. I was not drawn into it as I had been when I was a teenager, when I would listen alone in my bedroom at night, held in a web of maudlin dreams. There was a distance now, imposed by the practical necessities of the work ahead, and by changes in my own heart over the years. I was surely not immune to sentiment, far from it, but I had become more discerning, or perhaps more reticent to allow myself to be manipulated.

Greg came in again. This time he crouched awkwardly by the tub, balancing with his hand on the rim. He said in a soft voice, "Dina called. She says that we can go ahead with the move tomorrow." He hesitated, as if finding his place; I had an urge to look away, but I remained still while he continued, "She also had some sad news. She wanted you to know Erik Bruhn has passed away. Apparently he had lung cancer and was in the hospital."

He touched my shoulder gently, then walked out.

The sorrow found its way under my ribs and stayed with me, along with a consoling thought I knew Eric carried with him. He was one of those rare dancers who attain a kind of immortality on the stage. The truth he brought into the dance was not something that came to an end with a particular performance, nor would it end with his life. His successors would have to reckon with what he left behind in all his roles. He acknowledged his own debt to the tradition inspired by the great nineteenth-century Danish choreographer, August Bournonville, whom he once described as "a man whose creative force and genius gave him courage to survive himself. . . ."

In his devotion to that tradition, had Erik not revealed the same courage? Unlike those who win fame with the height of a jump, he elevated ballet to art; his nobility was never a pose.

Later, when Greg and I were bundled in bed, I told him, "Erik was a prince—Danish, like Hamlet. He was a consummate actor. He taught us what it's supposed to be like when it's—"

"—alive," suggested my husband, finishing my sentence with sleep about to overcome both of us. I was going to say, "great."

"I keep thinking of his Madge—the witch in *La Sylphide,*" I said, closing my eyes. "I wish you could have seen him."

I woke up feeling anxious without knowing why, until I saw the suitcases and boxes piled around the flat. Then I remembered last night's mad rush to pack. We were moving this morning, or rather Greg was going to move us while I was in class. This afternoon, ready or not, I was scheduled to have a run-through of the whole ballet, and Kenneth was going to be there to pass judgment.

At the first sign of light, I pounced on the mattress and awakened Greg, the springs in the couch thrumming beneath us. After a cup of coffee had revived him, he watched as I sat seemingly motionless, going through Juliet's scene on the bed. I concentrated on my diaphragm, allowing my breath to lift me, coming forward in a way that would be almost—if not quite—imperceptible to an audience. Rising swiftly to my feet, I took off across the room. Then I turned back suddenly, and asked him, "What did you see?"

"I couldn't take my eyes off you." He took a sip from his cup and tried to wriggle out, "But it's awfully early for this, isn't it?"

"Oh, come on—what did you think?" I pressed him.

"You looked . . . like you were in turmoil. Distraught at the beginning. But at the end you were shifting your focus, and the rest of you seemed to follow. There's obviously a lot of motion going on inside, like a spring that's winding up . . . and when you finally got up, I thought you were going to cry out."

Satisfied, I turned and walked toward the bathroom. Greg called after me, "Wait a minute! Was I right? Was that it?"

"Close enough," I said, without breaking stride.

Later in the morning, on my way to the school, I detoured to a dentist's office to take care of a tooth that was giving me trouble. My dentist back in New York was a saint and I was leery about entrusting my mouth to a stranger. A taxi left me in front of a huge, white Victorian, and upon entering, I was told to have a seat and wait. I continued practicing my scene on a small sofa in the waiting room, attracting curious glances until the dentist came out to fetch me, extending his hand and introducing himself. He wore a wispy beard and colorful necktie, and seemed pleasant enough, though I did think his smile was a little crooked for a man in his profession.

Once inside I tried to get comfortable in his chair, and he put on a surgical mask. Then he placed one of those plastic vacuum cleaners in my mouth and began to probe with a shiny hooked instrument. The sound coming from inside my mouth was enough to permanently curl my hair. While I strained to open for him, he tried to draw me into conversation. I managed to say I was dancing with the Royal Ballet. His face, what I could see of it above the mask, showed a sudden interest. He exclaimed, with a loud voice that startled, coming so close to my ear, "You don't say! What role are you performing?"

He paused long enough for me to give my reply, which was the opening he was looking for. "Oh, that is a prodigious role," he said, his accent thickening. "I must tell you of a production I saw some years ago, at the Old Vic. Before your time, I should think. . . ." As he went on with his review and continued to work on the teeth, I tried to find some interesting spots on the ceiling where I could focus my eyes. It occurred to me that I would be seeing both dentist and choreographer today—a combination that seemed perversely apropos.

"Have a rinse," he said, handing me a paper cup the size of a thimble. He had been going on about painting for some time and spoke fondly of Edgar Degas and his fascination with dancers. "What I've always found most curious about ballet," he continued, "is the anachronism. It can be lovely, of course, but our more modern artists have opened another path, haven't they? More freedom, I should think."

"I'm not so sure about that," I said. "It depends on what you mean by freedom, doesn't it?"

"I mean," he asserted, while returning his attention to my mouth, "the rules and rigid framework of the classical arts must have been rather stifling for those artists."

As he withdrew his hands, I asked, "Do you think Mozart or Rembrandt felt stifled?" I was touchy on this point and lifted forward, adding, "How about Shakespeare? Would you say that he lacked freedom?"

He ignored my questions, instead asking me to tilt my head back. There was a hint of irritation in his voice. I suspected he was not the type who liked hearing his opinions challenged, and I was in no position to quarrel.

He finally replied, "No doubt they seemed quite daring, in their time, of course."

With that he had the last word, and I was ready to bolt from the chair.

I had almost blotted the dentist out of mind by the time I arrived at the school, or almost arrived—having chanced to catch a cab driven by the only nasty driver I ever encountered in this city. Most of the London cabbies seemed to have come out of a school that equipped them with more than a fair share of humor and compassion—chivalrous, they were. This one happened to pass my stop and then refused to turn around or even give me a receipt. "You'll jus haf ta walk, woncha?" he taunted.

I slammed the door, then yelled at him through his window, "What are you anyway—a Capulet or a Montague?"

That made me feel better, and the walk did me good. The weather was still on the damp side of dismal, but change was in the air. April had the effect of raising body temperature, with hope for spring no longer quite so dim. My head and even my bag seemed lighter. If I were not yet in what I would describe as "fighting condition," at least I no longer felt as if I were lugging my corpse around with me in little pieces.

I was late. On my way to class, I was overtaken by the company's General Manager, Peter Brownlee, an amiable man whom I met once a week. Peter invariably brought along a joke and an envelope of cash, six hundred pounds expense money. Which seemed like a lot until it went, and it always did—thanks in no small part to the fleet of cabs I kept in business with trips to the opera house, the school, the toe-shoe factory, the company doctor, the osteopath, and God only knew where else.

I warmed up as always and took class in a small studio with Oliver Symons, a gentle soul who had grown accustomed to the varied repertory of groans, grunts, and grimaces with which I usually entertained him. Today I had in mind my first scene in the ballet, a lighthearted romp during which Juliet and her Nurse played catch with a doll—establishing the childhood innocence. Oliver and I worked on coupe jetés, a string of spinning leaps that had me darting across the studio with the same playful abandon I intended to bring into the scene.

I did not count the steps, instead linking them together into larger chains of movement, always thinking first of the dramatic idea, and then of the quality of the phrasing. Counting music was a necessary evil, to some extent, but over the years it had become a popular disease among dancers. This "dance-by-the-numbers" approach was made worse by music composed as if by the same method, to say nothing of the ballets. A dancer could be tone deaf and still fit into a modern repertory, or most classes for that matter, with nothing more required than some sense of rhythm and an ability to count.

Making a hurried stop in the dressing room, I jotted:

> An idea and a feeling must animate each gesture—from the play—not from the "book of arithmetic." At the end of the first scene, when the Nurse takes my doll and I feel my breast for the first time, I am feeling what's inside—the progress of the heart is the only story. In the ballroom, when I first see Romeo, I can feel it beating wildly; and from the balcony to the bedroom—it's bursting with hope.

Giving up for the moment, I put on my shoes, leggies, and skirt, and headed for rehearsal, lost in thought. My husband caught up with me as I walked into the studio, my hand suddenly coming alive in his.

Kenneth was seated as if holding court, flanked by Monica and Anthony. This space had the feel of a stadium, filled with dancers warming up and milling about. The whole cast was here. Kenneth kindly gave permission for Greg to watch, and he seated himself on the floor. I left my bag with him and bumped into Donald MacLeary, whose ingenuity in the studio was exceeded only by his charm. I was reminded of his lighthearted comment on the moment when Romeo first removed his mask: "Oh, he's even better than you imagined!"

Anthony ambled over and offered a few droll words of reassurance. It could only have been a week or two ago that he had missed a rehearsal because of a shoulder injury. I had arrived to find a note of apology explaining "the disadvantages of having an ancient partner." Here he was about to shoulder my weight throughout the afternoon, and somehow he would make it all appear effortlessly lyrical. When I touched him, his expression changed, as if he had overheard my thought, and I sensed for an instant how proud he actually was of what we had accomplished so far.

While we waited to start, Kenneth asked, "Gelsey, are you ready?"

"Just one or two trouble spots," I said.

"Do you want to tell me," he drawled, "or would you rather keep it as a surprise?"

"I'll surprise you."

"Whenever you like," he said dryly, looking as though he might be wondering what I had up my sleeve.

I continued stretching and making mental notes through the swordplay of the first scene. This kind of rehearsal always took forever, with the million stops necessary to smooth out the rough edges. During the breaks, the conductor and pianist conferred in hushed tones. I wished I were a fly on the wall over their two buzzing heads. What little surprise did they have in store?

Gerd and I managed our opening scene without either of us being knocked out by the flying doll, but I realized during this playful interlude that I was going to have to figure a way to get across Juliet's infinite curiosity about life, as she ran circles around the old Nurse. That would come. We proceeded without any stops until the family entered for Juliet's first introduction to Paris. As I bowed to him, I hesitated for a moment, and glanced over at Kenneth, who seemed to sense exactly what I was asking.

"More formal, Gelsey," he said. "Cross your wrists."

With my wrists crossed and my hands placed just over my knee, there was just the right touch of aristocratic formality. I suddenly thought of da Vinci's angel, after all this time, and the moment could not have been more perfect. Now the scene moved from Juliet's playing with a doll to the first subtle hint of a more mature, feminine nature, when I bowed—spiraling invisibly within. The dynamic in the upper body suggested a sense of quiet dignity, and yet, as if to say, here was a woman to be reckoned with. I was pleased, and so was Kenneth, as far as I could tell.

A short time later in the midst of festivities in the ballroom, just when everything seemed to be flowing smoothly, we came to an awkward halt. Anthony had been supporting me in a series of arabesques. As I faced him, and he held me from the waist, I was to lean away from him. My head seemed to bend back all the way behind me. It may have been a pretty curve Kenneth was after, but that bend seemed excessive, and the strain was severe. I saw the line of my neck and shoulders distorting in the mirror, and had visions of me wearing one of those white neck braces that come up under your chin.

"Kenneth, I'm sorry, but I have to ask you," I sputtered, sounding as perplexed as I felt, "why is this step here?"

The room seemed to hold its breath while he pondered in his chair, allowing the suspense to build.

"Why are you dancing?" he came back, mimicking my desperate tone to hilarious effect. There were gales of laughter suddenly coming from all sides. I was laughing also, but I was not going to let him put me off that easily.

"I think I can answer that one," I said, "but can you tell me if there's some dramatic reason for this step? Can you give us a clue?"

"Well . . . not dramatic. She's just tried to peek under his mask, and now she's leading him on . . . isn't she? She's saying to him, 'Come here, come here!' "

His lilting tone seemed to say he wanted a flirtatious ingenue. I asked, somewhat incredulously, "You mean she's the one being forward here?"

"She's . . . luring him," he said, as if convincing himself.

"Oh, I thought she might be more cautious. Would you mind if I don't tilt my head so far back? I can keep my focus moving up and lengthen the curve . . . all the way through my neck, without breaking the line. Wait—I'll show you. Won't take a minute!"

I was off and running again, and with Anthony's support, able to demonstrate what I meant.

"That's fine, Gelsey," said Kenneth. No doubt he realized that emphasizing the noble line of the neck was more appropriate for me, given my proportions. Juliet was going to measure this love against the stars, and with my whole body arching up like a bow, I was now able to say as much with greater simplicity and without any of the strain.

I hoped Kenneth liked what I was doing, and I suspected he did by the time we ran through the family scenes in the last act.

He not only gave me free reign, but helped me clarify some of the mime and improve the timing. When my father, Derek, gave me his angry ultimatum that I marry Paris, Kenneth suggested that I take longer before giving him my refusal. This seemingly tiny detail heightened the impact of Derek slugging me to the floor. When he finally knocked me down, I hit the wood with quite a resounding thud. I looked up at Kenneth and said, "You see all the fun you missed?"

His laugh was encouraging, but after the family exited stage right, I was stymied trying to rise from the floor and begin that long journey to the bed. I explained to Kenneth, "I still haven't found the key to this moment."

"Well, remember," he suggested, "neither has Juliet."

"Okay," I said, taking a deep breath, "with that in mind . . . one more time!"

Unaware of the room full of eyes watching me, I found my place again on the floor. I started from my knees. This time, by making changes in Juliet's emotional intensity and pattern of breath, I was able to generate the impetus I needed to get to my feet. Once again, the scene moved from outrage to desperate hope, but the transitions were becoming more rapid and finely tuned, and there was a moment of absolute quiet, when I simply stopped breathing altogether and sensed her terror at the prospect of being alone. I heard Kenneth say in a soft voice, "Much better."

Afterward, I thanked him for his help and said, "You meant I should keep in mind she doesn't understand yet why her family can't understand. . . ." He was nodding distractedly as I finished, asking him, "That was your point, wasn't it?"

"Yes," was all he said, his expressionless face yielding no further enlightenment. I had intended to bring up the subject of love, which was, after all, the point of the drama, but something told me this was not the time. Kenneth had been more forthcoming than I had expected, and I decided to count myself lucky to have come through in one piece.

We had run late and quit with the tomb scene still ragged. After going through what seemed like a receiving line of parting embraces, I led Greg into the dressing room. Monica popped in to give me a few technical corrections. After she left,

I bent down to collect my shoes, and said with a giddy laugh, "How many more thoughts about this ballet do you suppose I can fit in my brain before it starts swelling up like my feet?"

Greg made no comment. Instead, he leaned over and kissed the top of my head; then he went out the door, saying something about calling us a taxi. I had almost forgotten—we were going to our new home. It took me another fifteen minutes to gather my things and meet him outside where he was waiting with a cab. As soon as the two of us climbed inside, he asked me, "You're not really disappointed, are you?"

"No," I said flatly, "I'm just drained."

As traffic flickered by out the window, I crossed my legs and pulled off one of my boots, saying, "But I still feel like I'm losing too many moments—and there's no time left!"

My lower lip was quivering slightly. I shut my eyes, and fought off the threat of tears, as I felt my husband's fingers slowly massaging the sole of my foot.

"I don't know quite how to tell you this," he said, "but you've already won . . . and so has Juliet . . . unless the two of you happen to draw an audience made of stone. The fact that she exists and moves with such clarity says you've done all the work that counts. She lives on your insights . . . and every new one gives that much more depth. You've won."

"Not yet," I whispered, tilting my head back, sensing only a sudden pleasure now coming from my toes.

Natasha's flat was like the wing of a Victorian palace that had been stripped of its past. The rooms stood huge and empty. Nothing belonging to the owner remained except for some boxes and bric-a-brac piled behind the locked door of one of the two bedrooms, and toe shoes, hundreds of them, stuffed in drawers and cabinets. Everything else had been moved. Natasha had a new place across town, and this older flat was now for sale. When we first moved in, we decided to think of ourselves as "squatters," as we had no time to even begin to furnish the place. The walls were white and bare. Nails poked out where paintings once hung. On that first night, we decorated with our fantasies, mounting masterpieces all around us while we surveyed the living room from a mattress in the middle of the floor. With a ceiling twenty feet over our heads, we were surrounded by space, as if inside a vacant theatre.

The austerity seemed to suit us—like a pair of monks, we were, ready for the last, week-long push toward performance. We had been given the keys by Dina, and taken her out to dinner, then returned to read her the last chapter of memoirs. I rested a little easier with her promise to help out backstage on the day of my opening, a day when anything that could possibly go wrong would go wrong, if left unattended. Dina was a woman who devoted her life to ballet behind the scenes. Having worked with Natasha over the years, she had an extraordinary talent for dealing with the pressures that accumulated in rehearsals and came to a head in the dressing room before a performance, when the slightest detail out of place might shatter nerves and concentration.

Rain pelted the windows all night and they rattled as if someone were outside tossing handfuls of marbles at them. This flat was on the ground floor and faced the street. I heard cars going by, their tires swishing over the wet pavement—and woke up without the alarm sounding, lifting my head from the coats we had gathered for pillows. The clock said five, which meant it was four because I set it an hour ahead wanting to get a jump on the world. But the warmth and smell of sleep nearly paralyzed me. If ever there were a temptation to quit, it came when I turned on the light and saw my husband's dreaming face. One more act of will had to be summoned to overcome my envy and crawl out from under the covers.

There was no turning back now. The final days passed as quickly as we were able to tear the pages off the calendar. The anxiety level occasionally shot up through the ceiling when I reminded myself this was only the beginning. My rehearsals for the next two ballets were about to start, and Anthony delivered a shocker with news that we had been invited to perform the balcony pas de deux for Queen Elizabeth II—at a gala celebrating her sixtieth birthday. This was an unexpected honor, but I had only two pairs of pointe shoes that were even close to fitting, and they would never last.

"I know galas are always a pain," said Anthony, "but you will do it, won't you? It's to be televised, and I mean, it is the Queen. . . ."

"I don't know," I told him. "If only I had shoes. . . ."

We postponed a decision on that one, focusing attention on the full evening and more immediate concerns. The conductor saved his bombshell for the dress rehearsal. This was the first time I was actually onstage, with the set, costumes, props, and a full cast and orchestra. A small group of photographers stood in the front rows of the audience snapping away. Kenneth was seated farther back near the technical people who were adjusting lights. I had managed to get through most of the ballet without making any stops. When I found myself lying on the tomb near the end—about to circle the crypt and discover Romeo's corpse and stab myself—I was confronted with a tempo I had never heard before. Slow, very slow.

Suddenly I had all the time in the world, and that might have been preferable, if not for the fact I had never rehearsed the actions with the timing now required. The tempo problem was complicated by the tomb itself. This prop was not what might be called "friendly"—at center stage was this gigantic slab over which Juliet had to climb in order to strike the tragic tableau, mortally wounded and reaching for Romeo. I was in a real fix, until Kenneth responded to my desperate plea for help.

He came up onto the stage, with this last rehearsal more or less over, and helped me map out the scene from beginning to end, taking time to show me how I might most effectively navigate across the tomb in order to finish on the right music and capture the dramatic idea—mimetically. The families may not have come together around us in a "glooming peace," but the image did bring Kenneth and me together for a fruitful exchange. By the time we were ready to leave, both of us had what we wanted. The only hitch was that I had still not actually rehearsed the scene according to this new blueprint.

Nor could I be sure the conductor would play the same tempo tomorrow night. But that was true for the whole ballet, to some extent. The only practical solution was to inspire the conductor and musicians through the dancing itself, shifting regard from the metronome to those more elusive qualities that seemed to come into play between the notes, as if the actions onstage could actually be read in such a way as to breathe life into the music and the phrasing that bound us all together. After expressing my thanks to Kenneth and to the conductor, I made my way to the apron of the stage, trying to find Greg.

He came up from behind, saying my name. When I turned around, I saw him standing with Madame Messerer—the Russian teacher who had given me my first class in London. I was taken aback at first, but then I saw tears in her eyes and a blush of joy in her face. She took my hand and exclaimed with a voice as tremulous as I felt, "Preeema! Preeema!" It was certainly a touching compliment, and I squeezed her hand, neither of us able to say another word.

When Greg and I walked away, I explained in a whisper, "I'm in shock. I was afraid she was going to try to correct my arm positions."

He let out a laugh loud enough to bring down the set, and wrapped his arms around me, saying, "Maybe there's hope after all."

The stagehands had ordered everyone to leave the stage. Monica caught me and passed on some written notes. These were mostly technical corrections, and a reminder not to enter in my first scene before the lights came up. She wished me well and said, "Perhaps more sensuality, Gelsey, when you come out on the balcony."

I had qualms about that piece of advice. Playing for any sort of sensuality other than the moonlight falling on Juliet's cheek seemed inconsistent with choices I had made earlier. There was a crossfire of opinion. Donald MacLeary made a remark about a certain ballerina who "looked like she had already been to bed with Romeo on the balcony." I had come to the point where the responsibility for the character was mine alone, and I would simply have to live with my performance, however it turned out.

That night I stayed up late with Greg, simplifying the mime on the balcony—so I was catching a single moonbeam in the palm of my hand—and reworking details in the tomb scene, using the mattress in our cavernous living room. I was thoroughly exhausted by the time my husband said, "You may as well go to bed. There are only so many moments that tell the story, and you've turned them all inside out."

"I have to get this right," I insisted. "I'm not exactly an expert with a dagger, and I want it to look as ghastly as it should." I started again, much to my husband's amusement. "Somehow, with two hands, I have got to get the blade in, and yet keep her heart turning out . . . trembling inside . . . eyes toward heaven and . . ."

While I was in the throes of final agony, Greg stood in for Romeo, lying corpselike at the foot of the "tomb" with his head lifted toward me. Staggering backward, I heard him say, "Great! I think you've got it. But remember, you're seeing everything through a microscope, and the audience is going to watch through a telescope. The gesture might be clearer if you get the dagger higher in the air before the thrust."

I slept on that one.

It was the story itself that carried me through the night and next day. Each time I felt an attack of nerves coming on, I turned again to the drama almost as a source of faith—not so much passages from the play, though I kept a copy with me along with my notebooks, but a sense of what I had to tell. There was a terrible urgency. The feeling was like I had witnessed an atrocity in Juliet's death, and was now preparing to testify.

I was deliberately silent, as if keeping my mouth shut until I were called. I took class as usual in the morning and then came home for a nap. Greg ran out to pick up his suit and hold off the family and friends, a few of whom might have still been wondering if the program at the opera house would contain an insert announcing Miss Kirkland had become indisposed and was being replaced in this evening's performance.

But I was already in the theatre by the middle of the afternoon.

I dumped my bag on the dressing-room floor and organized the jumble of things that fell out. Then I pulled on tights, socks, and shoes. The room was dingy, with a makeup table, a sink, and a little storage nook at the back. While I busied myself threading needles in front of the mirror, my mind started playing tricks on me. I was distracted by my feet, which were tingling, cramped in toe shoes to stretch the material. I imagined tripping down the shallow flight of stairs on making my descent from the balcony. This nightmare kept coming back like some sort of perverse news clip. When I accidentally pricked my finger, I was relieved and even glad to have a tiny focus of pain to occupy me.

Dina came in with tea and a light meal from the cafeteria several floors down. The truth was that I was trapped inside my dressing room because I had not yet learned how to find my way around this theatre. There seemed to be an endless number of winding halls and stairways. I told Dina, "All I have to do is go out and make one wrong turn!"

She never lost her calm. I was already beginning to panic, with the door constantly opening to well-wishers and deliveries of telegrams and flowers, the perfume of roses setting off alarms in my brain. Anthony came by with a *merde,* a gift he offered along with some gentle words of reassurance that I was certain he needed as much as me. I tried to make him know how I felt as he slipped away, for a while.

Gerd, who had the dressing room next door, was bustling in and out, saying, "Oh, Gelsey, you're going to be fine! Why don't we just go over our scenes again before we go out." We did just that several times.

At five, a countdown began, with the clock moving toward a curtain that would rise promptly at half past seven. I spent a half hour putting on makeup, as light and as simple as possible, and then another half hour having my hair done, pinned up so that I could take a warm-up class without wrecking everything with the sweat. Oliver gave me a forty-five-minute workout in one of the studios. This was sufficient to get my body and mind going in the same direction.

Afterward, I came back into the dressing room to secure my shoes and ribbons, and gulp down a last cup of hot tea. Greg breezed in for a final kiss. He was almost hilariously careful about not disturbing my makeup, our lips barely touching. His voice cracked and his eyes moistened as he said those three words we all long to say, and I said them back softly.

Then he was gone.

When the stage manager called fifteen minutes, I touched up and rechecked everything, including a tray of essentials to be placed in a changing room just off the stage—where I would repair between the scenes. I ticked off each item I would need: mirror, brush, powder, lipstick, pancake, hammer, sponge, needle and thread.

At five minutes before curtain, the wardrobe mistress, Maureen Male entered to help me on with my costume, and another gracious woman, Danuta Barszczewska, who had done my hair, now took down the ponytail. They were both so composed, I tried to absorb their secret.

I was led to the backstage area, which was crowded with stagehands and dancers in costumes. I had to keep my body moving now. The wings were claustrophobic, full of strange equipment and pieces of set that I was warned not to lean against. I found a quiet corner where I had just enough room to stretch while I waited.

When the first scene of the ballet finished, there was a set change, which threw the backstage area into a hushed flurry of chaos. One of the stagehands led me by the hand to that spot where I would make my entrance. I stood, concealed between heavy, black curtains, and started measuring each breath, ever so slowly—waiting for the lights to come up. Juliet was racing down this corridor to find the Nurse, racing faster than her feet could possibly carry her. The joys in that heart had to be visible in her body from the moment she first set foot in the room and called out.

I tried to wiggle my ears, stretching all the muscles in my face. I knew the conductor was going to wait to see me enter, and I was already mentally skipping ahead of the music. There was a silence while I poised. I found the level I needed in my body, taking another couple of breaths, my nerves almost put to rest by the idea I was holding steadfastly in my mind. I repeated these words to myself over and over: *Oh, Nurse! Oh, good sweet Nurse! Where are you!*

Then I felt the warm glare of lights.

3.

IF
THE
SHOE
FITS

Light surrounded by darkness—that was the sensation I experienced as I entered, on the run, as if Juliet had just burst into the room. Crossing diagonally downstage, I was only aware of the audience as a kind of void on the other side of the glare. Out of the corner of my eye, I caught sight of the Nurse napping in her chair upstage. *Oh, there you are!* In my mind, the tone of Juliet's "voice" rose in excitement, as did the level of my body. But as I dashed behind the chair, I heard another mental voice, one that seemed to speak without words, telling me I had worn the wrong shoes.

This pair was too tight. I could feel the toes of my right foot cramped inside the shoe even as I gripped the back of the chair and lifted through my torso, whipping the left leg into the air behind me. At this point, surprising the Nurse with a kiss on the cheek, I was guided entirely by reflex and the rush of adrenaline; my body was outracing my mind. There was no time to stop and listen to what that wordless voice was saying. In a flash, as the Nurse rose to her feet, I darted in front of the chair, then merrily twirled her around.

I was teasing her, snatching the doll she held idly at her side and then skipping away from her, trying not to be too precious. Juliet was too old for dolls. Why else would she be so quick to fling this one into the air? *Catch!* My arms said exactly that just before I let go, hesitating for a split second as I took aim. Juliet dearly loved the Nurse, and loved to make her ancient heart flutter, but it was my own heart that seemed to stop, momentarily, as I willed the doll across the space between us and into Gerd's outstretched arms.

Suddenly, I was in the air, crossing the stage again, leaping, spinning, pushing myself like there was no tomorrow. The hours in the studio were paying me back now. I was taking control, if only for this brief passage of coupe jetés, allowing my breath and momentum to turn each leap into the preparation for the next . . . and the next. The set, though scarcely cluttered, had the feel of an obstacle course. With each spin, just as my head came around to spot in front of me, there was a sound, like the beating of wings over the music—a fleeting impression of my own constantly moving shape. The motion of the body was so continuous it may have concealed my effort, as if Juliet were simply whirling with joy.

What seemed spontaneous was surely something of an illusion, and yet the feeling was real—inseparable from the movement itself and the idea of the character. As I approached the far corner of the stage, propelled by that same joy, I turned along a sharp curve, coming back toward the Nurse. Resisting the turn, as if I were suddenly moving against a strong wind, had the effect of softening the curve, ever so slightly, enabling me to stretch the outer edge of Juliet's world beyond those square boundaries of the proscenium.

This was really a trick of perspective, as when the eyes of an actor, by changing focus, direct the audience's attention to some imaginary site offstage. For an instant, I was able to glimpse a boundless world, curving away from me as far as the eye could see.

I came out of the turn with a little jump off one leg—a kind of sauté, or temps levé—though I paid no attention to the name, or the step itself in any formal sense. The beauty of such a step was that no one would ever see it. It vanished in a burst of exuberance as I changed direction and kept my momentum going back to center stage, where I made a quick feint to the side before rushing to the Nurse.

She was playing along now, lifting the doll above her head, out of reach, as I flew into low arabesque and tried to capture it from her hands; then she lowered it behind her back, out of sight, and I flitted about, as if momentarily exasperated trying to peek around her. Again I heard Juliet's voice inwardly urging me on to my toes, *Where are you hiding it? . . . Oh, there it is!* Here, the scene called for me to take the Nurse by the waist and twirl us both around. I remembered Gerd asking in rehearsal not to make her dizzy by turning her too fast—although the character, quite overcome by this time, would fall back in the chair after I spun away.

The mischief was to end with Juliet hopping up and on to the Nurse's lap, establishing a warm intimacy just before the parents made their grand entrance with Paris. Gerd and I had taken pains to work out the timing, which had to be perfect because there was barely time for me to finish the business with the doll, skitter away, then come back to find her lap.

Everything seemed to go well until that last moment. Up close, Gerd was all costume, and I could feel the padding beneath its ruffled layers as I turned her between my two hands, her huge white headdress bobbing as she went around. Letting go, I took the doll with me and ran several steps away, then raced back swiftly toward the chair, ready to spring onto her lap and the soft cushion of that costume. But there was no lap and no chair. I was already in the air when I realized that Gerd was not sitting, but standing in front of me, hunched over slightly.

I never even saw the broken chair, knocked down while my back was turned. It was Gerd's face that told me something had gone awry. Her lips were puckered and her brows knitted together as if she had just heard the most shocking piece of news. I came sailing into her with both legs tucked up under me, like a little cannonball, feeling her shudder as she took my weight. I curled my right arm around her neck, the same way we had rehearsed the scene with Gerd sitting. But I now found myself sliding down the front of her body, groping to find the floor.

It was like one of those falling dreams, when you wake up in terror trying to catch yourself. My feet met the wood abruptly, at a weird angle. Still holding the doll with my left hand, I swirled away from Gerd, as if all the excitement had caused Juliet to become a bit giddy. I was desperately trying to recover my balance and stay in character. I had to sustain the shape—at least not allowing my ribs and shoulders to pull up and distort my neck—otherwise, all would be lost.

As it was, I wound up out of place, scolded by my own inner voice, as if some part of me had been watching over the whole scene. Sensing the Nurse in back of me, I managed to get the doll to her hands, passing it behind with a furtive gesture to elude the eyes of Mother, Father, and Paris, who had already entered. But I was late. Surely they had seen. The look on Mother's face told me I would hear about this later, or so I interpreted the chill of her greeting.

I put the mishap out of mind for the introduction to Paris, though the sense of dismay stayed with me, as I bowed, crossing my wrists over my knee. Moving with assurance, Julian placed one arm around my waist and with equal poise took my hand. Then he walked me slowly toward the front. I lingered behind him and the music—enough to give some hint of Juliet's uncertainty and inexperience, confronted with her first suitor and aware of her parents watching. Rising onto pointe, I broke away from him gently, both feet fluttering under me, betraying the outward calm with which I now regarded him.

I'll look to like, if looking liking move. . . . Juliet's little tongue twister kept floating through my brain even as my feet continued, on their own, with rapid beats of pas de bourrée. How I dreaded this next passage . . . the simplest steps! Backing up and turning away, as wary as I was flirtatious, I snuck a glance at the stretch of floor below—endlessly black, covered with bumps, ruts, and cracks—made all the more hazardous by the patches of glare thrown down by the lights.

It occurred to me that my legs were bound to wobble, as they had in the dress rehearsal. I felt my way forward with my toes, stifling the impulse to lift my arms, not looking down, not liking the message coming from those feet. I was trying to bring some mystery into this encounter, placing accents in the phrasing with special care—sweeping through low arabesque, then turning soutenu with arms curving above the head, and gliding through another arabesque. Changing direction, I retreated on tiptoe toward the Nurse, walking briskly and very ladylike—all the while feeling as if I were dancing through an earthquake, no longer able to distinguish large and small disasters.

This was only the first leg of the journey, and already I was winded, pausing for a hushed exchange with the Nurse, yet not allowing myself to relax. What began as cautious flirtation had to become still softer and more lyrical as Juliet performed a few formal steps she had prepared for the occasion, crossing back toward Paris, then retreating again almost wistfully. Encouraged by the Nurse, I started toward him, faltering on the first flurry of bourrées, my ankles threatening to buckle. The floor seemed to have taken on a life of its own, and as my feet skidded over the surface, I could feel the heat of a blush rising into my face.

Balancing on the left leg while unfurling the left arm, I met Julian's gaze from afar and deliberately averted my eyes. The ensuing sequence had me travel a long figure eight, covering the entire distance between us. Out of sheer desperation, I kept my composure—all fluttering coyness as I came near him, almost face to face, and turned away again. What intent lay behind that smile of his? I hurried back to center stage, hesitating —hovering on pointe as if suspended in thought, lifting the right foot a few inches off the floor behind me, and bringing my right hand nearly to my cheek—not looking back, but sensing his eyes with my neck and shoulders.

Staying on pointe, I circled the Nurse, coming around in time for a final bow with Paris. Then I watched him leave with Mother and Father. *Oh, joy! They're gone!* came Juliet's voice as I scooped up the doll and held it high over my head, ready now to resume the game, backing away from the Nurse and whirling into arabesque, allowing her to overtake me. But this time, she would not play along. We simplified the last exchange so only a brief look passed between us, her expression gently upbraiding me as I took the doll into my arms, and very slowly lowered it to my waist, saying good-bye to something once cherished.

I was still looking down when I felt the Nurse reach around from behind and place her hands softly over my breasts. Letting the doll fall to the floor, I reached up quickly with my own hands, then lifted my gaze into the light—as if astonished by this sudden revelation of womanhood. I was actually startled to feel my heart pounding right through my costume. Then came a total blackout, followed by panic: the scene was over.

Bending down to pick up the doll at my feet, I stayed in character, uncertain whether the audience was able to see me in the dark. I heard, or perhaps only thought I heard Gerd whisper behind me, "Quick! Quick! This way!" We had rehearsed the exit a number of times because Gerd was concerned that the "dolly," as she called it, and I might find ourselves trapped in front of the curtain when it came down; I had darker visions of being caught under that great crush of material as it fell on top of my head. Braced for such a calamity, I scurried backward, doll in hand, squinting my eyes, unable to make out anything more than the ghostly silhouette of Gerd's costume.

"Good! Good! Come along," she said, ushering me into the wings, where the atmosphere became even more dreamlike and unnerving, with dancers and stagehands squeezing every which way to get by each other. The changing area was a makeshift room one step up and off to the side, a bright enclosure that offered only temporary refuge, like the hold of a ship in a storm. As soon as I was inside, Maureen moved behind me and began unhooking the costume while Danuta grabbed a handful of hairpins and started to remove the ponytail. Working around me and each other, these two women had their own amazingly efficient choreography. With less than ten minutes to go until the next entrance, I was relieved to place myself in their hands. Mine were still trembling.

I stepped out of the heavy blue velvet outfit I was wearing, dabbed the sweat off my body with a face towel, then slipped into a gold ballroom dress—the first of four costume changes in the ballet. I pulled a pair of woolies over my calves and went for my tray, not sitting down but sneaking in some pliés to keep warm—driving Danuta to distraction as she tried to pin on another hairpiece, this one dotted with pearls, some of which, I told her, were bound to find their way onto that stage floor. While I touched up my makeup and took a few sips of hot tea, she quietly sprayed the last curls into place, as calm as ever, keeping an eye on the clock for me.

There were just a few minutes left to attend to the toe shoes. Stooping over awkwardly, while trying to make as little noise as possible, I hammered the pointes and scraped the shanks, then applied another layer of rosin. "Monsters!" I muttered out loud, uncertain myself whether I was referring to the feet or the shoes. There was a slippery spot, a bit of grease on the sole of the right shoe, over which I was still fretting when Gerd came by to suggest that we go through our new bits again. I figured she was giving me a taste of my own medicine, having the two of us rehearse right up until the bitter end. No doubt I had it coming.

But how were we to make up for the break in continuity caused by the fallen chair? That was the pressing concern in those last seconds as I prepared for the ballroom. An intimate moment between our two characters had been omitted, tearing a tiny hole in the emotional logic running through the rest of the story. The audience was going to have to see how close I was to the Nurse to really feel the full impact of her later betrayal, when she sided with the family against me. But how was that closeness to be established now with one of the key images missing?

Taking her role to heart, Gerd nursed me through the back-stage area and up a steep flight of stairs that led to a platform overlooking the stage. Here, in view of the audience, we started our descent, traveling down a long staircase, pausing to take in the scene already underway below. As my eyes adjusted to the lights again, Juliet's emotional state seemed to come into focus, and her voice returned, as if she had been speechless but suddenly could no longer contain herself at the sight of so much dazzling finery and so many guests. Nearing the bottom of the stairs, just when those who had been dancing cleared the way in front of me, I rushed ahead into the ballroom.

Romeo and Juliet, Act III,
Bedroom Scene, with Anthony
Dowell as Romeo.

Bedroom Scene, with Anthony Dowell as Romeo.

Family Scene, with Derek Rencher as Lord Capulet.

Family Scene.

❧ ──────── ☙

Flight to Friar Laurence.

With potion bottle.

Family Scene, with Sandra Conley as
Lady Capulet.

Family Scene, with Julian Hosking as Paris.

Potion Scene.

Tomb Scene, with Anthony Dowell as Romeo.

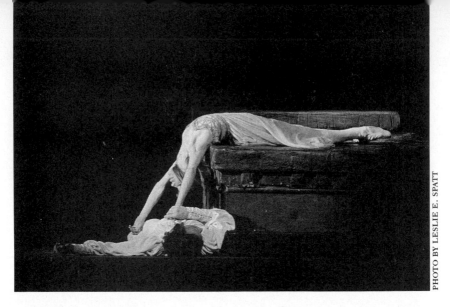

PHOTO BY LESLIE E. SPATT

Tomb Scene, with Anthony Dowell as Romeo.

Curtain call.

PHOTO BY DINA MAKAROVA

The great hall of the Capulets had been embellished by my imagination, and enlarged—so the set created by Nicholas Georgiadis had become even more lavish and expansive, continuing in all directions. Above me, candles were blazing in an immense chandelier, and in front, a vast archway opened into a courtyard extending beyond the audience. There were gardens arranged in a maze, and fountains, and even a few glittering stars. Yet none of this was actually visible now as I came to a stop near center stage and peered into the distance.

There was never really time to imagine such details in a performance. If that sublime vista existed at all, it was only because I knew how and where to look. Facing out, I drew a deep breath and rotated invisibly through my torso, altering both the intensity and direction of my gaze—as if moved by the wonder of it all. In this way Juliet's inner world shaped the space around me.

She was thrilled by the splendors that lay before her, and had to see and experience everything. This was her first ball, her first foray into the society of her parents. Having been fussed over for hours, she was anxious to test her charms. Was she aware all eyes were watching her? Not yet. What came to mind was a wish to share the adventure with the Nurse, and with that wish came a telling gesture that enabled me to add some clarity to the relationship and recover at least some measure of the confidence I had lost.

With my attention still riveted to the front, I reached back for the Nurse, who was at least twenty feet behind me. Even as my face registered Juliet's astonishment at entering this new world, my hands were seeking the Nurse—one following the other as I started around—with palms open like my heart, and fingers trembling with joy. At that instant I had the breath I needed to cross the floor between us. Rather than retreating like a timid child who had become discomfited at finding herself alone, the way the scene was taught, I was racing to the one friend who had to be with me on this night of nights.

That one gesture seemed to set the rest of this scene into motion for me. Rejoining the Nurse near the foot of the staircase, I nestled my head on her shoulder and let out a long sigh. There was no need to exchange words because I trusted her to read my thoughts, our quiet affection posing a subtle contrast to that exhibited with my mother. I accepted Mother's light kiss on the forehead, as I thanked her for the beautiful gown she had given me, and after having made one skittish attempt at evasion, I politely acquiesced to her wishes, that I dance with Paris and look him over as a possible husband.

Surely Juliet had practiced for the ball. The careful attention she devoted to dancing ultimately led to the quality I was after, though my efforts would have come to nothing had it not been for Julian's attentive partnering. This pas de deux was full of delicate pointe work, interspersed with several supported jetés. Our dancing had to answer the question of whether or not Juliet was capable of loving Paris. By constantly moving to the next step ahead of the beat, we strove to draw one long, fluid line of movement, creating a rather chilling sort of beauty, without the slightest possibility of passion.

Paris proved himself to be an expert at handling women. Yet Juliet's heart remained untouched. The clincher came just after the dance, when Julian approached to kiss my hand. Rather than focusing on the hand, he drew my eyes, with a seductive look that went beyond anything he had done in rehearsal. His glinting audacity almost took me aback. Juliet was a fast learner at this game of courtship, and she had no desire to lead Paris on or hurt him, so she pretended to be overcome by a sudden fit of timidity. I withdrew my hand and turned away, feigning shyness, only to find myself face to face with Romeo.

The setup was perfect. Just when Juliet was beginning to wield her feminine wiles to advantage and exhibit some sign of having a mind of her own, she ran headlong into fate. I came so close I nearly bumped into Anthony, who loomed over me in his mask. My body and all the world around me seemed to freeze for a moment as our eyes met for the first time, his unflinching intensity a mirror of my own.

That stillness had to capture the cataclysm of this love. Juliet was stunned by the absolute mystery of him. Who could he be? As he moved away from me across stage, I followed him intently with my eyes until others moved between us, and I remained enthralled even as Paris continued to bestow his attentions upon me. At last there came a break in the rather ceremonious

dancing which had been going on throughout, and I was released from the suitor's company. Already falling under the
spell of enchantment, I was now called upon to play the mandolin.

This interlude served as a pretext for Romeo's solo, but it was
also a chance for me to reveal Juliet's grace and sensitivity to
music. I seated myself on a small bench, stage right, pointing my
feet beneath me and supporting the instrument on my lap. The
mimetic challenge demanded more than plucking the strings.
While Romeo performed his lyrical variation, Juliet was to accompany him, seemingly absorbed by the music yet not unaware of his romantic overture. I tried to sustain a certain ele-
gance of posture, inclining my ear as if bearing down during the
more delicate passages, not allowing my eye to stray outside this
sphere of thoughtful repose.

At the angle I was sitting, almost facing out toward the audience, Anthony was outside my field of vision. Occasionally I
heard his impact on the floor, but I was listening to the voice of
the character, as if he were courting me through the eloquence
of his dancing. Unfortunately, while Anthony was putting himself through the paces, I could feel my muscles slowly tighten-
ing, and by the time he circled around me at the end, I suspected I was in for trouble. Juliet acknowledged Romeo with a
subtle look, which I managed, gritting my teeth. Having finished my little recital, I rose to my feet, giving up the mandolin
and pressing forward with some trepidation to start my own
solo.

It was one of those variations that look so deceptively simple.
Juliet would have been in her glory, shining alone in this dance.
About midway through, I started to waver, my nerves making a
sneak attack. I had been sitting too long and failed to pace
myself. Now skimming the floor, I felt the level of my body drop,
as if I were being tugged down by some diabolical change in
gravity. Coming out of a turn, I tensed up suddenly and stopped
breathing, the fear finding its way into my legs. Resisting all out
panic, I forced a smile, not wanting to let on this stinker of a solo
was getting the better of me.

There was no time to catch my breath when I was already in
the middle of a phrase—stepping up onto pointe with arms over

my head, and swinging the right leg back through rond de jambe. This step had to be repeated three times, moving back diagonally, with each step becoming more joyous than the previous one. I was losing definition in my upper body, unable to hold on to the shape and breathe out for that extra second that would make the moment really exciting. By the third time through, that swinging leg had become something dangerous, throwing my weight back and off the supporting leg, as I gasped for air.

The founder of the Royal Ballet, Dame Ninette de Valois, was known to chide dancers for "catching flies"—that is, for dancing with their mouths wide open. I had now become Gelsey the Flycatcher, or so it seemed. I tried to assure myself I would be forgiven. If this were really Juliet's first ball, a moment of awkwardness would probably go unnoticed . . . or might even seem charming.

Love reaching for the stars—that was the idea that I was going for, though it seemed absurdly unattainable under the circumstances. I passed Romeo standing off at the side and tore into a long circle of jumps, all of them connected by rapid hairpin turns on pointe. I told myself not to hold back, just to breathe and relax a bit, at which point I relinquished any control over my body. It was like an endless chain reaction, one tiny fluff following another. With my ribs and shoulders lifting up, I was off-balance, pulled away from the floor, the metatarsals in my left foot straining every time I pushed off.

Passing near Anthony again, I came around for one last treacherous diagonal and three arabesques traveling downstage. How did everything go so wrong so fast? Perhaps Juliet had been too eager to please. If she seemed somewhat nervous turning that circle, at least she had been willing to take a few risks—that was the best rationalization I could muster. But how was I going to meet Romeo with any kind of grace? I summoned whatever there was left inside for those arabesques, holding the last joyous moment only through what seemed like the most excruciating exertion.

Then a miracle happened.

Just when I was about to teeter over, I was swept off my feet and lifted into the air, the lights all of a sudden very bright and close. It was Anthony who had come from behind. The grip of his hands tightened around my back as he moved me, not up and down but in a semicircle, with all the guests looking on. I spiraled forward, and at the same time pushed down as though I were still on the floor, resisting the direction he was turning me —once again, opening my heart. The curve, like his effort, was unswerving, beyond perfect, making up for everything that had come before.

There were three of these lifts that swept an arc in the middle of the ballroom. I gave Anthony all my weight, perhaps contributing to the physical stress that might one day land him in that fanciful museum he had once mentioned. If I were to jump to help him with the lift, we would break the motion and lose the shape. This was the first time Romeo had touched Juliet. I sensed no tension in those hands upon which I balanced, but I knew he had to be straining. It was the only way to bring both the feeling and illusion to life.

And did he ever!

The rush of exhilaration carried me through the scene and, after the ballroom was cleared, all the way through our pas de deux. Alone with him for the first time on that immense stage, I was almost dazed—the space around us shimmering when he seized my hand and brought it to his lips. Nothing could stay the course of this love—not even Juliet's discovery that Romeo was a Montague, made only too clear when a brutish Tybalt, danced by David Drew, came between us and tried to start a fight. From then on, with the Nurse confirming my worst fears about Romeo's identity, a sense of foreboding intermingled with my joy and stayed with me, until the lights came down.

I scrambled offstage, then into the changing room to ready myself for the balcony, trying to set a record for the quickest of quick changes. Off with the gold dress and on with the pale green. There was only time to slap one more layer of rosin on the shoes before I found myself being led along by a stagehand to the back stairway. I knew my legs were bound to catch up with me sooner or later. The darkness seemed to drag against my feet as if I were wading through an undertow. Even the most exalted emotions and all the moonlight in the universe could never make up for such a lack of stamina.

Had I not already jinxed myself for this scene?

As I climbed the stairs, I heard Kenneth's voice, at its most abrasive in the back of my mind, saying what he had said during dress rehearsal, *We can't see you, Gelsey. You're not in the light!* It was a correction that meant I should come out far enough onto the balcony to be fully lit. I was jarred as much now, waiting behind a curtain to make the entrance, as I had been then. I tried to aim my thoughts elsewhere and took a few deep breaths, holding my hand out in front of me—the same hand Romeo had caressed only moments ago in the ballroom.

Juliet's voice returned: *My only love sprung from my only hate!* That line got me through the curtain. I walked slowly into the light and put both hands on the balcony rail, steadying myself and listening to the soft strains drifting up from the orchestra. This time, as I raised my hand and started to draw it in to my breast, a shadow fell across the palm, providing a real mystery for me to solve as I lifted my gaze to the sky, with Romeo about to steal into the garden below. What accident of moon and wayward cloud could be casting such a shadow?

I carried that little omen with me when I did, finally, rush down those stairs. Three steps from the bottom I felt my feet slipping out from under me and made a desperate leap to the floor, somehow catching myself without breaking either my neck or my stride. No one was more astonished than I was when I made it, but I was doubly astounded when this pas de deux surpassed even our best efforts in the studio. Anthony's confidence gave us the freedom to take every sort of risk.

At one point, as Juliet ran toward the edge of the garden, so overjoyed she no longer even knew where she was going, I was about to race right into the wings and out of the theatre—and might have done so had he not caught my hand just as it swung up behind me. But he did, bringing me to a sudden halt, an almost magical stillness falling between us as I turned to him, ever so slowly, his eyes pinning me to the spot.

It was more than timing. There was something so urgent and utterly fearless in all his gestures from beginning to end. The way he enfolded my hands and clasped them to his cheek as he knelt in front of me, with the side of his face resting on my open palms, and the long curve of his spine aimed as if to pierce my heart. He seemed to be saying this tenderness was the only form of courage left in the world . . . and he said it with such a passion I believed him and took it as a vow.

Plunged back into darkness after finishing the scene, I heard applause coming from dancers in the wings, and felt encouraged enough to think Juliet might somehow outlast my body. My luck held out for our brief wedding, midway through the second act, with the good Friar, played by Christopher Newton, directing the whirlwind ceremony. Instead of fawning over Romeo, I quietly knelt at his side, listening to the Friar as if he were saying something on which our lives actually depended, the solemnity disrupted only by a steady throb coming from the big toe in my right foot.

Then came a long period during which I was offstage. Tybalt had to slay Mercutio; Romeo had to do away with Tybalt; and the audience had to have an intermission.

That interval was my undoing. Shortly before Anthony and I were to perform the bedroom pas de deux at the beginning of the third and final act, my feet seized up, the first wave of spasms coming while I was in the dressing room. First the right, then the left. My feet were pointing on their own as the muscles under the arches contracted, like two fists clenched inside the shoes. I pulled my heels out and squeezed my fingers inside to get at the knots, silently agonizing.

After the pain subsided, I spread a towel over the floor and did some gentle stretches, until the muscles released. But another wave of spasms took hold soon after the dresser helped me into my costume, the beige nightgown I would wear for the rest of the ballet. Danuta happened to be standing over my shoulder in front of the mirror, finishing my hair. All I could do was shift my legs under me and try to keep still a little longer, fixing my eyes on the last pin she held between her lips at the corner of her mouth. She was done for the night and ready to go home. So was I unless those muscles unlocked.

I remembered a performance of *Don Quixote* that took place in 1978, when Anthony and I were dancing with American Ballet Theatre at the Kennedy Center. He had suffered an attack of cramps in the final act and been forced to make an early exit. I figured if I were unable to continue this performance, he would certainly understand, though the idea of my pulling out at this point was more than mildly appalling.

By the time I left the dressing room, I had taken that train of thought as far as envisioning how an announcement that I was being replaced might go over with the audience. While the curtain was still down, I went straight onto the stage, which was set for the bedroom scene. When Anthony found me, I was near the foot of the bed, pushing through a few careful barre exercises to warm up again. I decided not to mention the cramps. They seemed to be under control as long as I kept moving. With only minutes to go, I coaxed Anthony into running through the scene. He was still recovering from his grueling duel with Tybalt, but went along without hesitation, perhaps sensing my distress.

We worked through several sections of the pas de deux, until we ran out of time and had to take our places on the bed. The curtain would rise with the two of us partially under covers, blissfully asleep. We waited, sitting upright, side by side with our legs stretched out in front of us. As Anthony leaned forward reaching for his ankles, I turned sideways to fluff up one of the pillows in back of me, telling myself not to get too comfortable. What if I actually fell asleep? Seeing the curious look he was giving me, I said in a low voice, "It is past my bedtime, you know."

His expression brightened. "Oh, I'm keeping you up, am I?"

But I never had the chance to reply. At that instant my feet seized again as if somebody had come sneaking up on me and yanked those big toes. The shock must have contorted my face as I stared down my body. Two spastic feet! This could not really be happening. How could both of them cramp at exactly the same time? The light seemed to go dim. I vaguely heard Anthony's voice asking, "What's wrong?"

"Look at them!"

"What? What is it?" His tone was one of pure bewilderment, both of us now looking at my pink toe shoes, which were poised at the end of the bed, pointing almost perfectly.

"But I'm not doing that," I told him.

His brows shot up. "Oh my God!"

The next thing I knew he was bending over my legs, massaging the calves and working his way down. I felt like a boxer between rounds, my eyes rolling around in their sockets.

"How much time?" I asked him.

His grimace said none, but he kept at it with his hands long enough to get the blood moving. I tried wiggling my toes and was somewhat reassured when I was able to feel them rubbing against the insides of the shoes. As soon as we heard the first muffled notes coming from the orchestra, we pulled the covers up over our legs, and laid down quickly, settling our heads on the pillows. As Anthony sidled closer, curling his arm around me, I closed my eyes and whispered to him softly, "Better say a prayer."

I sensed the curtain going up, the lights and music both brightening, and the air around my face moving gently, as if the stage had drawn breath, perhaps some morning breeze. By the time I felt Anthony stirring next to me, I was slipping back into that peculiar double awareness which seemed to divide all my thoughts. There was Gelsey and there was Juliet, the outward distinction now disguised only by the mask of sleep.

This pas de deux was one of the more exacting, with so many lifts and spins and abrupt changes of direction we needed a road map to get through it. But the challenge was to make the choreography capture the whole range of emotions that would pass between us in those moments before Romeo was forced to flee. He had already been banished and was under threat of death even as he rose from bed, wrapped his cape around his shoulders, and checked the window for the first signs of daylight.

When I opened my eyes, the beauty of our wedding night still enfolded me, like a dream from which I refused to awaken, the senses yielding through those hours of rapture what the heart had known all along. But Romeo shattered that dream, standing in front of the window and pulling aside the curtain, letting in the cruel realities of this morning. Somehow I found my legs, just when I needed them, and moved off the bed, backing away from the light, away from Romeo.

Against that backdrop of terror, how were we to keep hope or dreams alive? Without actually lifting the arms, I reached out to draw Romeo back to me, to hold back the dawn, with Juliet's voice becoming a single breath, coiling in the body and held like a note of music: *It was the nightingale, not the lark!* But the impulse was suddenly desperate, uncontainable. I flew across the stage as he started toward me, my arms finding his, sweeping them all the way around behind my back as we came together, an ecstatic embrace—marred only by a realization that I had misjudged the placing and landed on the wrong foot.

Anthony offered me encouragement under his breath, while he whisked us through the next couple of steps. I dared not point the toes as strenuously as I would have liked, though I kept working through both feet, rolling up onto pointe and compensating with the rest of my body whenever I sensed the muscles straining. It seemed for a while as if those prayers might be answered, the two of us moving together as if through some medium other than air, concealing the one tiny lapse. But fate was simply lying in ambush, waiting to pounce when we least expected.

We were well into the scene when I broke away from Romeo and ran to the other window, upstage right. Without opening the curtain, I spun around to him and froze, the thought now becoming unbearable: *He must go, or die!* We had changed the timing, so Anthony waited before he rushed to me, speeding up the steps that followed and heightening the suspense. Grabbing my wrists, he pulled me toward him, both of us arching back in a brief tug of war, unable to tear ourselves apart.

I suddenly whirled around to the window, swinging the right leg into arabesque as he took me by the waist. Then he whipped me back around to him . . . and back to the window, staying in tight behind me as I swung my left leg into another arabesque. Feeling his hand slide under my thigh, I braced myself, the floor dropping out from under the supporting leg as he lifted me across his chest. I pointed my feet by curling the eight littlest toes, and watched the stage go spinning into a total blur. Unable to spot in front of me through nearly four spins, I was unable to avoid becoming dizzy. Yet we had planned it this way, as a kind of whirling outcry to the heavens.

I came down on one foot, with the stage still whizzing around me. My first step was shaky, but he had placed me down at an angle that would hide my disorientation. I was already on my way back to him, at full speed, as if my legs knew where to go before I did. The climax of this sequence was a rather acrobatic underarm lift. He would catch me just as I turned into him, then hoist me high over his head behind his back, with his arms fully extended under my biceps. The worst was behind us. I was sure we were home free. This was one of those moves not nearly as difficult as it looked, and we had done it so many times.

But it never happened—at least not the way either of us ever imagined. We missed, one of my underarms somehow proving too elusive for him to handle securely. I found myself slung across his back at a perilous angle, sliding down his spine until he managed to flip me over and bring me down into the carry that followed. There was, almost miraculously, no fall or break in the movement. We simply kept going. Most likely the audience would never even know, although a few eagle-eyed critics might be wondering about the "choice" we made back there. But still, it grated, teasing the edges of my brain like a missed note, or a flubbed line. Only worse. The thought could never be completed.

I almost wished I had fallen. At least they would have known they had missed something. Juliet's anguished *Why?*—that question of all questions she was to have hurled at the stars themselves—had remained locked in my throat as I lay paralyzed on Romeo's back. Only my entire body arching up into the lights could have made that climactic utterance felt. But there was no getting it back now. The moment was long gone.

I knew Anthony had to be disappointed, as aware as he was of that image created by our two bodies. Nothing escaped him. Yet I sensed only his fierce resolve. He never let down or lost sight of the story we were telling, even guiding me through one grief-stricken arabesque as we approached the finish. I was in a slightly awkward position, swaying as I swung the left leg behind and slid my hands down his arms, pulling away from him, my grip latched around his wrists like a pair of handcuffs.

I heard him hiss softly, "Left! Lean left!"

Any words spoken by dancers onstage are actually rare enough to be quite startling. His warning found my ear just as I was rising onto pointe, balanced on my right leg. He saw what I felt: my left shoulder was pulling up, so I was tilting to the right. His hands no doubt turned blue as mine tightened another notch around his wrists. I strained to adjust, and let go, my arms slicing above my head. Then I tipped over toward him, lunging forward, the two of us slowly collapsing into a graceful sprawl.

Which was, fortunately, the intended outcome.

Our parting embrace seemed to be the last chance for us to salvage this scene. As Juliet broke down, and tumbled on to that hopelessly rutted stage floor, I was asking myself whether she or I had the strength to endure Romeo's departure. I tensed the muscles along my spine, not dropping my head, hearing myself gasp when he seized my arm, yanking me to my feet. The shake he gave my shoulders was brusque and felt almost as if he had given me a bracing sort of slap. I closed my eyes, conscious only of the sensation of his body pressing against mine . . . and my lips taking the shape of his.

Then I stood quite still, until I knew he was gone.

I knew what to expect in the end—the numbness, the surge of recollection, the tears of joy and sorrow, the sense of moments irretrievably lost. How could my experience onstage possibly measure up to the ideal vision I created in the studio? The disparity had overwhelmed me in the past, so much so that I became inwardly wretched when confronted with compliments or the inevitable question, "How was it for you, Gelsey?" If I were not clever enough to escape my own torment, I might at least turn the question around tonight.

I had scribbled down all of my fears and confided them to Greg, knowing the performance itself would inevitably wipe out any sense of perspective. What I dreaded most was leaving the stage and returning to the world in such emotional disarray I was unable to share any thoughts with anyone. Greg had suggested, not quite seriously, that I try staying in character until we left the theatre. There was no chance of that, though I did hope some of Juliet's finer qualities would stay with me long enough to ease us through the ordeal. If only I had the presence of mind to see with the eyes of the audience, and really know how much came across.

The last line of a play, it is said, can sometimes save a performance from indifference or bring an otherwise inspired effort to ruin. The same thing may be true of the last gestures in a ballet, and I was more than aware of both possibilities when I crawled on to the tomb in the final scene. Juliet was already dying and her voice cracking with grief, as I inched my way to the very edge of the tomb. From here I could see Romeo's lifeless body: Anthony was stretched out on the floor below me. I reached for his hand and slowly pulled it all the way up, feeling what no one saw, as he helped me lift his arm.

Then I clasped his hand to my cheek and held it there as long as I could, as if the simplicity of the gesture could make this one moment last forever. Turning over onto my back, I kept my focus moving up, allowing the movement of my eyes and torso to create an arc, sweeping from my heart and forehead all the way to heaven. I felt infinitely vulnerable as I lay across that naked slab of wood. Still I held on to Romeo's hand—not letting go until the final breath was spent—until there was only the quiet of our bodies, and the music passing over us.

When the curtain dropped down, I heard Anthony whisper, "Don't move! Picture call!" But I had slipped a fraction of an inch too far over the edge, my head and shoulders threatening to pull me to the floor. Only my pointed feet, pressed against the surface of the tomb, kept me from going over. The curtain went up again as I struggled behind closed eyelids, sustaining the stillness as if caught in the middle of Juliet's last desperate prayer.

When I heard the first wave of applause, my doubts were already clamoring to be acknowledged. Had I lifted the dagger high enough into the air? Was that death believable? No sooner was the curtain down than I was on my feet. Anthony was standing in front of me, suddenly, taking my face into his hands. He held my gaze for a moment, his eyes shining through exhaustion. Then he slipped his fingers in back of my neck, with gentle urgency fastening his cheek to mine. The blush of affection sent my heart tripping into my throat.

Neither of us said a word. The tomb was quickly cleared, and we found our places center stage, flanked by the rest of the cast, linked hand-to-hand. There was no way to tell yet with any certainty how the performance had been received. The heat of the lights hung in the air, as did the lingering scent of sweat. The atmosphere was hushed, charged with a strange mixture of anxiety and relief—like a battlefield, I thought, after the dead are carried off and only the ghosts remain.

Anthony was on my left, and Julian on my right, with the huge red curtain rising up swiftly in front. We walked forward into a tumult of applause. The ovation was like something alive, swirling around us, gathering force with each step. I felt tears welling, and both hands being squeezed tight. My eyes kept going out of focus, adding yet another soft layer of unreality to what was already unreal. The presence of the audience and all those clapping hands was unfathomable. Had they actually been out there the whole time?

After our first bow, the conductor joined us onstage, and several enormous bouquets of roses were carried from the wings and ceremoniously presented, the first of which I placed on the floor as an offering to the company. The formal gesture seemed almost pitifully inadequate, but it was all that could be done for the moment to convey some hint of the debt of gratitude I owed. The uproar continued unabated even as the stage manager lowered the curtain again. With only the final calls remaining, I hurried offstage to wait, already overcome by my own riotous emotions. The thought of my husband and mother shot through my mind. I wondered where they were sitting, and whether they were pleased.

While some of the other principals sallied forth to take their bows, I stood in the wings, trying to get a grip on myself. Bending over to check my shoes, I was dismayed to see they were no longer pink, but black—coming apart at the seams and scuffed beyond redemption. Tiny holes had worn through the pointes, so the lining under the silk was visible, peeking out at me as I rubbed my fingers over the material and imagined the surprise in store for those unsuspecting balletomanes who trained their opera glasses on my feet.

When I came up for air, I was descended upon by Kenneth himself, who seemed to come out of nowhere, materializing over my shoulder like an apparition. His smiling face beamed as he took hold of my hands and leaned toward me, heedless to any risk my makeup may have posed to his gray suit. He announced with a rapid whisper in my ear, "I'm coming out with you, Gelsey. It's Juliet's twenty-first birthday."

Twenty-first birthday? What on earth was he talking about? I had no idea he meant the anniversary of his ballet, and only later would I learn that the actual birthday had gone by unnoticed three months before. I was still bewildered as the three of us—Anthony, Kenneth, and I—moved quickly onto the stage. The presence of the choreographer came as something more than an unexpected honor. I took his enthusiasm to be a sign of approval; and as I was always somewhat apprehensive about the audience, I figured there might be safety in numbers—with the reaction from the house divided between us, at least temporarily.

But the curtain calls were another story. After our improvised tribute for Kenneth was over, I followed Anthony into the wings, and then through a narrow passageway that led to the apron of the stage. From here, only the orchestra pit separated us from pandemonium. I felt like I was in the path of an approaching subway train, the sound obliterating all but the most fragmentary impressions. The galleries went up hundreds of feet in front of us, and from the balconies overhead there came a continuous shower of daffodils, raining down until we found ourselves ankle deep in their petals. Shouts rang out over the din, and bouquets of roses were thrown from the front rows, landing at our feet.

From one of the bouquets, I plucked a single rose and presented it to Anthony, eliciting another boisterous roar as the two of us embraced. Perhaps the lovers were still alive after all. We carried their dreams in our bodies—in the very shape we had been fighting for all along. But it was Anthony who kissed my cheek, not Romeo. I recognized a familiar mannerism as soon as he stepped back. He had a way of cocking his head, with a slightly impish smile that seemed to spill over his face from one side to the other. He was no longer acting, and neither was I, though our gestures emerged from the same wondrous form out of which the story had unfolded.

To face each other now was to enter a realm of pure feeling, which had to be turned out so the audience might enter as well. My eyelashes were batting away uncontrollably as I moved toward the front and tried to avoid being blinded by another flurry of daffodils. One of the stems was bound to poke an eye, sooner or later. With arms at my sides, I set my gaze at the center of the far balcony, and looked beyond, to the left and right along its golden façade, as if to embrace the whole theatre at once. Then I swept forward into a bow. My vision was swamped with tears, but I could see people out front suddenly rising to their feet. Were they leaving? Lifting my focus to the balcony again, I spotted both sides before turning around to Anthony. Whatever doubts I may have had, they were banished by the ovation and his luminous smile.

I heard a chorus of "bravos" when we left the stage. The remaining calls took on a kind of frantic levity behind the scenes as Anthony and I tried to make our entrances and exits, together and apart, without bumping into each other in the tight passage that ran between the curtains. I was never really sure whether I was coming off or going on—and yet, each time the moment arrived to face the audience alone, I was amazed by the calmness that came over me. I had the feeling I was stepping into some fantastic mirage.

It was my mother, the former actress, who, years ago, taught me the purpose of the bow was not to bask in praise or milk applause, but to conjure an image of sublime reverence for the theatre. At that time, I had only started to appreciate the challenge of mastering the dramatic repertory, and had no idea what it might mean to open one's heart at the end of a performance and draw in the entire audience. Between the rather awkward showgirl curtsies I had seen at the New York City Ballet and the mannered poses of the Russians, there seemed to be little room for natural gesture. It was not until I saw what Margot Fonteyn was able to do simply by lifting one of her graceful arms into the air that I realized another approach might exist. Her secret, however, was not the arm, but the simplicity—the emotional thread that extended from her heart to the tips of her fingers—before she ever bowed her head.

Between calls, just before I ventured out for the last time, I was approached in the wings by an elderly woman whose unexpected appearance caught me somewhat off guard. She walked with the aid of a cane, and with the sort of fearless conviction that should have been enough to tell anyone this was her theatre and her company. Indeed, Dame Ninette de Valois—"Madame," as she was called—had more or less willed the Royal Ballet into existence, and it is probably not too much of an exaggeration to say that without this remarkable woman, tonight's performance would never have taken place.

Tonight, like so many other nights, was a part of her vision. At eighty-seven, she was still teaching and coaching, writing and lecturing. There was something in her manner that always reminded me she had started out her career as a pantomime as well as a ballerina. In fact, she had become a star by the age of fourteen. Irrepressible, and Irish, she had worked everywhere from the opera to the music halls, from Sergei Diaghilev's Ballet Russe, to William Butler Yeats's Abbey Theatre. As far as I was concerned, Dame Ninette was the best living record of ballet in this century, if only because she had drawn the best from the Italian, French, and Russian schools, combining it all with her own roots and rich tradition of British drama.

She was petite, even smaller than I. Wisps of gray hair were set off by a dark silk scarf she had wrapped around her throat. When she smiled, her whole face lit up, and a fine web of wrinkles fanned out from the corners of her eyes. "You see, dear," she said, leaning on her cane and gesturing toward the other side of the curtain, "Everyone loves you here. You must stay with us."

I was floored. She was surely being kind, but no one of her stature had ever said anything like that to me before. I stammered something about my catching flies in the ballroom, but she was a bit hard of hearing. A look of confusion clouded her face. She drew closer, her voice rising an octave, becoming more emphatic—as if she had decided to lay down the law: "But you simply must stay!" Her expression softened again as I offered assurance. Then she encouraged me toward the stage with that cane of hers.

I was still glowing inside when I made my final exit. Closed off by the curtain, the set was already under seige by stagehands. I tried cutting through, anxious to get back to my dressing room. But it was hopeless. The backstage area was now a hive of excitement, and I found myself surrounded by the crowd that had gathered. The numbness was setting in. I felt nothing below the waist, as if my legs had been lopped off and I were standing by some miracle of faith. Each time someone grabbed my hand, I was surprised to see my arm rise in front of me, still attached.

I managed to keep my smile flying, though my mind kept moving out of the picture. I was standing on that spot where the tomb had been in the last act, and I humored myself with the thought that those warring families had come together belatedly in the jubilant scene taking place around me. I noticed Anthony, hemmed in a few feet away, graciously accepting compliments from a group of awestruck admirers. The director of the opera house, Sir John Tooley, came toward me, bringing an exuberant sense of moment to the occasion. Always the most refined gentleman, there was an air of quiet authority and a certain aristocratic opulence about him.

He also exhibited that dry British flair for flattery, whispering in my ear, "What a genius you are." He sealed the accolade with a kiss on the cheek, and then he hurried away, as if the blush might be contagious. A few years ago, I probably would have made a dash for the nearest exit, not even aware of the embarrassment I might have caused. But tonight I held my demons at bay. It was almost as if Juliet were in some way making up for my lack of self-esteem.

And so it went, with each brief encounter calling up a jumble of conflicting moods, all of which filtered through fatigue and endless amazement. The adulation was certainly at odds with my unspoken reservations; and yet I was touched, and proud beyond words. I drew a panicky mental blank when it came to remembering names and making introductions, but one familiar face put me instantly at ease. He went all the way back to my childhood—to the New York City Ballet. And what a star he had been—before making a more lasting mark in the world.

"Arthur, what are you doing here?" I blurted as he came through the ring of onlookers.

Arthur Mitchell was the founding director of the Dance Theatre of Harlem, though I still remembered him as Puck, from George Balanchine's version of *A Midsummer Night's Dream*, and as one of those older dancers whose laughter had once inspired bouts of self-conscious torment on the part of that serious little girl I had been at the awkward age of ten. He happened to be in town tonight. Dressed for a formal evening and grinning ear to ear, he pulled me into his arms, exclaiming, "Now that was really good stuff! You know what I mean?"

His warm, fatherly hug worked wonders, leaving no room to reply or even breathe.

There were so many voices and faces, so much affection coming from so many directions at once. Anthony's assistant, Iris, held on to my hands, quietly beside herself. Her reaction gave me a double pleasure because I knew her joy was yet another measure of his. A congratulatory kiss from the company's general administrator, Anthony Russell-Roberts, carried with it a special significance in light of the risk the Royal Ballet had assumed on my behalf, giving me the chance to dance again. This Anthony was a nephew to the Royal Ballet's most venerated choreographer, Sir Frederick Ashton; but he was also the charming man who handled the business side of things—the "money bags," as he put it. He was the one who had negotiated for me to appear, and his relief had to be almost as great as mine.

The knot in my throat tightened a notch when I spotted a small group of friends and family heading toward me, with my brother Christopher and my mother leading the way. The pride shining in her face was enough to erase the memories of those nightmare years; she was radiant—and I felt like the prodigal daughter returning to the fold. I managed to thank my lawyer and my editor, who had made the trip from America to lend their support. The set, what had been fair Verona, was coming apart all around us; and the stagehands were issuing orders to leave the stage, jostling everybody out of the way. When I finally saw my husband's tear-bright eyes, I rushed ahead of myself, so wobbly I almost flopped over. With my head pressed against his chest, I heard only the words—"so beautiful," as if they had escaped from his rib cage. I thought I might never move or dance again, but spend the rest of my life on this spot, held fast by the arms around my waist. Lifting my face, I found his bow tie, lopsided and dangling in front of my nose like a mischievous butterfly; and I could feel laughter tickle the back of my throat, trying to get out even as we kissed . . . his tears mixing with mine.

My lips were tingling with pins and needles, and I was in love with the whole world. My husband helped me introduce my mother and brother to Anthony and to those who supported me in the studio, Monica and Donald. My family was being included in my life for the first time I could remember. This had never happened before, not like this. I had shut them out, my mother especially, as if I were hiding the darkest of secrets. For a few years, of course, I had been doing exactly that, but even during the happiest times, I had never really been able to share such a blessing.

The winding halls that led back to the dressing rooms were filled with dancers racing around in and out of costume, and members of the technical staff trying to keep up with them. Greg steered us along the corridor. Running into Julian, I made sure he knew just how beautifully he had partnered. He donned a modest grin, obviously pleased, but was quick to say he intended to improve his next performance. After being side-tracked into a few last good-byes, I was hit by the finality of it all. Tonight was over; and the shock was going to take days to wear off. My muscles would twitch as they replayed every movement; the score would haunt me, like an infernal ringing in the ears. Such was the curse—having to accept the fact that our actions on the stage were as irreversible as those of the characters we had portrayed.

Turning the last corner in the maze, I asked Greg, "Did you think the death really worked?"

"Like a charm," he said. "There were people all around me sobbing. But you just can't imagine how I felt, watching you die up there, and knowing . . ."

"The bedroom scene was pretty shaky," I told him.

"Not from my seat," he insisted.

Outside the door to my dressing room, more people were waiting. Before we could enter, a dear friend, Patrik Moreton, introduced us to the English actress, Jean Marsh, well-known in America for her work in public television's "Upstairs Downstairs." She was a striking woman with sharp, etched features, and a pair of eyes that seemed to rule out any dissembling. My voice sounded terribly scratchy, and apologetic, as I confessed I had missed a few steps. She gave me a knowing look, as if she recognized some shared foible. Patrik jumped in, with his white suit and characteristic brand of zeal, "Oh, dear, fuck the steps! I mean . . . what an actress!" I was at a loss, trying to explain how a dancer acts through the steps.

Jean, looking more like Greta Garbo by the minute, came to my rescue, kindly inviting us for a visit to her home in the country. Then I felt a gentle tug at my arm. My husband gave me the "hook," so to speak, pulling me into the dressing room, which now resembled a funeral parlor, with flowers strewn from floor to ceiling. After stripping down to a pair of tights and pulling on a robe, I plunked myself into a chair at the makeup table. From here, I did my best to greet a steady stream of friends and fans, who came in two and three at a time. Unfortunately, between all of those flowers, the hair spray, the makeup, and a thick haze of cigarette smoke, our cramped, little room soon began to smell as if someone had actually died.

The only window was jammed shut. I sensed some of those old insecurities bubbling up inside of me, along with a passing twinge of resentment—which I directed at the mirror. Between visitors, my husband came from behind and stroked the back of my neck, saying in a soft voice, "I know everybody wants to see you, they're only trying to be kind, but it's beginning to feel like a freak show in here. You've fulfilled the obligation to the audience. We can go anytime."

"No," I told him, "I'm fine. Really." Which was not quite true; I was running out of patience as well as oxygen. "I keep hoping," I added, "someone will ask me why I was pointing my toes even after Juliet was already supposed to be dead. You know, that ironic touch of grace." Which was true; I was curious to know how many of those details the audience had noticed.

Two of Greg's old friends, Barry Laine and Stephen Greco, brought a draft of fresh air into the room. They had gone to college with Greg, and both were, coincidentally, critics. I was fond of them and happy they had been able to finagle the airfares to come from New York. Barry had been a consultant on my memoirs, and we had become close over the past two years, despite my longstanding misgivings about critics. By the very nature of our callings, we tended to look at ballet from different, and sometimes opposing, points of view; but our exchanges were stimulating and always marked by the warmest affection.

Of the two friends, Barry was more restrained in manner and cautiously thoughtful. Stephen was easier to read, exuberant, occasionally leaping ahead of himself, brushing a lock or two from his forehead as he groped for the right word. It was Barry who took the lead tonight, commenting, "Well, there's a lot to think about, but one thing I can say, your Juliet is certainly the most complex I've seen. You have so many things going on at once. Even in the ballroom, for instance . . ." He looked like he was picturing that scene in his mind, but held back, offering no further elaboration.

Stephen, standing beside him, used the opening to broach a more delicate subject. "Gelsey, were you pleased with your performance? Did you think it went well?"

My exhausted "yes" seemed not to convince him.

Moving closer and pressing on, he said, "But did you have trouble with the side of you that always demands such perfection?"

For a split second, I felt like I was being interviewed, though his concern was genuine and mirrored by Barry's intent expression.

"I gave the best performance I could give," I said, rallying myself. "Whatever flaws there were, I have time to work out. I do get support here, and I don't waste my time trying to perfect some of those superficial things I was taught when I was younger. I'm still as much of a perfectionist, but—"

"You give yourself a hug now and then?" Stephen was quick to interject.

"Right," I said, after a moment's hesitation, not quite catching his drift at first.

"Or somebody gives her one," quipped Barry, eliciting a bright ripple of laughter.

There were parting embraces all around; and both friends said again how moved they had been. I felt encouraged by their visit, but after they had gone, I wondered if the London critics would be as kind. The British press had a reputation for being notoriously difficult to please. The prospect of the reviews was a bit unsettling.

I glanced at Greg, who had piled several bouquets in the sink and was turning on the tap, saying something about letting them soak overnight. Dina had organized all of my telegrams and cards into a neat batch, and suggested we try a French restaurant which happened to be a favorite of Natasha's—Chez Solange. In my haste to leave, I decided against taking off my makeup; once again, I was a sight, with splotches of spirit gum on my face and false eyelashes weighing down eyelids already at half-mast. Overloaded with bags and flowers and more bags, we finally left my dressing room, only to find another crowd camping outside the stage door. These were mostly children and the truly hardcore balletomanes. I sat on a couch in the lobby and signed as many autographs as my empty stomach and addled brain allowed.

The streets of Covent Garden were blustery, and packed with the after-the-show mob, everyone hurrying helter-skelter to catch the last trains. Dina had a car waiting for us, although the restaurant was walking distance from the theatre. She had taken care of everything. I had passed the point where I was making any choices, and simply allowed myself to be guided forward, hugging my canvas bag to my chest, reassured by the arm around my shoulders. Eventually, a small, matronly woman with a French accent ushered the three of us into a cozy corner booth. We were sitting at the end of a long, rectangular dining room, with paneled walls that looked as soft as the cushion of my chair, into which I was slowly sinking.

I felt like an amnesia victim. The two familiar faces on either side of me were my only links to reality, though the smell of food offered some hope for revival. While I devoured a main course of sole, sticking to my diet of fish, Greg read aloud from the cards. The most touching were from dancers, including a group who had dubbed themselves, "Gelsey's Angels." One card was emblazoned with a black cat, which I was surprised to learn was a sign of good luck in the British theatre. One of those magical creatures must have crossed my path tonight, I said, though I was really not superstitious.

Dina, who had been my silent guardian angel most of the evening, prevailed upon me to try a French pastry. Over coffee and dessert, the first I had eaten in years, I opened Anthony's *merde*—Greg again performed the honors, reading the message.

> *Dearest Gelsey,*
>
> *To have you "back where you belong" makes me so very happy; I hope this will be the first of many performances with us.*
>
>

All my love,
Anthony
>

I could hear the emotion in my husband's voice, when he added, "Well, I think you've finally come to the right place." I was too moved to say anything. In slow motion, my hands tore open the neatly wrapped box. Inside the layers of tissue paper was a tiny glass bottle, an exquisite antique of cut crystal, with a silver cap.

A potion bottle!

It was almost too perfect.

Passed between us, it caught the light and glittered like a prism. Holding it up to my eye, I aimed it at my husband like a spyglass, but I was only able to see the colors that it captured inside itself.

"You know," he remarked quietly, "what sort of potion this bottle would have been used for when we first met."

"It's amazing, to think . . ." Dina agreed.

Replacing the card and the bottle carefully inside the box, I said, quite simply, "We have so much to be grateful for."

"A night to end all nights," said Greg.

During the cab ride back to the flat, he rested his head on my shoulder, while I squeezed my thanks into the palm of his hand. I watched all of London speeding by us outside the window, as the memories came rushing back to me. The fallen chair in the first act . . . the slip on the balcony steps . . . the cramps . . . the lift that never came off. Yet I felt strangely detached, as if I were remembering someone else's performance. I did know I had managed to fill the most crucial moments, but I had not yet come to terms with the experience or made peace with myself. The taxi rattled to a stop in front of our door. After settling with the driver and juggling the flowers, bags, and keys, we made our way into the flat, like a couple of inept thieves.

The lights were blazing as if we had never gone out.

Greg headed into the living room.

I headed into the bath.

We yelled, trading muffled endearments back and forth, and then we gave up. The task of removing my makeup was like taking a chisel to plaster. But the steam and bath water seemed to put everything right again, and I made myself ready for bed in record time. When I came out, I found my husband sprawled on the mattress, having removed his shoes and jacket, which lay over the back of the only chair. He was sound asleep with an arm crooked across his face and that bow tie of his resting at the center of his chest. He looked so completely serene, I decided not to wake him.

The flat smelled faintly of floor wax and boiled cabbage, the latter being a new addition to my diet. As I crept around the living room, padding across the wood floors in my bare feet, each step I took seemed to echo inside my head. I turned on the television; only one channel was still on the air, showing some old black-and-white horror flick. I killed the sound, then went to retrieve Anthony's potion bottle from the entrance hall where we had dumped everything. I wanted to find an appropriate spot for it in the living room. The problem was the bottle was so tiny, and the room was so huge.

At one end were windows rising to the ceiling, and at the other end was a fireplace, over which hung an ornate mirror, so high I had never even seen my reflection; the rest of the space was empty, except for our mattress and a few makeshift pieces of furniture. There was a mantelpiece above the fireplace, but the bottle, placed at the center, appeared so unstable I feared the slightest tremor might topple it. The idea soon possessed me to store the treasure under my pillow.

Maybe it was madness, or the sugar playing havoc with my system, but I found myself acting out the potion scene from the ballet. This was a favorite scene of mine, mostly pantomime, as Juliet prepared herself to take the sleeping potion the Friar had given her. I had motivated the movements with a number of her lines from the play, when she envisioned the terrors of the tomb in her bedroom; and I had used the narrow ledge of her bed—like a sleepwalker wandering the edge of a cliff—in order to heighten suspense.

God only knew what time it was. The world seemed eerily silent as I crisscrossed the floor and then skirted the side of the mattress. My husband never stirred, but just as I was about to slip the bottle under the pillow, I was startled by his drowsy voice, whispering in the language of dreams. I murmured my love in his ear and stretched out beside him, placing the bottle on the floor next to the mattress. I kept turning the ballet over and over in my mind. Too exhausted for sleep, I scribbled down a line in my journal: "I am safe, until my next performance."

Then I pulled the covers over us, and lay awake . . . for what might have been minutes, or hours.

"Raves!" shouted Greg. "Wake up, Gelsey!"

One of my eyes popped open, just in time to see a storm of newspapers and waving arms coming at me through the doorway. It was Monday morning, and Greg had ventured out early to collect the reviews. Paralyzed from the hairline down, I did not lift my head from the pillow, even when he pounced beside me and unfolded one of the newspapers under my nose. I would never rise again: my body was a mass of tangled, hot wires; and my lungs were on fire.

Bronchitis, laryngitis, the plague—you name it, I had it. I spent Sunday, the day after the performance, peeping out from under my covers at a procession of guests, while my husband scurried around the flat playing Florence Nightingale. He was in his glory, presently, rattling off the names of the London papers and roistering shamelessly. "The *Times*, the *Telegraph*, Financial Times, the *Observer*, the *Guardian*—they're unanimous. You were a sensation. If this were a Broadway play, you'd be running for years." One tubercular-sounding cough was enough to send him running out to the kitchen to fetch a thermometer and a glass of orange juice.

When he returned, I was propped on one elbow, over the *Times*. Either I was going blind, or I needed reading glasses; all I could make out was the headline: CLASSIC ROLE MAGICALLY

TRANSFIGURED. As Greg leaned over me, I rasped, "What did they say?" Ignoring my question, he waved the thermometer in front of me like a baton. While I lay muted, thermometer under tongue, he read the reviews aloud one by one, insisting that I keep my mouth shut until the end. The last was Clement Crisp's notice from the *Financial Times;* Greg broke off at one point, saying, "Listen to this line—'To watch Miss Kirkland running to Friar Laurence . . . is to see a being as flutteringly borne on the air as the silken cloak that flies behind her. . . .' Now you can't say your Juliet didn't come across. You've practically inspired poetry from a critic! What more could you want?"

I had actually written my own "review," making notes on each scene and going over refinements I hoped to bring into the next performance. What pleased me most about my notices was how clearly my choices had been read, those moments of stillness as well as the gestures that linked them. The critics said they had seen a Juliet moving from childhood fancy and adolescent passion, to a mature, even sublime love. They noted this was a departure from the dramatic reasoning seen previously. I was happy with the response; nobody enjoys being panned. But I also knew there was more painstaking work to be done.

And that was troubling.

At last my husband plucked the thermometer from my lips and turned toward the light slanting in from the front windows, which were open a crack, letting in a breeze. The curtains were blowing, billowing like fluffy gray clouds, then collapsing into nothing. "You've got a temperature," he said, sounding as if he were reading an ominous weather forecast. He was in his own way trying to cheer me up. The psychological letdown following the performance was natural after so much exertion. The decline in my physical health was more distressing.

How could I renew any sense of purpose lying flat on my back like an invalid?

"The trick," said Greg, closing the windows, "is to know the inspiration will come back when you need it. You'll find it in the story you're telling, or you'll find it in Juliet's heart. But you will find it."

The next day I was back in class, and the week progressed

rapidly from desperation to despair. I was a painful case, with my cough tearing out my lungs, sapping my stamina. I had visions of kissing Anthony, during the bedroom scene, and then collapsing into spasms. I took heavy doses of vitamins and antibiotics, and made daily visits to the company's general practitioner, Dr. John Creightmore, who offered wise, soothing words and was not averse to making house calls, or "theatre calls," when I was unable to come to him. But nothing seemed to help.

In the middle of the week, America bombed Libya, making my problems seem absurdly minuscule by comparison. This retaliatory air raid was a hot conversation topic among dancers who were normally oblivious to events in the outside world. The distraction had me asking myself what value the theatre could possibly claim in this age of terrorism. I felt remiss for not knowing the issues fully and not having time to find out what was going on, although the irony of my appearing in *Romeo and Juliet* was not lost on me. The world was still inhabited by warring families.

On the same day as the bombing, another order of shoes arrived, eight pairs—none of which fit, in part because my feet had swollen, and in part because these shoes had come from the wrong maker. With only one decent pair of toe shoes, I had to say I was bowing out of the Queen's Birthday Gala, which was scheduled for the following week. By chance, my former partner and romantic flame, Mikhail Baryshnikov, had agreed to appear on the program, along with Alessandra Ferri, who had but recently left the Royal Ballet to join American Ballet Theatre.

The administrators of the opera house and the company, Sir John Tooley and Anthony Russell-Roberts, respectively, were in a tizzy trying to persuade me to perform the balcony scene—shoes or no shoes. The extraordinary importance of the event could not be casually brushed aside: it was for the Queen; and it was for television. My husband advised the officials one night by phone that I would wait until after my regular performance to make a final decision.

I advised my husband, "There's just no way!"

The whole business was becoming a royally embarrassing situation for all involved. Greg was having a difficult time, attempting to explain the problem of my not having any properly fitting shoes. I heard him saying over the phone, in his man-to-man voice, "Well, you see, it's really quite different for you or me. Not having the right pair of shoes for that special evening out, we might get away with a tight fit for a few hours. Or, we might simply run home for a quick change. But for a ballerina, it's far more complicated. It actually comes down to safety. Toe shoes are not at all like sneakers. Surely the public and Her Majesty can understand that."

The days seemed to have their own trying choreography. By the end of the week, I learned that Julian was ill and had to be replaced as Paris. This meant giving a crash course to a stand-in, Ross MacGibbon, a young man who had decided he was going to give up ballet and attend college. He was probably all the more anxious to depart after our first couple of rehearsals. But he did make a steadfast effort and, it was later said, gave the performance of his life. Little did anyone realize, at the time, that Julian's illness was actually a rare degenerative disease (which would prove fatal in three years). Julian's appearance on that first night was to be the last time he would dance. I was honored to have known and worked with him.

Anthony and I had little time to rehearse, but as things turned out, the second performance went better than we expected. There were no falling chairs, and most of the scenes were tighter, more polished, at least from my point of view. Donald MacLeary had helped me work through a few rough spots in my variations and in the tomb scene. My bedroom pas de deux with Anthony was heavenly in an almost literal sense: I assumed angels had to be watching over us because I never so much as sneezed. There were more daffodils, more ovations, and more happy tears.

In my euphoria, I told Anthony I would find some way to do the Queen's Gala, which was fast approaching. This led to a few minor outbursts of hysteria the following day, as I tried on every pair of toe shoes in the Royal Opera House—testing every shoe worn by every ballerina in both the Royal Ballet and Sadler's Wells Ballet. It was a kind of maddening twist on the Cinderella story: nothing fit. I finally decided to clean and powder the same pair of shoes I had worn for that second performance, and prayed I could get another six minutes out of them—just enough time to dance through the balcony pas de deux.

The gala, "Fanfare for Elizabeth," took place on Monday, April 21, honoring the Queen's sixtieth birthday with a program of ballet, opera, and dramatic readings. Baryshnikov canceled at the last minute, eliminating any chance for an uncomfortable encounter or an incident the media might blow out of proportion. I had enough to worry about with those shoes and the unexpected change of set. Our balcony scene was to take place against a sterile powder-blue backdrop, which seemed more appropriate for an afternoon siesta, rather than our romantic evening tryst.

As Anthony put it later, "We are fish out of water, aren't we?"

Only minutes before we were to perform the scene, I was in the dressing room with my husband, making a frantic attempt to rework the opening mime to fit the new set. Well on my way to panic, I fumed fitfully, "Just how am I supposed to catch a moonbeam in the middle of a goddamn desert? The lighting is like something out of Lawrence of Arabia."

Greg, remaining calm under the circumstances, told me, "I wouldn't worry too much. From what I've heard, the Queen isn't particularly fond of the ballet. She's said to be more interested in horses." Then he said more seriously, "Forget about the set. Romeo will be there for you, and I'll meet you when it's over."

I gave him a look I instantly regretted.

He gave me a good-luck kiss on my cheek.

My husband was right. Even out of context, the balcony played passably well in the theatre and was warmly received by the audience. For the audience watching at home, however, the television cameras distorted the dance illusion each time they moved in for a close shot—breaking the body and the shape. This was truly unfortunate because the renowned classical actress, Judy Dench, had given such an inspired reading from the play to introduce our scene.

Still, it was a festive occasion, and perhaps something of the romance came through even on video. At least the home viewers had the advantage of watching the Queen and royal family seated in their box at the back center of the theatre. After the long program concluded, I joined my husband and Anthony along the receiving line to be formally presented to Her Majesty the Queen, and His Royal Highness the Duke of Edinburgh. A reception took place in a lounge outside the first level of boxes—an area appropriately known as the "crush bar."

Greg and I found ourselves at a loss in regard to matters of protocol. I unwittingly made the mistake of offering my hand to the Queen, wishing her happy birthday, before she had formally acknowledged me. I told her, "You must be exhausted after such a long day!" She said she enjoyed the program, and for a moment, I was overcome by the strangest feeling—with me still wearing my Juliet costume, and the Queen wearing that crown. It all seemed so make-believe—as if we were captive to some extraordinary illusion.

After I had moved along the line, and greeted the Queen Mother, feistiest of the royal party, a somewhat humorless and nondescript face came out of the crowd. He informed me that it was quite improper either to address the Queen or take her hand before she had recognized me—the man was evidently some sort of official stuffed shirt. Greg cautioned me, lightheartedly, not to cause an international incident. Anthony assured us, "Americans are always forgiven."

In the week that followed, I began rehearsals for both *Giselle* and *The Dream.* The latter was Sir Frederick Ashton's version of *A Midsummer Night's Dream;* Greg and I began to pore over the Shakespeare play. I wanted to have at least an initial conception of the character of Titania before I started the work in the studio. I discounted a brief experience I had performing the pas de deux from *The Dream* back in 1980; I wanted to start fresh. With Juliet behind me, I knew I had only begun to hit my stride, and I was looking forward to finishing this season with a strong showing in ballets that would require me to extend my dramatic range. Giselle was going to be a special challenge as I intended to refine my own interpretation of the role, despite the Royal Ballet's unusual staging.

The snag in my plans appeared about midweek. I had taken

class as usual and entered one of the rehearsal studios to work on one of my solo variations in *Giselle*. I was having difficulty with a certain sequence of steps—glissade into arabesque, then extending into a soft plié. Each time I pushed off the left foot to move into arabesque, I fell over; and the pain in my foot was becoming excruciating, to say nothing of my embarrassment. After about six tries, I finally asked the pianist to stop, and made a closer inspection of the foot, which had blown up so much that I had a devil of a time removing the shoe.

I asked my kindhearted teacher, Oliver Symons, to have a look. The foot had by now inflated, like a gigantic balloon. Oliver approached with caution, then gave the ankle a little poke with one of his fingers. "Well, no," he said, "that doesn't look at all right to me. Now that's very odd indeed. You better have Leslie Bailey take a look at that."

From this point events moved swiftly. Leslie Bailey was the company's physical therapist. I made an appointment to see her straightaway, and she, in turn, made an appointment for me to see Mr. John Strachan, the company's orthopedic surgeon, who, in turn, made an appointment for me to have a bone scan.

A "hot spot" was revealed on the scan. A hot spot meant a stress fracture, a hairline fracture which in my case was located on one of the metatarsals of my left foot. Most likely, I was told, I had danced the *Romeo and Juliet* performances and the Queen's Gala with my foot already fractured. I was advised, given my natural inclination to move around, to have my foot placed in a soft cast for at least three weeks. The upshot of it all was that I would be out for the rest of the season.

I was crestfallen. On my way to the hospital to have my foot put in the cast, I read a touching note from Anthony:

Dearest Gelsey,

   I am so terribly upset about the diagnosis on your foot—please hurry up and get better soon. I have not much time left to be behind you!!! (Selfish on my part).

                                        Much, much love,
                                        Anthony

When at last I settled into a chair back in the flat, and held my cast up in the air, toward Greg, he tried his best to humor me: "Well, at least you've finally got something that fits!"

I didn't know whether to laugh or cry.

4.

TO
DANCE
WITHOUT
ARMS
OR
LEGS

As soon as the Royal Ballet informed the press that I had been injured and would be missing the remainder of the season, a photographer from the *Times* telephoned, requesting a shot of my fractured foot. "Just the foot," my husband inquired, playing for time, "or the whole body?" Greg stood in front of the living-room windows, cupping the mouthpiece with his hand, while waiting for me to make up my mind. I gave him the go-ahead with a reluctant nod. "She'd be delighted," said Greg, after a pause adding, "No time like the present!" He turned away from me, and I heard him giving directions to the flat, trying to explain to the photographer that we lived in a house which had no street number: "It's the big, white Victorian monster . . . right next to the gardens. You can't miss it."

After hanging up, he swung around and started toward me,

saying apologetically, "Well, the guy promised it would be for the front page. At least the public will be able to see why you're not dancing. Photographs don't lie."

"They may not lie," I cut in, "but they sure as hell never tell the whole truth, do they?"

He stopped short, his long arms dangling at his sides, his smile gently disarming me. "Not even your memoirs will be able to tell the whole truth—not with this world the way it is."

The telephone interrupted again; I hobbled into the bathroom to ready myself for the photographic session, while Greg answered the call. The publication of my autobiography was now set for October, and pressures were already starting to mount, especially during these days of convalescence, when I had time on my hands to think about things like editing and publicity and promotion. I had agreed to be interviewed by Diane Sawyer on "60 Minutes," although that was still some months away, timed, I was told, so the airing would coincide with books arriving in bookstores. The prospect of doing press interviews always daunted me. I placed little trust in the media to report my story accurately, if only because I had such little faith in myself to communicate adequately those artistic issues which were my passion—to speak outside my own medium.

It was one thing to put me in a ballet studio, quite another to confront me with a camera. I reacted like one of those primitive tribesmen who fear losing their souls to the lens. Yet I fared no better with interviews for print. I hated seeing my words changed or pulled out of context to fit into some journalist's clever notion of an "angle." Faced with impertinent questions, I knew how easily my tongue might slip. The publicity people continued to badger my husband and me with requests, which we turned down. Our editor and lawyer were sympathetic allies who seemed to understand. I was not cut out temperamentally for that sort of exposure—book or no book. I was surely not a talk-show "personality."

I shuffled back into the living room. Greg was perched on the windowsill, his hands in his pockets and the telephone replaced on its black cradle near him. He was a silhouette, with kneecaps up to his ears, the last light of this afternoon falling like a bright cloak over his shoulders. "A piece of good news," he announced.

"That was Merle Park. She wanted to know if you might like to teach some classes at the school, if you feel you're up to it. I said you'd give her a call back right away. . . . What do you think?"

A happy spastic, I hopped, bounding on my one good leg, all the way across the room. I flung my arms around his neck, almost unseating him. The Royal Ballet had been so generous and supportive, beyond anything I had ever expected. After my first Juliet performance, I had posted a note on the bulletin board outside of Anthony's office, thanking the company for the most rewarding experience I had ever had in the theatre. Merle's invitation, coming on the heels of misfortune, was yet another kindness, another blessing. Yet, it was something more —an opportunity to see if my talents were limited to performing, or if there were something that might be passed on.

Since writing the memoirs and reckoning with my life, I had been asking myself how it actually happened that I had become a ballerina. Why would anyone ever choose to devote an entire lifetime to dancing? It sometimes seemed like the curse of the Red Shoes. I recalled my earliest joys in the classroom, but they had little to do with becoming a ballerina. At the age of nine or ten, I had experienced a kind of pure satisfaction in discovering I could take on so many challenges with my body. I could mold myself to conform to the outrageous demands of a technique which, as far as I could tell, had no apparent purpose. None of my early teachers ever actually enlightened me—and yet, I took it on faith, such a purpose had to exist.

My intensity, what most distinguished me in the studio and on the stage, was as much a search for meaning as it was a quest for perfection. Was it not my only real gift? Could such a thing ever be taught?

What had seduced me was the mental challenge: I loved the daily battle of wits and those special moments when I shared my natural curiosity with other students, who were kept as much in the dark as I was; and later, after I had been recognized as a ballerina, there were similar moments, when other dancers asked me how I did what I did with the steps—some simple turn, or a more intricate combination. I became intrigued and fascinated, trying to explain the process, but there seemed to be no words. The repetition of classroom corrections meant almost nothing as far as making that transition to the stage. I saw enough dancers who were able to execute technique, but they were as lifeless as marionettes in performance. No language existed in the ballet world to tell them what they were doing wrong.

They were, actually, doing exactly what they were told to do. Some of these dancers were far more gifted than I was, or could ever hope to be, at least physically. They watched my performances, and they watched me demonstrating this or that bit of technique, hoping to imitate whatever it might have been that had attracted them. I had done much the same, trying to imitate Margot and Natasha, and a host of others. But such efforts were for the most part fruitless. I had gone so far as to slow down films of those ballerinas who had inspired me. Analyzing their movement had afforded a few limited insights into what was going on inside their bodies; however, their deepest secrets were never really apparent, either on film or in the flesh.

"Well, what do you think?" repeated Greg, looking for some sign of conviction in my face, as he slowly lowered himself from the windowsill.

"I guess I'll find out if I have anything to teach, won't I?"

He stepped past me, saying, "I wrote the number by the phone." Then he went for the door, calling back over his shoulder, "I'll meet you in front. I want to make sure our photographer doesn't get lost."

After returning Merle's call and setting a date to start a series of "master classes," I hurried outside the flat to wait for the photographer. When he arrived, the sun was already going down, lost somewhere out past the end of our street. He tried to reassure us, a glossy English voice suddenly booming, "Oh, plenty of light . . . for a few quick ones." He directed Greg and me toward a spiked iron fence. It ran along the edge of the garden, which was closed off to all but the most permanent residents, we explained, by way of apology for our being barred from posing on the inside.

The photographer was a strange fellow, with shaggy hair and the habit of scratching his head and then squinting—as if neither his eyes nor his brain were able to make any sense of the world. My hair was being whipped by a stiff breeze. I looked up and swore I saw the first stars appearing. The man advised my husband to pick me up, and asked me to point my cast toward the camera.

And so we posed.

Not long, but long enough for Greg to complain about his back going out. "Maybe," he said in my ear, "there's a museum for the spines of writers as well as dancers." I clung to his neck, while the fellow scurried all around us trying to cover every angle before nightfall.

After he left, we sat on our front steps, shielded from the wind as dusk faded to darkness, and lights appeared in the windows of homes up and down our quiet street. I hooked my arm inside Greg's elbow and leaned against him, listening to sounds of other lives coming from apartments in our building, an opera singer's voice breaking the silence as she practiced some aria neither of us recognized, and minutes later, a child howling at the top of its lungs. Then, silence again.

I asked Greg, "Will you help me with the classes?"

"Of course," he said, with a long sideways glance.

"Do you remember that conversation? . . . I must have told you. I was with Anthony and he was telling me about his young dancers. It happened one afternoon in his office. Do you remember that?"

"Vaguely."

"The young ones just don't have that love of the theatre we had—that was what he said, and he told me how awestruck he was when he first went inside the theatre . . . 'awestruck' was the way he described it. But he made it sound like the first time he had fallen in love, like an enchantment. Everything for him came out of that love. Then he said again, 'But they don't have it. . . . For the young ones, it's only a job. It's very sad,' he told me."

"Sad," echoed Greg. "Not hopeless."

"But how can I reach them?"

"The same way you reach the audience."

"It's not the same. How am I going to get them to fall in love with the kind of work it takes?"

"The same way you did," he said, adding so softly I was barely able to hear him, "You'll find a way."

As the mood changed, something inside me was slowly vanishing, like breath on a mirror. What I had to do was clear enough. Nothing more was said. Nothing stirred. There was only stillness, until the chill in the air drove us back indoors.

Neither of us was surprised or disappointed during the next few days as we realized our photograph was never going to be printed—nobody ever told us why, and we never bothered to ask. As April turned into May, the newspapers were filled with horror stories of the Russian nuclear disaster at Chernobyl. A ballerina with a bum foot was no match for a radioactive cloud drifting toward the West, according to some reports, heading straight for London.

"The radiation must have destroyed the film," Greg said.

"Or, some angel," I suggested with a laugh.

I prepared to teach in much the same way I prepared to dance a role, as if I were entering the unknown. I wanted to impart to my students an inkling of the kind of exploration they might use one day to make the transition from the classroom to the stage. That seemed the most I could hope to accomplish, and so I racked my brain, trying to think of ways I might help them make some connection between the technique their teachers had been drilling into them for years and the purpose of that technique, as far as telling a story onstage.

I had only my own experience to draw on, and spent a week feverishly jotting down notes, which were for the most part the simplest questions imaginable, questions children ask and teachers sometimes prefer to evade. I was aware of certain confusions about the teaching of ballet, apparent even at the company level. On one occasion in the cafeteria, I heard a clever fellow make the outrageous statement: "You can't teach anyone to turn. Either a ballerina can turn naturally, or she can't." I knew without doubt I had not come into the world knowing how to turn, or how to dance for that matter, but I had somehow managed to learn.

Of course, I had been highly motivated, and I had run around picking the brains of various teachers to acquire the knowledge I needed. "But that sort of motivation is not to be found among the dancers of this generation," the fellow was only too quick to inform me, which was yet another twist in the same argument—assuming today's young dancers have been so poisoned by the televised evils of the modern world, they no longer know how to learn. Even when shown how a step is done, they supposedly lack the sensitivity or wit to do it; and when blessed with the natural coordination that enables them to manage the step, they somehow fall short on feeling or intelligence.

Had the hearts and minds of this entire generation simply been lost?

I loved these informal skirmishes, and usually came off as the unbridled idealist, so certain was I that anyone could be taught, or inspired, to do virtually anything.

During one of my encounters with Gerd in the dressing room at the school, she had voiced her frustrations trying to coach "her girls," as she called them, in their solo variations for Sir Frederick Ashton's *Birthday Offering,* a ballet he created in 1956 as a tribute to Dame Ninette, when the company officially received its royal charter. The cast at the time had featured an extraordinary group of ballerinas—Margot Fonteyn, Beryl Grey, Violetta Elvin, Nadia Nerina, Rowena Jackson, Elaine Fifield, and Svetlana Beriosova—and the choreographer had turned the ballet into a showcase for their unique talents.

Ashton had tailored the movements to suit each ballerina, encouraging each to make a personal imprint onstage. Gerd was able to offer brilliant imitations, even in the confines of the dressing room, demonstrating bits from each solo for me, humming along to accompany herself. But she complained that the dancers she was coaching were unable to perform their variations in the "correct style." With eyebrows and voice on the rise, she exclaimed, "Oh, they just can't do it!"

She seemed as flustered as she had been playing the Nurse, those cheeks of hers reddening, as she abruptly sat herself down in a chair. "Back when this ballet was first done," she told me, "each solo had a different personality . . . and each ballerina was different. But now, they're all the same. Why, they're dead! Gelsey, they've no personalities at all."

"But, Gerd, you just demonstrated those solos so beautifully for me. You've got to take the dance apart for them, because they can't see the problem. They don't know what you're do-ing."

"Oh, I don't know," she said, with a long sigh.

"You must know!" I insisted.

I coaxed her to get up and repeat one of the variations, to look more closely at what she was doing. Gerd was a delight to watch —prancing around herself, her feet fluttering through some sort of pas de bourrée. Her entire upper body revealed the personal-ity implicit in this particular role, as if she were calling up another version of her own identity. As she moved, every ges-ture seemed to emanate from her torso.

She was in her way telling me a story. The focus of her eyes shifted from her lovely hands, as they flitted in front of her, to her imaginary audience. This character was very feminine and a bit of a coquette—a grand young woman who knew she had great merchandise. She was preening and flirting, as if suddenly finding herself in the presence of royalty—Gerd's expression was priceless, as she looked down her nose with just the hint of a smile. All blushing audacity, she was.

When she stopped, I told her what I had seen. The problem was not so much one of style, in a purely technical sense, as it was finding the dramatic keys, to unlock and animate the danc-ing.

"But why don't they just do it?" she chirped at me, as she dropped back in her chair.

It might be said that Gerd was a performer at heart, but that heart would have to be opened up and turned inside out if her students were ever going to be able to make their roles come to life. "How can they?" I asked her. "They've only been taught to count and execute the steps, in the correct style, as you put it. But that's not the same thing as finding or expressing the charac-ter of the variation, and that's what you're doing when you demonstrate . . . isn't it?"

She seemed to understand what I was getting at, though her features hinted at some inner distress. I was trying to put her gently on the spot. I knew that she knew much more than she was yet able to say, and the same was true for so many of those dancers who seemed to move and act as if by magic.

"Look," I continued, "you have a great sense of theatre and

mimetic gesture, and you know how to phrase the steps in a special way. So did all of those great ballerinas you remember dancing the roles. That kind of thing can only be recaptured by asking ourselves what it was about that generation of dancers that enabled them to invest so much quality in those steps Sir Fred created for them. What did they know? That character you just showed me did not come out of nowhere!"

"Oh, I don't know," she said, repeating her pet phrase and raising those lovely hands again, as if to fend off any further cross-examination. Yet Gerd was not about to give up.

It seemed a telling sort of irony that even with so much technical progress in recent decades, Gerd's students were somehow unable to master those roles. Even in a ballet like *Birthday Offering,* a plotless divertissement, there was an underlying sense of drama, which, however elusive, begged to be explored through the dancing. The overall grandeur of the ballet, hearkening back to nineteenth-century Russia and the famed French choreographer Marius Petipa, as well as those formal elements wrought by Ashton—with his supreme dignity and clarity of spirit—all seemed to me like so many pieces in a magnificent, unsolved puzzle.

Certainly, the original ballerinas had grown up in a far different age, when books were still being read, when theatre in London was in its heyday in this century. But could the age alone account for what those dancers brought to the stage? Or had they been taught, as a matter of course, that magic enabling them to speak and act through the dance?

Another time, Merle joined us. As she was still trying to finish the school's official syllabus, she often brought up more specific technical questions. I was not surprised when she asked, in her typically ebullient manner, "Now, Gelsey, how would you teach a port de bras bending forward?" She stood with one of her hands on the rim of the basin, using it as a barre; and then she bent forward, her slender figure curling over slowly toward her legs. She repeated the same simple movement two different ways. Upright again, she pulled a few strands of dark hair back into place, asking me, "Which would you say?"

Now I was on the spot.

Her first try had been one long, graceful stretch, with her

head coming over and almost touching her knee. The second had been carried off with a more controlled, noble line through her back, neck, and head; and her eyes had followed her free hand as she moved. These were fine distinctions, but she seemed to be looking for a definitive answer, as if one way might be more correct than the other.

"Well, Merle," I replied, "it would really depend on your reason. Each of those movements could have a different purpose. Either way, the main thing to think about is keeping your heart and mind always above your limbs, as you go over, so your coordination is fluid. If you pinned me down, I could say that second way you did it might have created a more beautiful image. But I can see why both ways should be taught, so the dancer can discover the range of expressive possibilities, if the body is ever to become a voice. . . ."

"Well, yes," she agreed, "of course."

She may have been hoping for something less complicated, as a means to decide how the exercise might be done in classes at the school. After all, she was trying to implement a system of training. Yet Merle had been a great ballerina herself, and it occurred to me that her own experiences onstage made for an intuitive bond between us, however different our backgrounds, and our methods.

Our sessions in that dressing room had gone on endlessly throughout the period I worked on *Romeo and Juliet*. When Merle eventually offered me the opportunity to teach, I was especially pleased because she was aware my ideas about ballet did not fit exactly into any of the formal systems; yet, she was receptive enough to appreciate what I had to offer through my unsparing approach.

She promised I would have free reign with two classes of teenage students, who would soon be graduating and with luck entering companies. These girls would already have taken their regular class in the morning, she had explained, so I might concentrate on things other than their daily workout at the barre and mirror. Many of the students I had seen had not yet mastered certain fundamentals, so I knew I had some work cut out for me. I asked myself: if I were in their shoes, what would I need to know to go on?

The day before I was to start the classes, my husband and I went on an afternoon shopping spree at Harrods. We braved the crowds in the toy and sporting goods departments to pick up a few special items I intended to use with the students. I was able to get around quite well these days despite the cast, so we made a side trip to add a few more temporary pieces of furniture to our temporary home. These seemed like set pieces, lugged by cab back to the flat where they were easily swallowed up by the insatiable emptiness of the living room and those bare white walls. I was nevertheless relieved to replace our tired old mattress with the latest in a Japanese futon mat.

Greg handled the heavy lifting. Dragging the mat into the center of the floor, he said, "It's like a mattress filled with lead!"

"It'll be great for our backs," I told him. "Just give it a chance. You'll see. . . ."

"We're living in the lap of absurdity," was all he said as we surveyed the premises, his computer having been relocated from the floor to a small table in the corner. Anthony's potion bottle found a secure resting place on the windowsill, where it captured its tiny share of moonlight; and for a final touch we filled the fireplace with flowers—an arrangement of roses—marking our first wedding anniversary.

"Love demands everything of us, and rightly so," I later wrote in my journal, stealing a thought from one of Beethoven's letters, intended perhaps for his inner Muse. My husband brought the line to my attention, and it gave me a lesson plan, the theme upon which I would base the first classes. I didn't have to make a journey back to adolescence to know the one subject, not likely to be included in any syllabus, that might motivate some of these aspiring ballerinas—unless romance were no longer a concern to this modern generation. But I had seen enough starry eyes and furtive glances in the hallway of the school to know that was not the case.

And I had watched enough classes to have a fair idea of the challenge I would face. *They are me when I was young,* I thought as I lay awake that night, while my husband rolled about silently in his sleep. I was disquieted, feeling unequal to the task ahead, suffering an attack of nerves much like those that come before performance. Light from the street was shining in through the windows, making shadows like black stripes, which revolved around the room every time a car went by. I scrambled over the floor and pulled a drawstring to close the curtains. Then I switched on a lamp and set down a few last thoughts, giving up on the idea of sleep and turning again to the demands of love.

> The greatest artists develop that same theme . . . infinitely varied and played out. But is there still a place in this world for such simple beauties? All of these young ballerinas have the necessary physical attributes, and personalities—but they have yet to develop the kind of facility they need to create both the dramatic and musical qualities that can move the audience . . . or touch the soul.
> The stage demands their laughter and tears . . . yet how can they know what that means? How can they make their roles their own? They have scarcely begun to discover the discipline of the barre . . . the deceptions of the mirror. Their feelings and ideas are trapped inside their bodies—they are like children who have yet to find a way through the looking glass.
> They are like . . .

I must have fallen asleep with the pen in my hand.

When I opened my eyes, my husband was leaning over me.

The room was bathed in pale light. It had to be morning. Was I still dreaming?

"Today's the day!" he bellowed excitedly, his face hovering inches above mine.

I kept still, longing to draw back into the dark and into my privacy, trying to catch hold of my dream before it slipped away. I could feel the hard lumps in the mat and every aching muscle in my back. After a halfhearted effort to lift up my head and look around, I let myself go, dropping back onto the pillow. Had I been talking in my sleep again? He said he had heard me murmuring earlier. Nothing he could fathom.

"We were in space," I told him, in a foggy, faraway voice. "Just the two of us in empty space. And we were going up in the air on two white balloons. Like globes . . . under our feet . . ."

He found a spot beside me, making a show of settling down on the mat. He was always prepared to listen. But the details were already eluding my grasp.

"I was scared I was going to slip off . . . or you were going to fall. I tried to yell to you, but there was a mask clamped over my face . . . and the balloon was spinning under my feet, so I had to keep moving . . . and I couldn't breathe with that mask. . . ."

"What kind of mask?" he asked.

"One of those white plaster things. You know, with frowns and smiles."

I broke off, trying to remember more. But it was like a story without beginning or end.

"I felt a push from behind . . . someone was trying to push me off! And my legs came out from under me! But I was strapped to the balloon, and landed on my back. I couldn't see you anymore, but I knew the same thing was happening to you."

"And . . . ? What happened?" Greg asked after another long pause.

"Nothing," I replied, looking at him as if to prove I were really awake. "The only other thing I remember is the two of us falling through space—on those white globes—and the feeling of being so powerless, strapped down like that."

"Must have given you a fright."

"But there was more to it," I said, my hands absentmindedly closing my journal, still on my lap.

"Sounds like another one of those scary, airy nothings," he remarked lightly, trying to shake me out of my mood before it had a chance to set in. Then he sprang to his feet and reached out a hand, saying, "What next, do you think? Shall we get ready for class?"

He pulled me up, with the spirit of an alley-oop, his acrobatic enthusiasm sending me toward the bathroom, my progress slowed only by the cast. After my usual bath and coffee, I spent the rest of the morning reading over everything I had written, as if I were cramming for a test. Between the anticipation and the caffeine, I came down with a case of stagefright, and soon took to the floor to breathe and stretch.

I made daily efforts to keep up a semblance of muscle tone, working hours around the lame foot, much of the time on my back. Otherwise, I knew I would have no hope of dancing again.

I was collected by the time we walked out the front door, hand in hand, joined by the thrill of our shared purpose and the unexpected shower of sunlight—both of us blinded as we crossed the street. Greg adjusted his giant strides to stay in pace with my tiny steps. We had a block to go for the best place to hail a taxi; many of the old Victorian houses on our street were having face-lifts—a lot of painting and sandblasting was under-way to restore them. Scaffolding blocked our course on the sidewalk, so we walked by the curb, squeezing between parked cars.

When we were halfway down the block, I sensed something fly past, like a flash or disturbance in the air. Even before that sensation had a chance to register, I heard a loud clank at my feet. When I stopped and looked down, I saw a monstrous piece of metal. God only knew what it was—something heavy and jagged that had been torn from the building and dropped acci-dentally by someone above. Greg was suddenly yanking me by the arm into the middle of the street and crying out in a fury. It all seemed like a scene out of a movie. Such was the unreality and my numbed reaction.

I had never seen him really lose his temper. He let loose a torrent of obscenities aimed heavenward, at a workman who was barely visible standing on the scaffold. The man merely leaned over and gawked at us from his perch several stories above our heads; and after listening to my husband's rather heated lecture on warning signs and the dangers for pedestri-ans, he called down in the most unruffled, almost pleasant voice, "You and the bird best mind where ya' walk, right, mate!" Greg's gesticulations, as he hopped around, might have con-vinced anyone the origins of dance were in human speech.

I stood gaping at him, my breath gone as I felt my legs start to tremble. With his arm around my waist, he practically carried me the rest of the distance to the corner. We lucked out flagging down a cab, and after we climbed in the back, he held up his hands between us, saying flatly, "You would have been killed. It missed your face by six inches." He sat staring straight ahead as if measuring that space between his palms, his expression frozen in disbelief.

"Where to, guv'nor?" asked the driver, sounding as though he were miffed we had invaded his taxi without first telling him our destination, as was customary etiquette here.

I gave the directions. Once underway I grabbed my husband's hands and tried to humor him, saying, "Calling me a bird . . . of all things. . . . That was a low blow! A bird . . . ?"

"Below the belt," he agreed, his laughter somehow making the world safe again.

The rest of the journey was happily uneventful. A false spring had descended upon London, and there seemed to be lovers everywhere. They crossed the streets oblivious to traffic, as if their condition gave them the right of way. Even our taxi driver seemed to exercise special caution, at least turning around those treacherous corners. Colors were brighter and shapes more vivid, as though the city were falling under a wondrous spell, from which neither of us were immune. We sat with the windows open, the warm air lapping at our faces.

Our little scrape with death was all but forgotten after we entered the school. Over his shoulder, Greg carried what we were calling my "bag of tricks." Catching sight of a few of the younger students changing classes, he whispered in my ear, "They all think they're going to live forever. They have such a naïve look about them." I knew how his mind worked well enough to realize this was only his way of putting the incident behind him.

The studio was on the ground floor. The first arrivals, the eager beavers, were already waiting for us as we descended a short flight of steps that led into the room. A row of windows ran high along the wall, and a small crowd of curious faces could be seen peeking in. While my husband pulled three folding chairs to the center, I closed a black curtain to shut off the view to my uninvited guests, gesturing apologetically as I did so, as if to say this class would have to be private.

These young dancers were not ready for an audience.

Master classes are usually conducted much the same way as are regular classes, with the exercises at the barre followed by combinations of steps in the center. A master teacher may choose or order the exercises somewhat differently, and perhaps offer corrections meant to emphasize a specific aspect of technique, such as pointe work. But I had something else in store for these students. As far as I could judge, they were not likely to benefit from yet another lesson on the finer points of technique.

They came in wearing their tights and leotards. Several of them were crouching, putting on their toe shoes and looking around to see if I were watching. I was surprised by the variety of body types, from plump to svelte to scrawny. Most of these students had passed through the same system of training, and yet each face and figure was unique. Before going further, I wanted to be sure they could feel that floor under their feet, and quietly advised those who had arrived to change shoes: "You won't be needing hard pointes. Today, we're going to be doing something different, and we don't want to be distracted by those bunions and blisters. Put on some old shoes, something soft and comfortable, a pair of toe shoes you've already broken in . . . and find a place to sit on the floor for now."

They appeared slightly awestruck. Were they as jittery as I was?

Greg and I sat in front of the class, with the mirror at our backs and an empty chair conspicuously between us. I asked the students closest to me, "Is everyone here yet?"

For several moments, all wore the same dutiful expressions, looking around at each other and counting heads, figuring out who was missing. Then a few tried to explain why the others might be late. Several of the stragglers came charging through the door, offering breathless apologies.

While we waited on the latecomers, I noticed this group of students did not seem to have acquired the habit of checking their images constantly in the mirror. It may have been that the strict emphasis of Royal Ballet training, demanding the "correct" positions for both head and arms inside the classroom, diminished the hold of the mirror—if only when the atmosphere became more informal. This was worlds away from my early experiences at the School of American Ballet. As a teenager, I undoubtedly would have been scanning the mirror even had I been seated on the floor, as they were now.

Their poise struck me as quite remarkable. But perhaps it was simply characteristic of their very English reserve and modesty.

The challenge to me and my peers had been to dance as fast as light and come up with that rare bundle of idiosyncracies and vanities that would please our master, George Balanchine, who was the ultimate authority at the school as well as his company, the New York City Ballet. The upper body had received such scant emphasis in class that we students depended more and more on the mirror to imitate the personal mannerisms of those ballerinas who were most favored. The cultivation of a personal image to match the stylized choreography became a full-time preoccupation that had its reckoning each day in our lives.

Yet, during class, the Royal Ballet students seemed attached to the glass in a different way, I had noticed. They faced a daily challenge of executing positions and steps in a more conventional, academic manner. While the technique provided tenuous links to a dramatic tradition of ballet, the mirror nonetheless held them in sway, encouraging a kind of stiffness and artificiality, as long as they remained fixed on their outward images. This was most apparent in class, when they were moving and peeking at their reflections.

There seemed to be flaws on both sides of the Atlantic, whenever beauty was regarded simply as an aspect of form.

"Are you comfortable?" I asked them.

There were a few nods and timid attempts to answer.

Were they scared of me? Did they think I was going to scold or punish them? Perhaps they were simply afraid of the unknown.

I said, trying to put them at ease, "We're going to do some talking, so you might come closer. I promise I won't bite. Why don't we start by introducing ourselves, since I don't know you, and you don't know me."

I told them my name and introduced my husband, offering as explanation for his presence one lighthearted comment, "He's good to have around sometimes." Then I added, "I've asked him to join us ladies because he knows some mime, which may help us along the way."

They seemed more curious about that empty chair between us than they were about Greg's role as my assistant.

"Now, tell me your names."

There was a sudden shifting of derrieres on the wood floor. No one volunteered. I turned to my far left and picked out one innocent face, saying, "Why don't we start with you."

She was long-limbed, with her dark hair brushed back neatly into a bun. In the midst of tying her ribbons, she was startled to find herself in the spotlight. Her hand shot up to her chest as if to say, "Who, me?"

"Yes, you there . . . what's your name?"

She answered in a whisper. I was reminded how terrified I was at her age when anyone asked me my name—or any question, for that matter. I had been afraid of my own voice.

"Can you say it louder? Like this . . ." I repeated my name in full voice, trying for humor, exaggerating like a singer or an actress, booming from deep inside my torso.

The class erupted in fits of giggles.

Her second effort brought only a slight improvement in volume. I encouraged her and suggested some changes in posture to all. "Why don't we try lengthening through our backs, right along our spines . . . so our voices don't get trapped. What do we use when we speak? Can anyone tell me?"

An eager student in back raised her hand, and piped up, "Our vocal cords."

"But what actually makes our vocal cords work?" I asked.

"Our breath?" came a tentative chorus.

Returning to the first student, I asked, "And what happens when we don't breathe?"

With a bewildered titter of amusement, she raised her voice, louder than before, "We die!"

"Right! That's what happens to us onstage sometimes, isn't it? So breath must be pretty important for us. Does anyone know another word for breath?"

They were puzzled, buzzing among themselves, no one daring to hazard a guess.

"I'll give this one to you. To breathe is to inspire. Does that make any sense? If your breath isn't strong enough to carry your voice across this studio, how do you suppose it will ever carry your body across the stage?"

With the rapt silence that followed, I knew I had at least captured their attention.

Their speaking voices, as with many dancers, seemed to die in the air; a few of the students were unable to project beyond their noses. I continued around the room with introductions, the clarity slowly increasing as each started to breathe, lifting the pelvis, and opening the chest around the sternum. There were one or two stubborn cases who resisted all of my cajoling— but at least this group as a whole no longer looked like it was about to sink into the floor.

I was not trying to turn them into fiery orators, nor was I trying to memorize their names. One of their obvious problems was an inability to breathe with their diaphragms, causing them to lift their ribs. I told one of the more stubborn cases, a raw beauty who seemed the most listless in the group, "Try breathing all the way down to your toes. Most of us women want to use our whole chests when we take in air, and that makes us lift our rib cages, doesn't it? Then we lose any hope of finding the shape we're really after onstage."

I got up and walked toward her, adopting a lighter tone as I prodded her, "Let the air swirl right into your face, and into your brain, and down into those toes. We don't want anyone to think we're bored—and none of us ever gets bored in class, do we?"

Her smile lit up the room for a moment, as she told me her name, and I exclaimed, "Great!"

Returning to my chair, I reminded myself to offer them constant encouragement and play no favorites.

The semicircle of sixteen dancers closed around me; their curiosity was now roused enough for me to try another tack. I told them, "I'm going to ask you a few more questions, and some of them might seem dumb to you. I don't mean to insult your intelligence. I don't know how much you know, and I need to find that out to be able to help you. So you might think of it as a kind of game . . . not a test. Do any of you have any questions before we start? Is there anything at all you want to ask me?

No one said a word, though they did appear to be intrigued,

and several glanced more openly at my cast, and at the mysterious empty chair. I checked the wall clock, which told me I would not be able to accomplish as much as I had hoped, at least not today.

"First off," I said, "I'd like to know . . . what are your favorite ballets?"

A few brave souls instantly cast votes for *Giselle* and for *Romeo and Juliet.* As several other voices chimed in, these two ballets quickly won a consensus. Even those quiet students too shy to offer an opinion beamed in agreement.

"So you like stories . . . is that it? Or, is it the steps in those ballets?"

"The stories," cried a few, almost in unison.

"Both," blurted a slender blonde near the front, caught up in the enthusiasm, becoming embarrassed as she looked around at her classmates.

"Can anyone tell me what those two ballets are about?"

After a flurry of whispers, several students said at once, "Love . . . ?"

"Right! Exactly." My bright tone was enough to tell them, "Now we're getting somewhere."

"How many of you, I wonder, saw me dance Juliet?"

All of them raised their hands. Their heads were bobbing up and down; and their faces told me I need not worry about any bad reviews. "Can you say what it was you liked about my dancing, or what you didn't like?"

They were more comfortable now, eagerly volunteering answers to my questions, though asking none of their own.

One of the bolder voices started things off, "You never stop moving. I mean, nothing ever stops."

"The steps flow . . . from one into another," said a brunette in the front, too close and too demure to meet my eye.

"And your feet," cried another, one of the more petite types in the room, "the way you use your feet when you go up on pointe is always so smooth."

"She goes right through her whole foot," one of her friends said, sounding very definite.

Others were quick to agree.

"Your gestures are so . . . clear. . . ." came a voice from the back, trailing off.

I stood up abruptly. "And do you think," I asked, pausing for emphasis, "those qualities you saw, the way I moved, helped me tell the story of Juliet's love?"

The silence was longer than I expected. All of their faces were looking up at me, their expressions quizzical and even a bit wary.

Had my sudden movement spooked them?

Several finally answered, "Yes, it helped," while others nodded in agreement.

By this time, all of them knew this was not just a haphazard conversation. But where was I leading them?

Circling around behind my chair, I asked, "Did it look like I knew what I was doing?"

They thought so, not quite sure of my meaning.

"What was the most important thing Juliet said to Romeo in the ballet?"

They were thrown a bit, glancing at each other, though none of them sinking back into the floor.

My husband offered a rather blunt hint: "What are the three most important words that any one of you will ever say to anyone in your life?"

A chorus of "I love you!" broke out around the room.

"But how do we say that without speaking?" I clarified the question before they went astray. "What do we say that with— what part of the body?"

While a few made cursory attempts at the standard ballet mime, bringing hands to breasts, the demure brunette at my feet said, "The heart?"

"Good! The heart!" This time I managed to catch her eye, and she flushed for an instant, before looking away.

"Now suppose," I said, returning to my chair, "just suppose I had to dance Juliet sitting in this chair. Let's make believe that I have no arms and no legs. What would I use to express my love for Romeo?"

That same voice at my feet piped again, "Your heart."

"But how is my heart going to do that?"

They were stumped.

"What was the first thing we were taught, all of us, when we first started ballet? To . . . what?"

Several hands rose, and I acknowledged all at once.

"Turn out," came the reply.

"Right. And what is turnout?"

"Opening our legs from the hips," they tried to explain. A circle of several friends was taking the lead; and I allowed them to continue the dialogue for a while, as long as I could see the others listening.

"But why do we turn out?" I asked.

"So we can do steps and positions," they replied.

"And so we don't knock our knees," one girl was quick to add.

"So turnout helps us dance," I said. "Good. But why do we dance?"

After a short whispered conference, they agreed, "To express ourselves."

"But . . . to express what?"

The little chorus, uncertain what I was asking for, abruptly divided.

"Love," tried one of them.

"Characters . . . and emotions," guessed another.

"Feelings," decided a third.

A freckle-faced blonde from the back broke into the circle, saying, "What's inside of each of us."

I gave them my very best cat-who-swallowed-the-canary grin, pleased for the moment with their confusion. Their curiosity was a joy to behold. Even their faces had come to life, perplexed as they were. A few were looking at me as if I had lured them into a trap with my trick questions.

"Watch me. Let's say I'm Juliet again, sitting in this chair, like I sat on my bed in performance, and I want to tell the whole world I love Romeo. But I have no arms or legs. I've been strapped in by my father. Just watch. I want you to tell me what you see, if you see anything, okay? Those of you in back might scoot closer. . . ."

The room went silent again.

They were with me.

For a minute or so, I was working as hard as I had worked onstage, on that infernal bed. When I broke off, I noticed some of them had been trying to imitate me . . . coming forward with their torsos, settling back now as my gaze fell upon them. I could see something quiet and precious in their faces, a kind of yearning, as if they had read my thought and tried to absorb it in their bodies.

"Well?" I asked.

A hand waved in front of me. That demure brunette again. "You said, I love you . . . Romeo."

"How?" I asked her. "Did you see anything move?"

"Yes," she murmured. "Your face . . ." Then she added, "And in here." She was pointing to her chest.

"Good. What else?"

"Your heart?" she asked.

"But I created an illusion, didn't I? After all, I was only sitting in this chair. . . . Do you think Romeo believed me?"

Her shyness returned; and while some of the others laughed, she turned her face away, saying softly, "I believed you."

"What work do you think I was doing in here, to express that love?" I asked everyone, first indicating my breast, then my forehead.

Silence again.

"What's that first thing we were taught?"

"Turnout," they repeated.

"So what was I turning out if I wasn't turning out my legs?"

"Your heart," the chorus resounded, anticipating me.

"Right. I turned out my heart, and I turned it out again and again, notch by notch, breath by breath. But what muscles do you think I used to do that . . . and how did I use them?"

They were at a loss.

I told them, "Well, now it's time for us to find out. What shape is turnout? What do the words tell you? Turn . . . out . . . ?"

"Round," came a marvelous wild guess.

"Fantastic! And what is round?" I asked them.

Another silence.

"What's under your rear ends?"

"The floor," declared several voices.

"And what's under the floor?"

"The earth." They laughed, seeing some absurdity in this line of questioning.

"And what is the earth?

"A globe?" blurted one.

"The world," cut in another.

"Right. A world. Isn't that what we try to make when we dance? But how can we make a world? What shape is the world?"

"Round," came the voice at my feet.

"It's a circle," added another.

"But what shape is the stage?"

They settled on "square."

"So how can we make a round world on a square stage?"

Stumped again.

"I want to tell you a little story. It's a kind of love story. When I first started ballet school in America, I was the ugliest ballerina you ever saw. I had a big head, a pot belly, a swayback . . . and skinny legs, like a mosquito . . . and hips that were too narrow. I was so turned in that my knees pointed straight forward in plié! I was angry with my teachers, because it hurt whenever I moved. But all they ever told me was 'Turn out those legs,' and none of them ever really told me why."

I gave them a caricature of myself at the age of eight, and they stayed with me, giggling.

"So, you see," I said, "there's hope for all of you."

That seemed to silence them.

"When I was about your age, I was already dancing solos, and some pretty big roles. But, I was unhappy because I didn't like the way I looked or felt. I was all arms and legs," I said, imitating myself at sweet sixteen. "The pains on the inside told me something had to be going wrong. Then one day I saw the Royal Ballet in New York . . . and I realized there was another way. Those dancers actually looked like human beings onstage—I mean, like real characters. That was the first time I saw Margot Fonteyn, and she moved with so much love, I cried out of sheer joy . . . and you might say I fell in love, because she gave us something in the theatre that was so rare."

I knew for most of these students, Margot was a legend they had heard about through most of their schooling; and I wanted to confide to them something about her part in my past. But was she anything more for them than a photographic image floating on a screen? Had she become their unreachable ideal? Or, was she already old-fashioned?

"So I thought, maybe I can look like her, too, but my body was nothing like hers, and I looked like a fool trying to imitate her. One day, after I had broken my foot—it was a bit worse than it is now—I found one teacher, David Howard, who told me, 'You don't really want to look like her, Gelsey, but you might want to be able to do what she does.' Well, this was big news to me!"

It seemed they considered my imitation of David's British accent hysterical—tittering away, they were. Maybe they were now free enough to laugh at themselves because I had been poking so much fun at my own self all along. I wanted them relaxed for what I was about to spring on them, so I simply waited for the uproar to die down.

"He showed me an exercise that gave me a clue to finding out what I was missing, in here"—I gestured to my breast—"those secret muscles I needed to develop."

Greg rose and pulled his chair to the side, and I did the same with mine, leaving the mystery chair at the center. I came around slowly in front of it, all eyes glued to me. There were a few nervous glances at the chair as I continued, "Now we're going to try a similar exercise. I need a volunteer. All I'm going to ask you to do is stand up, out of this chair, without using your arms to help you. We're all going to try it. Who wants to go first?"

A few students already had their hands in the air, while a few others were looking at me as if I had just invited them to have a spin in the electric chair. Most were content to wait and see what was really being asked of them. I chose one who had her hand at half-mast. She was a willowy creature with fair skin and huge eyes. Her blond hair was pulled into a bun, accentuating a high forehead. She had a chin that was almost invisible—it seemed to disappear into her neck, as if she were so downcast she had no jawline—because of the way she held her head.

But that was not the most immediate concern.

She sat down poker-faced and placed her hands on her lap, waiting for her cue. I simply told her to stand up without her arms. At first she was completely stuck in the chair, straining to find a way to bring her weight over her legs; then she tipped forward, head and chest inclined awkwardly over her thighs. With a heave-ho, she managed to lift her rear a few inches up, only to fall back onto the seat, letting out a groan of frustration and giving me a quick sideways glance. She knew what she was doing could not be right. Her face was reddening from the exertion, but she was determined.

She moved closer to the edge of the seat and then made a desperate effort, pulling herself upright, with her ribs jabbing out like so many knives. She managed to stand, but she had lost control over her upper body as she tried to do all of the work using her outer thigh muscles. Although her face remained taut and expressionless, I knew how embarrassed she was.

I told her, "You have the same problem I used to have with this exercise—because we both have such long legs and short torsos. We just don't have much between our necks and hips."

I could see she was relieved, a faint smile appearing.

"Let me show you what you did," I said. Taking her place in the chair, I continued, "At least, you've shown all of us the body has a voice. You've just told us you had a long hard day at the office." Tipping forward, I mimicked her voice, "Well, I can finally go home!" Then, struggling to rise as she had, I gasped, "If I can just get up!" She laughed, and I said, "Now watch me as Juliet again . . . rising to say 'I love you.' "

As I sat down in the chair, I saw my husband reminding me of the time. I scowled affectionately. Then I rose once again, creating that illusion of passion and grace.

Turning to the student, I asked, "What was different about what you did?"

She said, with a slight accent, "Well, I had to go way over just to stand up."

I asked the others what they had seen, and they were ready, like critics, to pounce on the innocent victim.

"She was stiff. . . ."

"She was too fast. . . ."

"There was no movement in her chest like you had."

Before their daggers had a chance to sink in, I put my arm around her shoulder and said, "Now we're going to show them how it's done. But first, just catch your breath a minute."

I asked the others, "What's the second thing all of us were

taught? Your teachers are always telling you to turn out those legs and . . . what?"

"Pull up!" returned the chorus.

"Now let me show you what I look like if I try getting out of the chair and think of pulling up."

My chest inflated, and my ribs lifted. I was suddenly the most graceless ballerina—or perhaps one thoroughly exhausted secretary at the end of her day.

"You see," I explained, "your teachers are asking you to do what they want to see. But when I'm dancing Juliet, or any role, I'm thinking of pushing down, using the floor—not pulling up."

This seemed to astonish them.

"Many times what we're asked to look like as ballerinas is opposite from what we need to feel and the way we need to work our muscles. Sometimes our teachers may not realize, but if we don't ask them, then we never find out, do we?"

Returning attention to my willowy, bewildered student, I said, "Now, you're Juliet . . . okay?"

She was certainly willing, a resilient spirit. I had her push against my chest, much as I had done with Julian during the rehearsals, and told her, "It's like climbing a mountain. That's how hard you have to work to get out of that chair. Can you feel these muscles, here in my chest, above my breasts? What do they feel like compared to yours?" As curiosity overcame reticence, she placed her hands where I told her.

"Yours are like steel cords," she said, "and I can't even feel mine!"

"Don't worry," I told her, "you still have a few years to find them and figure them out."

She took her place again in the chair.

As soon as I saw her poker face, I pulled a spray bottle of Evian water from my bag and surprised her, showering her cheeks with mist.

Her smile was amazed, and genuine.

"Can you feel that? You have to use all of those muscles in your face! They follow the same circular patterns as those muscles in the rest of your body. Try wiggling your ears, and rolling those big eyes of yours!"

Unbeknownst to me, Merle had entered the room and quietly

taken a seat by the piano to observe. She had been watching for some time and couldn't resist offering a short anecdote about the renowned Russian ballerina, Tamara Karsavina. "Oh, yes, Gelsey's right, you know. Karsavina used to do her eye exercises while on the tube." Merle stretched her own face into a kind of mask to demonstrate, rolling her eyes, then saying, "Those muscles are important for us, aren't they?"

The student's mind must have been completely beleaguered by this time. I hoped she was not going to become inhibited, aware as she was of the head of the school being in the room.

But she was game to continue.

I told her, "You're going to make a circle . . . pushing down, out and away . . . through the floor. Keep those arms and ribs down, and start to push down, as you breathe out. Turn out your heart, notch by notch, and imagine an arc. . . ." The trick, so to speak, was to bring her upper body slowly into play.

I began by making her aware of the circular path she was to follow, and eventually I held down her arms, so she had to push against me and had no alternative but to reach out with her heart. After twenty endless minutes of grueling effort, for each of us, with me guiding, teasing, and exhorting her, she was able to get up from the chair, and say "I love you, Romeo," at least with some sense of moving from her torso and speaking with her whole body. She had to strain, calling upon muscles in her back and chest that were entirely new to her. And yet, for a few moments, she was radiant, holding on to a shape she had never experienced before.

The class was stunned, and I could hear excited murmuring behind my back.

I exclaimed, "That's terrific!"

As she rose in front of me, I kept encouraging her, saying over and over, "And how else can you say, I love you?"

Her feet opened out toward first position, as if by magic, her heels together and toes parting in a gentle V shape.

"Good! How else can you say it? Keep coming forward, and keep turning out that heart . . . with each breath!"

Slowly, without any further directions, and much to my own amazement, she went up on her toes; and as she rose, I reached out, taking her hands to steady her.

"Great!" I whispered. "Really great! Now look up and out toward the ceiling."

"Why?" she demanded. "Why do I look up?"

"So we can see your chin. Look way out in front of you, so we can follow your eyes all the way around the world you're giving us . . . because there's no end to your love, is there?"

Her gaze traveled out momentarily beyond the room. Reaching the end of her stamina, she relaxed back onto her heels. But she did not allow her head or chin to drop.

I asked her, "Did that feel different to you?"

"Oh, yes," she replied, her eyes moist and shining.

I said to her, loud enough for all to hear, "If you work on all of those muscles that are going to be sore tomorrow, they may help you someday, when you have to tell Romeo how you feel about him. You did really well."

Turning to the others, I assured them, "Don't worry, all of you will have your chance. Thank you for today."

Time was up. There was a burst of applause. We had gone a full two hours—a half hour over schedule. A crush of students surrounded me, asking some of those questions they had been holding back. But the willowy one had been the first to be drawn in, the first to demand an answer, and I could feel the pressure of tears building behind my own eyes.

Merle flew by, saying, "Fascinating, Gelsey!" She was never at a loss for enthusiasm. She invited my husband and me to the upcoming graduation festivities for the school's younger children, those who attended a separate facility, known as White Lodge. Then she hurried off, apologizing for arriving late, and promising to come to my next class. I was still thinking about the unexpected turn this class had taken: the urgent tone of that student's voice had reminded me of my own when I first found the nerve to ask why.

Later, as Greg and I walked into the tube station, trading the burden of my bag temporarily, he marveled, "I wish you could have seen them all watching you—and then watching her, when she went on pointe. They were riveted—and you were as relentless as you are in rehearsal or in . . ."

He held off while we bought tickets and descended to an outdoor platform to wait for a train. The sky had turned into gray slate, and the temperature had dropped. We sat on a wooden bench, going over the class again. I had loved every minute, and tried to recall voices and gestures, and let their faces reappear in my mind. Had I been clear enough? Had they really benefited? When the train approached, the two of us moved toward the front of the platform and tried to guess where the doors were going to stop and open.

Above the screech and roar, my husband said, "But none of them seemed to have your intensity."

We picked our way between the exiting passengers. Once safely inside, I said, "How can we know yet . . . what any of them have, or don't have? We didn't even know that one had a chin until the last moment."

As the days and classes progressed, I was amazed by my own happiness, which seemed somehow to stave off any awareness of past or future, if only for those hours in the studio and the time at home when the telephone left us in peace. My cast enabled me to remain more or less oblivious to other people's expectations of my returning to the stage; and my autobiography, while yet to be published, was actually behind me. I knew this period of bliss could never last, but at least for a few weeks I seemed to be blessed with favorable stars and a soaring spirit.

By chance, even the tragic fallout of Chernobyl brought good fortune. A tour of Russia planned by the London Festival Ballet (since renamed English National Ballet) was canceled after the journey was put to a vote by the dancers, who apparently placed little faith in official Russian assurances on safe travel to Leningrad. And so, with the company unexpectedly held over in London, I was invited by the Artistic Director, Peter Schaufuss, to coach a seventeen-year-old ballerina for her upcoming performances of *Giselle,* scheduled to take place in Spain during July.

I was not without reservations. I had known Peter a few lifetimes ago—first when he was a member of City Ballet, and later when he was a guest at Ballet Theatre. There had been one row between us in particular, during rehearsals for Baryshnikov's version of *The Nutcracker.* Peter and I had tan-

gled in the studio and had a vile exchange, after which I had
simply written him off as a hopeless adolescent, in spite of his
undeniable talent. He was a Dane, trained in what might be the
healthiest of schools, that of the nineteenth-century genius August Bournonville, whose ballets and system of training, if not
spirit, are still preserved at the Royal Danish Ballet.

I assumed none of that noble spirit ever rubbed off on Peter,
even though he had started out his career dancing with that
company. But how the years can sometimes change a person!
The fellow whom my husband and I met for coffee one afternoon at a nearby hotel hardly resembled the young man I remembered. This Peter, who kissed my cheek and then sat down
across our table in the hotel dining room, was mild-mannered
and charming, and even a bit bashful. My friend, Dina
Makarova, was the one who arranged this unlikely reunion. She
later joined us, as did Peter's amicable assistant, Colin Sharp,
whose immediate warmth was the kind you suspect may be
longlasting. The atmosphere was so pleasant I was reluctant to
bring up old times.

But during a lull in the conversation, I recalled for Peter our
last battles in the studio. If I were going to coach one of his
ballerinas, I felt I had to know if I could really count on his full
support. "Do you remember that rehearsal?" I asked, in a mild
tone. His face possessed wonderful character, made all the more
striking by a tiny scar just over his lip. His expression said his
memory was blank. I tried to jog it for him, saying only, "You
accused me of 'hating men,' and I must have said a few awful
things. . . ."

He was blushing, as if we were onstage and someone had
switched a gel on one of the lights. An embarrassed grin slowly
took over his face, softening the handsome features. "Well, you
see," he confessed, with endearing candor, that Danish accent
somehow making each word sound softer yet more emphatic, "I
was so tired in that rehearsal, Gelsey, and I didn't want to admit
it. I didn't want you to know. It took me a long time . . . to
grow up as a dancer."

This was not an easy admission for him, even now, almost ten
years later. I was astonished by the personality change, even as
we went on to discuss the dancer he wanted me to coach. Her

Coaching Trinidad Sevillano in *Giselle*.

The Sleeping Beauty, Act I, Rose Adagio, with
Derek Dean as the French Prince.

Princess Aurora's Act I solo.

Rose Adagio, with Phillip Broomhead (l.) and Antony Dowson (r.) as Suitors.

With Monica Mason as the fairy Carabosse.

With Derek Rencher as King Florestan and Sandra Conley as his Queen.

Princess Aurora's Act II solo.

The Awakening, with Stephen Jefferies as Prince Florimund.

The Sleeping Beauty, Act III, Wedding Pas de Deux, with Stephen Jefferies as Prince Florimund.

Wedding Pas de Deux, with Stephen Jefferies as
Prince Florimund.

Wedding Pas de Deux, with Stephen Jefferies as Prince Florimund.

name was Trinidad Sevillano. She was Spanish. Peter described her as his "baby ballerina," and filled me in about her background. She was apparently the daughter of a shepherd. She began her ballet training at six and left home at fourteen, having been more or less on her own ever since, guided by a Spanish manager through various international competitions and concert appearances. Peter had first seen Trinidad dance at a gala in Chicago, and soon thereafter, he invited her to join the company.

She had danced her first Giselle at sixteen, a year ago in Copenhagen, learning the ballet in three weeks and charming the audience with her youth and technical prowess. She sounded as if she were exceptionally gifted, perhaps a prodigy. Peter's tone became paternal when he said, "Well, she's going through a difficult time. Some of the dancers resent her because she is so young . . . and also, she has a weight problem." He explained she was now on a special diet—he had sent her to a nutritionist who worked with a number of the dancers. Again talking like the concerned father, Peter complained about her being lazy, unwilling to give herself to the discipline. I was more than intrigued and suggested that I first watch her in class before making any decision.

As the meeting broke up, I asked Peter, "Does she know the story? Of Giselle, I mean."

"Yes. She was taught the steps," he replied matter-of-factly. "And she watched films."

We hugged with newfound affection and parted, agreeing to meet tomorrow.

His last comment about the girl made me somewhat skeptical. No matter how prodigious a young ballerina's talents may be, Giselle is not a role that can be mastered in three weeks. I assumed Trinidad had been typecast and encouraged to play herself. Of course, her own story held extraordinary romantic appeal, and she had already drawn attention from the press. How many daughters of Spanish shepherds suddenly find themselves dancing Giselle? Indeed, Trinidad was roughly the same age as the tragic heroine; and if all went well, she would be the first Spanish ballerina to perform the role in her homeland.

What appealed to me about working with her, sight unseen,

was the opportunity to follow through on the work I had started in the Royal Ballet classes. I was anxious to see those methods tested onstage by someone other than me; however, my expectations were certainly modest. Trinidad was only a year or so older than the students I was teaching; and I knew none of them was yet prepared to take on Giselle.

Yet perhaps there was something else which attracted me to this young dancer. Had I not also been thrust into roles before I was ready for them?

"You managed, after all, didn't you?" said my husband, as we ambled back to our flat, moving erratically with the sun ahead of us, as though we were following a runaway balloon, steering clear of those scaffolds that lined our street.

"Yes," I admitted, "but not by figuring out how to dance the role while I was onstage. It was that terror of being unprepared that sent me running in every direction to find a way."

The following morning Greg and I hiked several blocks to Festival Ballet's studios to see this underage marvel. The office and rehearsal facilities were located in what looked like a warehouse not far from the Royal Albert Hall. Painters and carpenters were at work renovating the building—Markova House—named after the famed English ballerina Dame Alicia Markova, who had founded the company in 1950 with Sir Anton Dolin, another in the gallery of revered figures in British ballet. Peter Schaufuss had only assumed the role of Artistic Director in 1984 and had not yet proven himself.

Peter's position was similar to that of Anthony Dowell's, as both were still dancing and trying to guide their respective companies through the gauntlet of audiences and critics while at the same time struggling to balance the books. Even with the government support received by British companies, funding was an ongoing and frequently nightmarish concern. The Royal Ballet, as the more established and prestigious of the two, enjoyed certain advantages, and yet it too was increasingly strapped during recent years. Festival Ballet did not even have a permanent house in which to perform during its London seasons and remained essentially a touring company.

In the past, Festival had attracted various stars who came and went as guest artists. As the new director, Peter had recruited

Trinidad and several other promising talents. He was obviously committed to seeing her develop with the company, and perhaps could not help but attach his own dreams to her success.

Greg and I looked for her in class. The studio was a large one on the second floor. The familiar routine had already started, led by a woman whose personal manner was as brusque and flamboyant as a ringmaster. We slipped by, finding seats in a long row of folding chairs at one end of the room. This class was for the women in the company, and the ballerinas appeared far more varied than those at the Royal, not only in terms of physical types, but in the way they worked. It was obvious they came from different backgrounds, countries, and schools of training. But which one was Trinidad?

My friend, Dina, again playing the role of the go-between, came over and discreetly pointed her out.

I whispered, "You're kidding! That's her?"

She appeared at first withdrawn and distracted, like a tiny urchin who had wandered into the studio by mistake. She was dressed completely in black—with matching leotard, sweat pants, and leg warmers—virtually slumping at the barre, her thick black hair frizzing out in all directions. She was undoubtedly more rounded and curved than the slender image that has come to mean ballerina in the public's mind, and in the minds of most artistic directors for that matter; but as far as I could tell, her weight was the least of her problems. What I saw was a demoralized dancer who was working improperly, who had no motivation, who really had no idea how to work in class or how to make the class work for her.

Trinidad was not alone in this regard.

She surely moved, as the saying goes, to the beat of a different drum, but this was not a subtlety of phrasing she had chosen; rather, it was a comfortable tempo for her to look like she was in attendance, warming up. At least, I thought, she was not counting music. I noticed she had sturdy peasant legs, which were hyperextended, making them appear to bow slightly behind the knees—an asset for some ballerinas when that curve can be used to enhance certain positions. Her arms were moving haphazardly from one vague position to the next—too high, too straight, too far back. Her elbows were especially unruly, rebelling whenever they had a chance.

Meanwhile, her focus was either nowhere or glancing at the mirror, straying to feet and legs as they moved front, side, and back. Sometimes she simply gazed down, rubbing a hip or a thigh or any part of her body that seemed like a convenient place to rest her hands. Her face and neck remained hidden much of the time by that impenetrable curtain of hair. Yet I knew her frame of mind. I had seen enough bored and depressed dancers in my time to recognize her symptoms. I could see why Peter might think she was undisciplined and lazy. But how were classroom calisthenics going to inspire a young ballerina struggling through adolescence?

After class, she hurried into a changing room. When she emerged again, she had pinned back her hair. As she walked forward to meet me, she was hesitant, her lips pursed, tense and sad even when she smiled. I asked her how much English she knew, and she replied, with a thick Spanish accent, "Lit-tle bit." She actually understood quite a bit, more than she was able to speak sometimes. I asked her if she had a few minutes before her next rehearsal to try an exercise with me. She said, "Yeees, I have time." Greg volunteered to help with his rusty Spanish, pulling over a small bench.

We would repeat that same exercise I had used with the Royal students. Trinidad had no difficulty understanding *Giselle* was a story about love, though it was clear she had only a vague idea of the plot. So for the moment, this Giselle would tell Albrecht she loved him, seated on a bench, then rising without using her arms: the beautiful Spanish word for heart, *corazón,* seemed to make the point clear. With me holding down her arms and pressing against her chest, she eventually rose to her feet— turning out and opening herself in a way which seemed nothing less than a revelation, as if a completely different person had come into the room.

Her response was fast and intuitive, allowing a glimpse of that nature she kept hidden during class: she was suddenly angelic and vulnerable. Her puckish face became beautiful as her emotions broke to the surface, her dark eyes glistening as if on the brink of happy tears. As her shape changed, so did her proportions; the area from her waist to her neck had lengthened, making her appear to lose ten or fifteen pounds in an instant and revealing unexpected grace when she moved. She quipped, "Oh, I like dancing like this!"

She won me over in that moment, although I still had certain qualms. There was such a long way to go from this simple exercise to the character of Giselle, and we would have only a month to break down the story and reckon with the choreography. She would have to overcome a number of careless habits if she were ever going to fill the role from the inside and do justice to the poetry demanded by this ballet. I was doubtful that Trinidad possessed enough maturity to give anything like a great performance. Yet she might at least render enough moments to provide a promise of beauties to come. I made up my mind not to allow her to mimic my interpretation of the role. She would have to discover her own way to tell the story—however many years that might take her in the end.

Before leaving, I pulled a hammer from my bag, and as the two of us huddled in a corner, I showed her how to pound out the pointes of her shoes, in order to make them silent onstage. When I saw how soft the muscles were in her forearms, I knew she would never be able to deliver the mime with any clarity. I gave her a piece of putty and told her to squeeze it in each hand every time she had a free moment. It was about the size of a golf ball, soft and malleable, but resistant enough to start building a few of those muscles she would need. She had already slumped back into her slack posture.

But she was not brooding. Her face remained intent. She seemed keen to know what else I might have hidden in my bag.

Curious, shy, and easily amused. Those qualities alone were enough, for now, to recommend her in my eyes. Henceforth, she was Trini, as she was known to those in the company. We agreed to start work the following week. She would rehearse with two partners, who would eventually alternate in the role of the duplicitous prince, Albrecht: one was a young Swedish dancer, Matz Skoog, and the other was Peter himself, who had partnered her for her first go at Giselle. We would be working at night, after she had already finished a full day of class and rehearsals—which meant somehow contending with her fatigue. I

163

figured she was young enough to put in those hours, as long as I kept her mind engaged by the story.

The situation was not entirely ideal, but the encounter elated me. I left her in the studio that morning and tried to imagine what it must be like for her separated from her family, her home, her country. What could the future hold for such a waif, thrown before her time into the theatre and its illusions?

The next afternoon my husband and I were picked up by one of those London cabbies who seem to cruise along with the most unflappable life-is-a-dream attitude. He was the type nothing phases, not even passengers like us, about to leave him stranded in the middle of nowhere. Without complaint, he delivered us to the Royal Ballet's Lower School, where the youngest students, roughly between the ages of ten and fifteen, board and receive both their academic schooling and classical ballet training. Located in the middle of Richmond Park, the place seemed a cross between manor house and monastery. This was White Lodge, a palatial affair where Edward VIII first entered the world and where Queen Elizabeth II's parents once resided.

From here, our friendly cabbie had no hope of finding a return fare. Nor would we have much hope of finding a taxi when we were ready to leave.

We followed a long path toward the lodge, enclosed by acres and acres of dense greenery. I said, "This is what the ballet world is like. Once you're in, there's no way out. It's like that enchanted forest in *Sleeping Beauty*, after everybody goes under the spell."

"Oh, there's always a way out," Greg disagreed. "Even in that ballet, I think."

We were in a roundabout way broaching a sensitive subject: I had recently told Anthony Dowell I wanted to perform the jewel of the Royal Ballet's repertory, *The Sleeping Beauty*, in the fall season. I was already having second thoughts about the wisdom of my decision, coming off an injury. But it was the only ballet offered that season that held any appeal, and it was scheduled for November, by which time I hoped to be back onstage.

I changed the topic quickly. "I was just thinking how different this atmosphere is compared to the school I went to as a child. I mean, there was paint peeling off the walls and we were tossed into the streets of Manhattan after our classes. I doubt if any of these kids have any idea how lucky they are to have a place like this. But, it's how and what you're taught, I suppose, not where. . . ."

"Some people might say you were the lucky one."

"I was lucky—but not the way some people might think."

Passing through a large crowd of parents and teachers, we climbed a grand stairway to a stone terrace, which overlooked an enormous lawn where the festivities would be held. The air was bright and cold. The men had their hands in their pockets; and the women were trying to keep faces turned away from onslaughts of wind and sun, with each coming from different directions. All were here to celebrate the end of the school year, and they appeared to be part of the same social set. For a few minutes, standing around idly, Greg and I felt somewhat out of place.

But Dame Merle greeted us with the warmest affability, as though we were long-awaited, special guests. With that noble bearing of hers, she looked to be more ready for *The Sleeping Beauty* than I was. Coming from behind Merle, preceded by that familiar cane, was the woman who had made it all possible, Dame Ninette, who founded the school in 1931. Her spryness was almost alarming. She asked immediately, "How are you, dear?" As soon as I started to reply, saying something about my good spirits, she interrupted, gesturing to my head, "No, no, not up there," and went on, pointing to my feet, "down there!" All eyes were suddenly staring at my cast.

"It comes off soon," I said, raising my voice to make sure she heard me.

She smiled in recognition, as if determined on my behalf, her jaw set, and her unyielding eyes fixed on mine.

Merle generously offered me the key to the school's swimming pool, should I want to take advantage in working myself back into shape.

I thanked her for the offer and said, "I just hope this body can be pulled together again."

"Oh, you'll do it," Merle said.

"Of course, you will," Dame Ninette insisted.

The activities soon commenced on the lawn, with several short performances by the students. The youngest ones whirled through a spirited rendition of a traditional folk dance, led by an adorable cherub of a girl. I whispered to Greg: "It's a shame most ballet training doesn't manage to preserve those natural patterns of movement. Her gestures are so alive and coordinated with the steps. Give her ten years of classes, and most of her muscles will be in snarls. More than likely she'll turn out square and rigid unless she's—"

"She's like a sprite," said Greg.

We watched as she and her classmates, waving scarves in the air, circled around for their proud parents.

After some older students danced a number, which featured boys rhythmically banging sticks, we accompanied Dame Ninette on a tour of the school. The past was everywhere, the halls telling of bygone splendor and royalty—with museum displays of old photographs and programs, celebrating the history of the Royal Ballet through its various phases, going back to the Vic-Wells Ballet—where Dame Ninette first launched her grand vision. She said how important a sense of history was for the students, yet I detected a note of sadness and concern in her voice.

As we walked along the corridor, I asked her, "Do you think the tradition is breaking down?"

She halted, and said, "It's the choreographers. There's so little time to work, you see. The theatre has changed so, since we began."

"But how many dancers are there now who can even breathe life into the classical roles? Even if one great choreographer came along, where are the great dancers? In America they don't even learn—"

She laughed, cutting me off. "Well, yes, American dancers are famous for dancing from the waist down. Of course you only had one choreographer. That's preposterous! Look what that does to a company!"

She was clearly speaking of George Balanchine, not Antony Tudor, whom she considered a British choreographer who happened to move on to America. With extreme modesty, she explained how her company had been the "home" for several choreographers, who began with study of the classics and then went on to make their marks in the world.

Dame Ninette started forward again, marching ahead of Greg and me, asking, "What's happened to Balanchine's company? Who's in charge there now?"

"Peter Martins and—"

"A wonderful dancer! What ever happened to him?" she asked.

I was spared a digression into the history of the New York City Ballet as we came to a steep flight of stairs, which led to a lower level where the swimming pool was located. Dame Ninette was adamant that I see everything—and just as adamant that she show the way.

When my husband offered her his arm, she declined, making light of her infirmity: "It doesn't hurt . . . it just doesn't work!"

We visited studios and classrooms, as well as the swimming pool, all the while conversing. Then we joined a reception already underway. Sandwiches had been laid out on tables and drinks were being served. We continued chatting about the state of the art. I remarked, "But, Dame Ninette, you of all people can see the decline in quality, and you know these young dancers and choreographers are not being adequately prepared. Surely there must be—"

"Yes, I may have to speak out. But, you see, I'm out of the picture now. What can I do? It's your generation."

"Well," I declared mischievously, "I'll have to keep making trouble, stirring things up in the studio."

"Oh, yes, you will," she said, with her eyes glowing and the lightness of laughter in her voice, "but not too much, dear!"

A short while later, Merle rejoined us. She graciously offered us a ride, as she was about to drive Dame Ninette home. We were relieved and pleased to accept. After all of us settled into Merle's car, Dame Ninette related one more story from her infinite repertoire. She told us about the first time she saw the famous Nijinsky dance. Her mother had taken her to the theatre, when she was "quite a young girl"—which meant this took place very early in the century.

"When I first saw him enter," she said, "I hid under my seat on the floor. My mother looked over and asked me, 'What are you doing down there?' I told her, 'I don't like that man!' He seemed more of an animal than a man . . . and he frightened me. Purely a physiological reaction. He was like a creature, you see. . . . I liked everyone else onstage, but Nijinsky scared me."

I was suddenly all Adam's apple. The way she described him made me shudder a moment before I could share her delight in telling the story. We drove on in silence for a while. A vague feeling of uneasiness came over me. There was more to it than I realized at first.

We parted happily, exchanging thanks and good-byes. I took the key to the swimming pool from Merle, though I suspected transportation to and from the school might be impossible.

That night, recording the afternoon in my journal, I wrote of Dame Ninette: "She is a beauty of beauties—that spirit of hers!"

Then it came to me. I looked up and asked Greg, "Didn't you think Dame Ninette's story about Nijinsky was strange?"

"How so?" He was staring into his computer screen.

"Remember that nightmare I had about Nijinsky?"

He thought for a moment. "Oh, the one with your dying swan?"

"Doesn't that seem like an odd coincidence to you?"

"Well, in a way," he said. "Only Dame Ninette was put off by the real thing. She saw him in the flesh, and with the innocence of a child's eyes."

We let it go at that.

Still, I wondered about Nijinsky's madness and the hold he had on the audience. It was disconcerting to think he had found a way into my dreams. Would I too have hidden under my seat had I seen him on the stage? Or, would he perhaps seem rather tame in today's world?

Later, Anthony phoned.

I was half asleep, and listened to Greg try to explain to him why I might not be interested in dancing Kenneth MacMillan's ballet, *Mayerling*, the dreary tale of the Crown Prince Rudolph of Austria-Hungary. "Gelsey has lived in the lower depths, and with all due respect to Kenneth, his ballet is so unrelenting with the depravity . . . from syphilis to drugs to suicide. I mean, if

there were even a single beam of light or hope—but you really
need to talk to her about it, Anthony."

We did talk, and finally settled on *The Sleeping Beauty.*

My cast came off early one morning in May, and with a
strange, lopsided sensation from having shoes on both feet, I
headed for the Royal Ballet School, ready to lead my class of
older students into another mystery. But this class was not to be.
Arriving at the school, I was surprised to find Dame Merle
sitting in a police car parked in front. Apparently there had
been a bomb threat. The building had been evacuated, and a
bomb squad was now inside.

Completely mystified, I climbed into the back seat with Merle
and ballerina Antoinette Sibley. We had no choice but to sit tight
while the police conducted their search. I asked in my igno-
rance, "Why would anyone ever do such a thing? Terrorists?"

Merle, who seemed more annoyed than concerned about any
real danger, told me, "Oh, anyone these days. They just look in
the phone directory, you see, and ring anything that begins with
the word 'Royal'!"

The random madness of the outside world hit me again. Were
any of us really safe, or immune? Would our sublime ideals
protect us? Looking out the window, I could see small groups of
dancers huddled in front of a building just across the roadway.
On this side, police were everywhere; the entire area was closed
off. There was an occasional crackle from the radio inside the
car, and each time I heard it the skin of my cheeks seemed to
pull tight. Merle and Antoinette kept up a steady conversation,
their agitation apparent only in the tone and frequency of their
laughter.

My husband, with a stroke of good timing, arrived on the
scene just as the police announced there was no bomb. The
dancers trooped back in orderly fashion from across the roadway, their schedules for the day to be revised. What had been a
fright that no one wanted to admit, was soon dismissed as nothing more than a nuisance.

With the disruption of my teaching schedule, I was grateful to
have some extra time to think about the upcoming coaching

session for *Giselle.* The last time I had performed the ballet was with Baryshnikov in 1983. So I spent the afternoon devising ways that I might help Trinidad start to explore the character and fulfill the stylistic demands of the ballet.

I knew she would eventually have to solve for herself the mystery of mysteries—which that ballet has raised ever since it was first choreographed by Jules Perrot and Jean Coralli more than a century ago—why does Giselle go mad?

That evening, Greg and I schlepped bag and bicycle tires to Festival's studios. We did appear slightly suspect entering the building, but an elderly night watchman let us pass without so much as a quizzical look. He was apparently ready for anything or anyone who happened through the door—it seemed the first-floor studio had been rented to some rather colorful Buddhists, who could be heard chanting as we hastened up the stairs. Trinidad was waiting for us, alone in the same studio where we had seen her take class. She appeared ghostly in the half light. All we needed was some mist, and we might have run through the graveyard scene of the second act, when the spirit of Giselle returns.

Greg turned up the lights.

I asked Trini, "Are your feet sore?"

"No," she said. "Well, not too bad."

Her voice was not convincing.

"Put on some soft shoes, even slippers." Seeing her quizzical expression, I added, "You're going to have to tell me whenever you don't understand me."

We would work without a pianist tonight. I wanted to put her at ease, for now, with regard to the music. I had her get up from the chair once again, and then the three of us sat down facing each other, to start delving into the drama. I assumed Trini knew about as much of the story as anyone who had seen the ballet: the peasant girl, Giselle, unwittingly falls in love with Count Albrecht, who has disguised himself as a peasant. When she discovers Albrecht's deception and the fact he is already betrothed to Bathilde, Giselle goes mad and dies; but she returns from the grave in the second act to save him from the Wilis, evil spirits of women who have died before their weddings—who come back to take revenge on men by forcing them to dance themselves to death.

But Trinidad would need more than that simple action line to start on the first scene. I was hoping to bring both her feelings and her imagination into play. Giselle's story was going to have to become important, really a matter of urgency for her, if we were to see anything more than a cute girl romping through the steps.

I asked her, "How old is Giselle?"

"Very young, I think." Her face was still deeply flushed from the chair exercise.

"About as old as you?"

"Yeees," she said, suddenly smiling, "that's true."

"And how does she feel about Albrecht?"

"She love him," she said, sounding sure of herself.

"But, Trini, what kind of love does Giselle feel for him?"

"I don't understand. . . ."

"Has Giselle ever been in love before?"

"Oh, no. I don't think so."

"What about you, Trini . . . have you been in love before?"

Taken aback, she replied, "Yees, I have . . . been." Her eyes said she had also been hurt. She looked down, as though she were gazing somewhere inside herself.

"And what happens," I said, drawing her back, "to Giselle at the end of the first act?"

She paused, trying to remember. "She find out Albrecht to marry Bathilde."

"So he betrays Giselle, doesn't he? How does that make her feel?"

"Oh, bad. Very bad."

"What else? Just bad?"

She came forward to the edge of her chair and let out a nervous laugh. "Well, she go crazy. She is mad!"

"What does she lose when she finds out he has lied?"

She went silent, her eyes as wide as they could be.

"Does Giselle believe Albrecht loves only her . . . just as much as she loves him?"

"Yes."

"And does she think he will marry her?"

171

She hesitated, uncertain.

I stood up suddenly, playing Albrecht, miming his formal vow of love from the first act—my hand sweeping up from my breast toward heaven.

Then I asked her, "What does that mean? Is he saying he will love her forever?"

She nodded quickly, and I asked, "Do you believe him?"

"Well, I do. I want to believe."

"How much, Trinidad? How much does Giselle believe him?"

She held back.

"Can you believe that he has lied to you?"

"Oh, no! Is terrible. . . . I not believe."

"Do you dream of loving Albrecht forever?"

"Yes. I dream . . . forever."

"And what do you dream with?"

"My head," she said, smiling impishly.

"And what do you love with?"

"My heart."

"Right. So we need to see the beauty in your heart and mind every moment you're onstage . . . don't we? When somebody is as much in love as Giselle, is her heart big or small?"

"Oh, big."

"As big as the whole world?"

"Oh, yes."

"And what shape did we say the world was?"

"Is round."

"Right, like that shape you made when you got up from the bench. What else does Giselle love?"

I gave her a hint, gently lifting and rounding my arms.

Her eyes held the answer before she said, "To dance. I love to dance!"

"But why does your mother try to stop you from dancing?"

"Because I am sick. My heart . . ."

"Right. You have a weak heart, and you might die. But you dance anyway, don't you? Why?"

"It make me happy."

"Do you have to dance?"

"Yes. I must dance."

"What does Giselle express when she dances? What does she

172

tell us about? Something that must be even more important to her than death . . . even stronger than her fear. . . . What could that be?"

"*Mi alma?*" she said, slipping into her native tongue.

Greg translated, "My soul."

"So is Giselle fragile, or strong? What kind of spirit does she have? Will she be able to forgive Albrecht for his lies . . . ?"

"Well . . ." There was a struggle visible in her face.

"Well, now we have to find out. If Giselle dreams of love, of loving Albrecht forever, what do we need to see when you first come onstage? Let's set up the scene, okay?"

While we moved chairs into place to represent Giselle's cottage and doorway, and Albrecht's cottage, I started another line of questions, the sort that might be familiar to any actor but most likely not considered by dancers. These ranged from the season and weather and time of day, to the activity Giselle might be engaged in before she hears Albrecht at the door and makes her entrance. In the weeks ahead, I wanted her mind to be so full of the details of Giselle's story, she would dream of nothing else. The real task was to create that inner world for the audience, by carrying that beautiful shape, which she had so far only glimpsed, into the dancing itself.

The first entrance required some simple mime, followed by a series of skipping steps (glissade to ballonné) round the stage, all the while Giselle was trying to find where Albrecht might be hiding. Trini's first attempt was a travesty, as might have been expected. She was like a prom queen looking for her date, with a pair of arms flying into the stratosphere. All of those lovely ideas we had talked about had yet to find a way into her body.

I asked her, "Do you like to flirt?"

"Flirt? I don't understand."

Greg translated, and I went on, "If Giselle loves only Albrecht, or Loys as he calls himself, would she want to flirt with the other boys in the village?"

"Oh no, she wouldn't do that."

"Then we don't want to see a silly flirt flapping around, do we?" My tone was light enough for her to laugh at herself.

We started the scene again, with Trinidad offstage in Giselle's cottage, making believe she was at work with needle and thread. She mimed that action, then stopped, needle in air, when she heard me give a knock at the door. This was her cue to enter, and I had her say aloud, "Could that be him?" It took her a few tries to say the line with any excitement. I wanted her to make the entrance with the level of her torso poised—above her arms and legs, as it had been when she rose from the chair. Her whole frame had to be filled with anticipation as she opened the door. After laboring through the mime, making up lines to say as we went along, she tried the steps again.

Giselle was hunting for Albrecht: she knew he must be hiding somewhere—she had recognized that knock—but, where could he be? Trini tore around the stage, unable to keep those arms down, and as she turned, unable to round out the corners of Giselle's world. Nor was she able to pinpoint her focus so the audience would be searching with her. I gave her any number of exercises to deal with each problem.

First, I had her do the steps with her arms tied to her sides by a scarf. Next, I had her try to skip around the room while balancing a book on her head. Then I had her put on one of my old practice skirts and try looking for Albrecht while she held on to the hem of the skirt. Then I had her skipping again, with her two hands clasped, pushing down in front of her. Finally, I took one of her hands and skipped around the studio with her, as if we were two children on a lark.

I took her on quite a ride, staying just ahead of her. Each time we went around the studio, we covered more and more space— taking more and more time hanging up in the air, less and less time when we took off. I was forcing her to get into the air faster and faster, and stay suspended; and as she did, I kept reminding her to breathe and turn out her whole body, to push away from the floor. As her preparation disappeared, the movement began to look more effortless.

I kept her focus moving outside the circle, asking her, "Who are you looking for, Trini? Where is he?"

She was suddenly moving faster than she had ever dreamed possible, taking off into the air when before she had only been preparing to jump. Instead of thinking of doing six sets of two steps, she was soon thinking of one long circle of skips, like a single joyous step—which meant the movement would eventually be phrased imperceptibly ahead of the music. For the moment, we sang, and hummed, and imagined the score.

With that old clunker of a score by Adolphe Adam, the ballerina who fell behind or danced monotonously on the beat would run the risk of putting everyone to sleep. I told her, "You don't want to hear them snoring in the front rows, do you?"

The strain was beginning to tell, but she possessed the inexhaustible energy and stubborn will of a child—as long as she remained inspired and challenged.

Later, I had her do the steps while simultaneously spinning one of my bicycle tires around each of her arms. I showed her first, and said, "All I'm doing is letting my torso make them go around, so it looks like my arms aren't moving." This gymnastic feat intrigued her. It appeared so incredibly easy. But as soon as she tried, the tires went sailing across the studio.

"What happened?" she asked, giggling.

"Try again. You'll get it."

"Is so hard. What I do wrong?"

"Keep those arms low . . . use your back muscles."

She had already picked up the tires and was trying again, mastering the trick within a few minutes. Soon she was able to put the tires together with the steps. But now she would have to put the story together with the steps; and later in the week, she would have to put both together with a pianist. That would mean yet another set of obstacles to be overcome. And still later, she would have to deal with her partners.

Of course, she had difficulty absorbing so much in such a short period of time, but she never let up. The first time she was able to create that perfect circle of skips and jumps, with her arms down gracefully at her sides, I asked her, "How did it feel to you?"

"It feels strange, Gelsey," she said, wiping the sweat off her nose with the back of her hand. "You know, everything feels so different!"

Her hair had come loose, tousled like a gypsy's.

"I wish you could have seen yourself, Trini, you were so beautiful! As strange as it must feel for you right now, that's what it takes for us to see that heart full of love. And the audience has to see that too . . . so we really care later, when it gets broken."

"Really? You saw?"

"Yes!"

With her eyes brimming with tears, she said in a whisper, as though she were telling us her darkest secret, "I was going to quit dancing . . . stop ballet. Not now . . . I think . . ."

My husband said, returning her shy smile, "Oh, not yet, Trini. You haven't even finished the first scene!"

Our excursions out of London were rare, but one Sunday early in June, we accepted an invitation from Donald MacLeary to visit his house in the country—an hour or so north of the city. We were to drive up with one of the Royal Ballet's loveliest ballerinas, Lesley Collier, and her boyfriend, Guy Niblett, who had danced the role of Mercutio in those recent performances of *Romeo and Juliet.* It was late morning when they collected us in a little foreign car. Greg and I squeezed into the back, looking forward to the change of scenery, both of us realizing how much we needed a break from the studio and the flat.

We set out under threat of rain. Guy was behind the wheel, with Lesley acting as devoted copilot, reading the map. He was easygoing and ruggedly handsome, while she always seemed to me the personification of naïve innocence. Lesley was only a few years older than I was, but blessed with one of those angelic faces that never appear to age, not to mention her breathtaking grand jeté. She was the type, I imagined, who might very well dance forever, though I would never have wished such a fate on anyone.

The conversation moved rapidly from the directions to Donald's home, to the lack of direction we encountered in the studio, to the hazards of our profession. The miles flew by on an expressway called the M-1 or the M-15, something that sounded vaguely like a rifle. The London suburbs soon gave way to country landscapes dotted with quaint stone farmhouses set among pastures and lush rolling hills. Our small talk was constant, interrupted only by a few short gaps of awkward silence. I had never really known Lesley or Guy, except for occasional exchanges during class and pleasantries traded in the halls of the theatre. I was curious to hear their views about the company, as both were insiders. My impressions were those of a guest, and a privileged one at that.

Once I opened my mouth, I was off, regaling them with some of those stories from my checkered past. Lesley was the first to respond, making a sudden leap of empathy. She explained how she had learned about the harsher side of ballet rather late in her career. She had been one who had always done what she was told and gone along with the show, so to speak; but she was no longer quite the naïve innocent that her image made her out to be. I sensed no regret in what she was saying; rather, I was listening to a woman who had arrived at definite conclusions about what she now wanted from ballet and, more importantly, from her life. She was learning to assert herself, and it was easy to admire her.

Guy had been keeping his eyes on the road. Responding to a question from Greg, who was being his usual inquisitive self, Guy expressed what may be a universal grievance in the the- atre, at least for dancers. "But how can we get it bloody right, when we're rehearsing so many ballets at once? We haven't the time to develop a character, have we?" Turning sideways to look over the back of her seat, Lesley inquired about my foot. I could see Guy glancing in the rearview mirror. He asked with sincere concern, "What will you do if you don't dance again, Gelsey?" My heart sank. I felt Greg next to me, with his arms folded over his chest, waiting for me to say something.

Perhaps sensing the tension, Lesley broke in, saying, "Gel- sey's going to be the most fantastic coach. She has such . . ."

"I'm not so sure," I retorted, not doubting my ability, but realizing the theatres were more and more phasing out the very idea of coaching. "It's the same problem Guy was talking about. There's no time. All we get today are Russians running around from company to company trying to do a quick fix on what they call style—and for most of them, style becomes a picture im- posed from outside. Lift arms so . . . and look there . . . and turn like doll. Yet what perfect bodies! With those Russian backs! And their epaulement! But they rarely ask why, or what's going on inside. By the time they're teenagers, it's already been built into their bodies. So everything for them is either correct or incorrect . . ."

"Depending, whether you're from Moscow or Leningrad," piped Greg, facetiously. He knew I had steered away from the more troubling issue and gave my foot a playful thump with one of his knuckles.

The car was hugging a sharp curve in the road, throwing me into him. I shut myself up, saying, "Better not get me going on this one."

Greg tried to pick up the slack, inquiring about the absence of a stage director in ballet. "You have your choreographers and ballet masters and such, but nobody really directs the drama like you have with a stage play. Why is that?"

I retreated into silence.

His question was batted around the interior of the car and finally landed nowhere.

There were cautious speculations about company politics, and then some more comments about the Russians—were they athletes or artists?

As we hit the outskirts of a rural village, the map was replaced by Donald's instructions. Outside the window, I could see the countryside beckoning; but my mind was already far away. I had worked out a master plan for myself—to teach and coach through the summer, and get back into shape by the autumn. The necessity for me to be onstage when my memoirs came out, somehow, had been blown up out of proportion. Guy's innocent question had struck the nerve. If I were never able to dance again, would I lose everything I had worked so hard to win back?

Before I realized we had arrived at our destination, we pulled into the driveway of what appeared, at first sight, Giselle's cottage. Donald's house resembled a full-scale model of the peasant girl's home—as if transported from the ballet set and plunked down at the edge of this village. The grounds were kept immaculately, the gardens miraculously blooming with flowers, like some golden dream of childhood. Traipsing across the lawn through the sunshine, Donald himself led the welcoming party, a couple of the company's young hopefuls, Maria Almeida and Jonathan Cope.

My husband and I were about to have our first real taste of English hospitality, although Donald was Scottish, his trim figure jaunting ahead of the others, his arms open wide and his hands upturned, as though he were checking for rain. After a warm embrace, I volunteered to move in at once, to become one of his caretakers—an offer he pondered, and then with an airy gesture declared a splendid idea. He had already prepared an itinerary for the afternoon, which began with hors d'oeuvres and a tour of the house, a rambling country affair, larger inside than expected, rustic, and inviting. Then all of us embarked on a nature walk into the nearby woods.

Greg and I straggled along the path, lagging behind the others, and every so often Donald dropped back to check on our progress and fill us in on local lore. He drew our attention to a glade where John Bunyan, the author of *Pilgrim's Progress,* was said to have preached during the seventeenth century, around the time he was locked up for his nonconformist ideas. This glade was a kind of shadowy ravine. I had no idea who Bunyan was and had never read the book, but imagined a dark character in one of those pointy pilgrim hats.

"He preached from the hill there," explained Donald, pointing into the shadows, "while he was in hiding."

I asked, "But why was he put in jail?"

"Intolerance," suggested my husband.

We fell behind again, strolling side by side, sometimes holding hands, sometimes not. I told Greg, "The stage seems so far away out here. It must be heaven, to go to the theatre and work, and be able to return to this place." The wind was rustling in the branches above my head, while I scuffed my feet over the twigs and leaves that covered the path. But my thoughts were elsewhere, moving in circles.

This pastoral interlude came to an end at the side of the local cricket field where some players and fans were braving the weather, on the cool side even for spring. I had heard about the rowdy mobs who sometimes turned British sporting matches into brawls, but these were peaceful, rural folk, mostly families and children. There was an idyllic beauty to the scene, and the image stayed with me as we took the path back to Donald's cottage, passing that same shadowy glade.

No way out, I said to myself, once again reminded of that forest in *The Sleeping Beauty.*

A sumptuous meal was waiting for us. Donald presided at the head of a long wooden table, playing master of ceremonies. He had already planned the seating arrangements, placing me on his left, and Greg on the far side of the table. Each course was served as Donald rang a tiny bell. The formal atmosphere and odd assortment of personalities made me think of a play, some comedy of manners in which the characters find themselves at a loss to communicate, though our host, with his wit, managed to keep a conversation moving along at a brisk pace.

He mentioned one recent ballet by the company's rising choreographer, David Bintley, whose work, *Sons of Horus,* I had attended with my husband. Both Lesley and Guy had danced in the ballet, which was a modern esoteric piece based on some Egyptian mythology. I found this production wanting in so many ways I was almost speechless. The consensus around the table seemed to be a favorable one, which surprised me, because I knew the strain on a dancer's body when constantly being asked to move between modern and classical styles. With as much tact as possible, I voiced my opinion. "I thought the dancers' talents might have been put to better use."

The comment blew over quietly, as if it might be too early in the English day for spirited contention.

With my physical condition at low ebb, I was trying to eat as wisely as possible; this was not so much a diet as a safety precaution against having to put myself through any sort of crash effort once I went back to the barre. I glanced with curiosity across the table where Maria was seated. She was a lean, exotic-looking creature, originally from Angola, but it was impossible to tell how or what she may have thought about dance; and the same was true of her tall counterpart, Jonathan, who possessed a strong, noble line. They talked about real estate deals but seemed to avoid any mention of ballet. Yet, they were fledglings, soloists with obvious physical gifts, who were about to be promoted to principals.

I thought perhaps Donald, being something of an authority figure in the company, might be inhibiting them. Guy and Lesley seemed somewhat less reticent, when the topic of conversation did eventually become more controversial. Somehow we got on to the departure of Alessandra Ferri, who had been an emerging talent with the Royal Ballet before she moved on to American Ballet Theatre. I knew her exit was seen by some as a betrayal.

I also knew I had a tendency to blurt out my opinions, not always with the grace I was able to bring to my pas de bourrées. As with so many companies, the Royal Ballet had its social cliques and its unspoken rules of decorum—which meant you were not supposed to talk about certain people while in the presence of certain other people, unless you happened to know where everybody stood, and thus who might be praised or insulted under the circumstances. This sort of thing always baffled me. Unless all the right people were together at the right time, there was no way to avoid certain blunders.

When Alessandra's name first came up, I exercised some restraint.

My husband, on the other hand, jumped fearlessly into the fray, turning to Donald over dessert, querying him: "The press quoted or misquoted her, saying something about her deserting a sinking ship—which caused quite a storm. The official story was she was going to improve her technique. But what were the real reasons she decided to leave?"

Donald, not at all ruffled, explained that the company had been nurturing Alessandra, and carefully grooming her for the future. She had gone off to dance *Swan Lake* at La Scala for Franco Zeffirelli. "When she came back," said Donald, his tone changing, "she went on about how he told her the story while working on the ballet . . . as if we ignored drama here!" Allowing his eyes to glance around the table, he asserted, "You know I always tell the story, at the first rehearsal—always tell the dancers the story from the start." I inferred from what he said that Alessandra had gone to Ballet Theatre, ironically, for at least one of the reasons I had come to the Royal Ballet.

I gently reminded our host, "But we deal with the drama in *every* rehearsal whenever the two of us rehearse together, don't we, Donald?"

He gave me the most endearing grin. "Of course, we do, Gelsey!"

The atmosphere became more relaxed when we moved into a sitting room for coffee and tea. Donald owned a collection of pugs, scruffy little dogs that had the run of the place. One in particular, an old fellow named Captain, caught my fancy right away. He suffered from some lung disorder like asthma, so each time Captain drew a breath, he sounded to all the world like he was growling, and the more excited he became, the more he was heard to growl and wheeze. And yet the dog possessed the sweetest disposition, racing around like a windup toy under the furniture. He was a mascot, instantly adopted on my lap.

"Sounds like Gelsey," remarked my husband, "whenever she's working in the studio."

There was a round of laughter. Then, with dogs in tow, we followed Donald up a long, polished staircase that led to an upstairs bedroom, and there, seated in front of a television, watched recent videos of his horsemanship. After retiring from the stage, Donald had returned to a childhood passion for horses, and entered various competitions in dressage and jumping and the like. He had won his share of medals, and I saw a glow of pride in his face as he sat next to me, while the screen featured him, a truly elegant figure in his riding gear, jumping his horse over water. His enthusiasm called up more than a few memories of my own childhood dreams. Had I missed my calling?

Greg said, with mock seriousness, "Who knows? You might have been a great jockey."

Which elicited another burst of laughter.

I delighted in repeating a story Antoinette Sibley had told me about Donald. It seemed, some years ago, he had been called upon to step in and partner her at the last minute in some major production like *Romeo and Juliet*. Antoinette was impressed that he knew exactly where she needed to be supported and he was able to move with such grace, anticipating her movements in a way that was uncanny. She told me, "He's a great natural partner," and when I mentioned his riding talent, she exclaimed, "Oh, yes, Donald can partner anything that moves!"

Donald laughed and brushed off the adulation.

I pressed him about the source of his "natural gifts." He admitted an early exposure to Scottish folk dancing, and he credited a few teachers who helped him find his way onstage. Easily encouraged, he reminisced about trips across America when the company toured by train, and he taunted the younger generation, those present in the room, for having it so easy these days. "They'll never know," he said wistfully.

On our way home that evening, just before sunset, we stopped briefly at a pasture where Donald kept his horses. Gorgeous creatures. I thought of da Vinci's horses, but was too exhausted by now to embark on any grand theories about painting and dancing.

During our return journey to London, I planted my head on Greg's lap and tried to sleep. With my eyelids closed, I lay there listening to the steady drone of the engine, sensing the interior of the car being intermittently lit up by opposing headlights.

For an instant before I dropped off, everything seemed to clarify: the book would come out, Trini would dance her *Giselle,* and I would find some way through that magical forest in *The Sleeping Beauty.* I must have had some real doozy of a dream during that ride. As we felt our way into the flat and through the darkness, I was thinking only of going back to a carefree childhood of absolute bliss; and later on, when the two of us collapsed together on our mat, I told Greg, "Well, I think, I'm ready to retire."

As our two heads found the same pillow, I repeated the intention.

Greg assumed I meant I was ready for sleep.

"So am I," he said softly.

"From the stage, I mean . . . from the stage!"

He lifted his head for a moment, and then he curled an arm around my waist, gathering me in.

Neither of us breathed another word.

5.

WHEN
BEAUTY
AWAKENS

Had the web of hope and work that held me to the stage been unraveling in my sleep? Was my spirit faltering, or were my dreams being rewoven into some new shape? During those first weeks I spent teaching and coaching, the possibility of my moving into some area of dance other than performing had become more and more appealing, while the prospect of putting my body through yet another ballet had become a source of increasing distress. With my past about to explode into controversy, and with the future closing in, my confidence that I would actually be able to dance again was wavering.

The joys I experienced working with young dancers seemed to confirm what I had been hoping for all along, that there was something else I had to offer—something I had come to value as much as my own performances. And yet, that realization gave rise to further tension. I never thought it was possible or desirable to devote myself to performing and at the same time pursue the other roles I was just beginning to envision for myself in the theatre.

My husband tried to play my aspirations off against my insecurities, attempting to come to terms with what was, after all, a shared dilemma. Between us, some measure of faith always returned, though I was never sure what form it might take. There were times a quiet sort of resignation possessed me and I made an uneasy peace with myself—and other times, when his passion or humor would catch me unexpectedly, and I would strengthen my resolve, at least as far as following through with my performances of *The Sleeping Beauty.*

Even so, I suspected I might be in for more than one rude awakening. It was too early to say how my body would respond to the ordeal of conditioning; however, I had performed this ballet enough times in the past to have no illusions about what I was up against. What was perhaps a pleasant dream for an audience could easily turn into a torturous nightmare for the ballerina. Even Margot had admitted she usually went into a state of "terror" anticipating the role of Princess Aurora.

The night before I was to teach my final class at the Royal Ballet School, I entered a few more notes in my journal, taking a line from the company's illustrious choreographer, Sir Frederick Ashton, to serve as my theme for class. Sir Fred once advised choreographers to "deal with that which is spiritual and eternal rather than that which is material and temporary." His advice, lofty as it was, seemed equally appropriate for young dancers. I added one further thought, "How can our moments onstage speak forever?"

"That might be too deep for them," said Greg. We were on our mat, and he was reading over my shoulder. He had piled some pillows under him, and drawn a sheet around himself, so he looked like some character out of *The Thousand and One Nights.* I heard a false note, as he went on, "Won't that be over their heads?"

"I've been trying to go over their heads in every class. I'd rather leave them looking up at the stars than staring down at their feet! So far they've managed to get out of a chair and walk to the barre, but half of them are carrying so much tension in the torso, they're not even prepared for a simple plié. How are they ever going to create character, or one true gesture? And why are you being so—"

"All I'm saying is Ashton's ideas might be out of reach for these kids."

He seemed determined to draw me into an argument.

My voice suddenly got loud. "If they're going to dance his ballets, they might try to deal with his ideas, and not just his steps!"

"Or *someone* might," said Greg, feigning innocence.

"What do you mean . . . ?"

"Didn't Ashton add a few steps in *Sleeping Beauty?*"

He turned away abruptly, with an exaggerated movement, lifting his hand to his forehead. When he faced me again, his widening grin told me I had talked myself into a little trap. We both knew that the Royal Ballet production of *The Sleeping Beauty,* while staged by Nicolai Sergeyev and supervised by Dame Ninette, also contained additional passages choreographed by Sir Fred. In a roundabout way, Greg was reminding me that in this ballet I would have my own encounter with Ashton, however brief.

"You don't understand," I told him.

"Oh?"

"Most of the choreography is Petipa's, and it's a technical horror show! You can't imagine. It's more of a goddamned boxing match than a ballet! And what you actually have to do to make it work . . . to act the part. . . ."

He saw something hilarious in this. "You may be the first ballerina to give up the stage for the ring!"

I rose on my knees, his levity somehow rubbing me the wrong way. "You know that wasn't what I had in mind! I'm just saying I'm afraid."

After flinging my words, I slowly dropped down beside him, adding more gently, "I don't know why it is, but I can't seem to joke about it, even though I know I still have months to prepare. It's like stage fright . . . already . . ."

I closed my journal and leaned against him. Why had I chosen this ballet?

I told myself again, if I were encouraging my students in a certain direction, I had to be willing to travel farther along the same path. I was reminded of what Dame Ninette had described as "the painful business of acquiring knowledge." What was there about the art that made up for the more exacting and painful side of the discipline? What made it all worthwhile? This was surely a quandary I had struggled with most of my career. I had no love for the pain, but I had come to live for those flashes of insight in the studio, for those moments of breakthrough that ultimately gave me the shape in every ballet—wasn't that still another form of love?

What I was saying in class would have to be exemplified on-stage, even in a ballet that seemed less than appropriate as far as those lessons I had been trying to get across. Petipa's *Sleeping Beauty* was often cited by critics as the purest example of classical style—the apotheosis of the French school as it came to flourish in Russia at the end of the nineteenth century. This was certainly one ballet in which form appeared to triumph over content. How could a frivolous fairy tale possibly measure up to the dramatic complexities of *Romeo and Juliet* or *Giselle?*

"You can always change your mind," said Greg.

"No," I told him, "there are a thousand reasons—not the least of which is I gave Anthony my word."

The next afternoon, we found a studio on the first floor where I would give the last class. This space was smaller than the others in which I had taught, but there was a lot of natural light filtering in, so the room had an airy, intimate atmosphere that seemed to match my mood. Greg and I moved a pair of chairs against a wall, and sat with backs to the mirror. The students arrived early. So did Merle, who greeted us warmly, and took a seat by the piano.

I began quietly, "Since this may be our last time together, I thought we might try to recall a few of these things we've been working on. Okay?" A few heads nodded, and I asked, "What have we learned so far?"

No one volunteered. Some of their expressions said, "Oh, my God! I've forgotten everything!"

It was Greg who broke the silence. "Why do you think Gelsey has been asking you all of these questions in every class?"

Several hands rose, but one voice from the back called out, "Because she wants us to think for ourselves."

"And what do we use," I asked, "when we think?"

I gazed up as if I were searching the heavens for an answer, until the familiar chorus came to life.

"Our minds . . ."

And so we were off again, the endless dialogue broken by some final exercises. When it was over, I was overcome by sentiment and exhaustion, my heart seemingly everywhere at once, as they said good-bye. I met with Merle, who had attended many of the classes, as had a number of teachers. I told her, "I've only scratched the surface with them, but at least they have some idea how much work they have to do, how much farther they have to go. I have the feeling I sometimes get after a performance . . . that sense of incompleteness. There's always so much more, but I suppose that's a lesson in itself, isn't it?"

"Well, now we'll see what they can do with what you've given them. Sometime, you might like to work with five or six of the younger ones for a longer period . . . and take them through a couple of years, to see the progress."

"Yes. I'd like that very much. There's only so much value in this approach unless it's sustained, and you know how there's never enough time. . . ."

"Never," she agreed, with a sigh.

"The sad thing is," I said, "the older we get, the faster it seems to go. It's like they say—"

Merle laughed, and said, as if to admonish me, "But, Gelsey, you're still so young!"

I took her words to mean young enough to continue dancing.

"What you really need is a theatre," said my husband, tossing his words into the air as we slowly threaded our way through the morning mob at Victoria Station. We were about to board a train to Gatwick Airport. It was the middle of June and our flight destination was Granada, Spain—where Trinidad would dance her *Giselle,* as well as Balanchine's *Symphony in C,* and the Kingdom of the Shades excerpt from Petipa's *La Bayadère.* Trini's immediate needs surely overshadowed all of my concerns about the future. But Greg was trying to lure me back into a discussion he had started in the taxi. What was he saying? I tried to make believe his voice had failed to carry over the noise, until he took hold of my arm.

"Let's just wait," I told him, "and see what happens in the next few days . . . if Trini gets through this."

"You're going to have to start somewhere," he suggested, referring to an opening which had recently come up for Artistic Director at the Irish National Ballet, a small company for which Dame Ninette was the official patroness. Releasing my elbow, he added, "Sooner or later you have to decide what you most want to accomplish . . . unless you secretly want to spend the rest of your life as a ballerina." Sensing that he had pushed far enough, he relented.

Hoisting my bag between us, I said only, "You know I'm not married to that idea."

An hour later, we reached the airport, and caught up with our fellow travelers from Festival Ballet. We took off under a blank gray sky; and a part of me shuddered like the plane, until we broke through the clouds, and I knew the pilot could see where we were going. The dancers on board took up most of the seats in the cabin. They were a friendly bunch, apparently accustomed to touring, or perhaps inured as I was years ago, to the wear and tear on the nerves.

I might as well have been time traveling. I had my nose buried in my journal, doing the sort of "homework" Trinidad had not yet learned to do on her own, going over *Giselle* moment by moment. Leafing through pages and memories, I kept asking myself how much of the story she had actually absorbed, but there was no way to know. Our crash course had lasted less than a month; and we were not even finished rehearsing. She had already been put through the wringer. But was Trini even close to being ready?

How was she going to cope with the audience? I had seen her burst into tears when one of our rehearsals was unexpectedly turned into a promotional event for a group of two hundred of the company's financial supporters. She had been unable to carry out the action in the first act, unable to take verbal corrections in front of those strangers—and I could still see the pain in her face. Her inhibitions had paralyzed her. As gifted as she was, she had yet to develop those habits of mind and body that she was going to need.

My eyes ran across an admonition I had given her during a rehearsal when her concentration wavered. "It's Albrecht who's going to betray Giselle in this ballet . . . not us!" I had pursued an obvious strategy, making the same demands on her I would have made on myself, though certain allowances had to be conceded her youth. Fortunately, the choreologist, Lynn Vella-Gatt, and the ballet master, Kevin Haigen, an old friend of mine from my early years at Ballet Theatre, had provided constant support, and had been open to my direction, as far as how Trini might dance the role most persuasively.

Festival Ballet's version of *Giselle* was first staged by Mary Skeaping in 1971; out of personal loyalty, Lynn wanted to preserve the notated blueprint from that production. The version of the ballet I knew derived from a staging which David Blair had done for Ballet Theatre in 1968. There were at least a few steps and pantomimic gestures that had to be adjusted because they were uneconomical or inappropriate for Trini; however, my intention had not been to push either version of the staging, or change any of the standard choreography.

What I tried to do was open the realm of interpretation for Trinidad. For me, as always, the bottom line came down to dramatic logic, and so far, the simplicity of my suggestions had carried the day. Through some subtle alterations in phrasing and focus, Trini had been able to deal with most of the choreographic obstacles, but she was overwhelmed by the number of choices which had to be made—and which had to be recalled after she had made them. We had taken the ballet apart, but as far as I could tell, Trinidad had not yet put it back together for herself, and she seemed to think this was going to happen by magic. This was not the only problem.

When any conflicts arose in staging, the responsibility fell on Peter Schaufuss to resolve them, as he was the Artistic Director; but Peter had also cast himself as Trini's partner—which made for another sort of conflict. She had some difficulty seeing him as her romantic prince. Peter filled the role with an impressive physicality; however, at times, his Albrecht seemed not to have been thought through in a way that would allow him to respond to her needs as Giselle—and for Trini, this led to a simmering, unvoiced resentment, notwithstanding Peter's good intentions and best efforts.

The age gap was obvious.

I found myself caught in the middle, sympathetic to both sides. I could understand her anger when his directorial duties distracted him from the dance or left her waiting for him to show up for rehearsal; but I also realized Trini underestimated Peter as a partner. Peter's work on the second act adagio was in fact brilliant compared to what I had gone through with some of my former partners.

His lifts were becoming seamless, and caring. She had not wanted to hear how lucky she was. Trinidad was able to sense the dead spots in the dancing, when nothing was happening between her and Peter. These were like so many blanks, which had yet to be filled in.

I told her one day what no one had ever told me, what I had known intuitively—that the responsibility to make her partner respond to her character was hers.

She was going to have to make her Giselle felt.

There came a sudden, ominous change of pitch from the plane's engines, as if the exertion of the climb had been too much for them. The sound vibrated all around me, scattering my thoughts temporarily. My hand was pressing down on my husband's wrist, over the armrest. His eyes were closed. He could sleep through anything. Some loose pages slipped from my journal onto my lap. After the knot in my stomach untied itself, I gathered them up and read through my notes—these happened to be some of the images which I had given Trini, to guide her through the mad scene at the end of the first act.

I remembered Trini's earliest attempt at the scene, when she looked like one of the inmates from *Marat-Sade*—like many modern ballerinas who approach the action without asking how the scene links the two acts. Instead of investigating how Giselle's love might bridge the worlds of flesh and spirit, the tendency is to play a kind of loopy hysteria, the Romantic image of a "pretty death" going by the wayside. As an exercise, I had Trini try the initial walk with her eyes closed, and asked her to imagine what Giselle might see in her mind as she tried to hold on to that beautiful dream which Albrecht's betrayal had just shattered.

> You're suddenly lost, in a dark forest . . . everything is quiet and still . . . except for raindrops hitting the leaves around you . . . a gentle breeze. You're trying to find your way with each breath, with each step. You're searching for what you've lost. You can see a shaft of light through the trees now, and you follow it. Follow the light. You see a clearing ahead of you and there's a field of daisies. Pick one out of the air. Isn't it familiar? Can't you remember? This is that place you felt so loved. Pluck one of the petals . . . slowly . . . and now another, faster, and another! They're turning to dust in your hands! You feel yourself being lifted, but you can't see who's lifting you.
>
> You don't recognize Albrecht. You can't even see him when you look in his face!

Later, her body had sung Giselle's tragic melody. While the pianist kept strict time, Trini alternately lingered behind or rushed momentarily ahead of the music, never allowing herself to fall into melodrama. She had needed help, translating imagery and feelings into the muscles. Her hands and forearms were still not strong enough to pluck those daisies with great clarity. Yet she had been convincing. At the end of the scene, when she fell dying into Albrecht's arms, holding him fast in that instant of recognition, she had the love she would need to fight for his life in the second act.

To forgive him.

Trini knew what she had accomplished. I lauded her, and she had been overjoyed in her modest way.

But that was in the studio. Would she remember when she was onstage?

If she were able to give the audience even a glimpse into Giselle's timeless soul . . .

By the time I felt the plane bumping down on the runway in Granada, I had persuaded myself the heart of the story had to be inside her. As we taxied, warned in English and Spanish to stay in our seats, Greg said, "At least you don't have to dance this one yourself."

"Thank God," I whispered.

"Or Allah," said my husband. "This city was once under Islamic rule."

We had flown from spring to summer, and became instantly aware of the scorching sun. I had worn my heaviest sweater, as if expecting an arctic expedition. A bus whisked us through the rather shabby downtown, then climbed up the side of a steep hill and delivered us to our hotel. We soon discovered we were only walking distance from paradise. The centuries-old Moorish ruin of the Alhambra palace and the gardens of the Generalife were for us the dream of dreams.

During the next few days, my husband and I spent most of our free hours wandering this serene labyrinth, where there was no time, only a sense of infinite repose and mystery, everywhere we turned—from the ancient fortress, with its vaulted chambers and vast domes and delicate mosaics, to the royal gardens, with their rose-lined footpaths and endless fountains. It was here in this enchanted landscape we found the open-air theatre where the performances were to take place, a stage framed by a towering stand of cypress. "Can't imagine a more perfect setting," said Greg, on first sight.

"For the audience," I told him. "You can never tell what may happen outdoors for the dancers."

"Still," he said, swinging his arm around me, *"Giselle* under the stars!"

Our daily routine was determined by the weather. In the cool of the morning, we accompanied Trinidad, Peter, and a small group of dancers to a downtown flamenco studio—apparently the only studio in Granada that could be found for ballet class. The place was a dive, located in the basement of a rundown bar. Upon entering, we usually attracted curious glances from the locals, a clutch of old men, and some of the young flamenco dancers wearing their colorful skirts. Hurrying past, we descended a long flight of stairs into a pair of claustrophobic rooms, with low ceilings and a floor which seemed to be made of concrete. Kevin Haigen, always resourceful and spirited, limited his classes to barre exercises and light center work—any jumps would have put heads through the ceiling.

How relieved I was to be an observer!

On our first visit, I was captivated by photographs of flamenco dancers that hung on the walls. These gypsies had such a beautiful sense of proportion.

"Look at those upper bodies!" I enthused to Greg. "Now that port de bras is absolutely stunning—it's so passionate and concentrated. A gesture . . . not a position. Why don't ballet dancers stop in their tracks when they run across something like this? I mean, here . . . in this God-awful, dingy place, there's an amazing tradition!"

With a finger, my husband traced an outline of the figure in one of the photographs and said, "Almost a classical shape, isn't it? So much motion. But none of these pictures even shows their legs."

"They don't need to," I said.

That same day we listened to Trinidad giving an interview in Spanish to a reporter from one of the local newspapers. I stood nearby and watched Trini's eyes lighting up. She talked on and on, not giving the reporter a chance to ask his questions, as the two of them faced each other in a corner of the studio.

"What's she saying?" I asked Greg, in a whisper.

He was turned away, holding back laughter. "She's telling him the story," came the reply.

"What story?"

I noticed the reporter had stopped scribbling in his little notepad. A young fellow in a rumpled suit, he was loosening his tie, while Trinidad, still in her practice clothes, was becoming more and more animated with her gestures. Her voice was musical, but I was unable to understand a single word.

"What story?" I repeated.

My husband leaned close, and said in my ear, "She's telling him the story of *Giselle* . . . and very eloquently, as much as I can follow her Spanish."

I had never heard her speak so long at one time. The pride and intensity in her face was almost like what I had seen in the faces of those dancers pictured on the walls.

Of course, it was one thing to relate the story verbally, and quite another to tell it with the body. I was not about to ease up on her. With that blistering afternoon heat and lack of studio space, our coaching sessions sometimes had to be held in a reception room at the hotel. Occasionally, we were able to steal time onstage, either before or after the company took its regular class. This was in the late afternoon when the whole motley cast of dancers took to the stage to warm up—decked out in bathing suits and all kinds of practice clothes, sunglasses and visors and floppy hats—the sun and temperature beginning to drop, slowly.

Greg and I usually lounged in whatever spot of shade we could find in the bleachers of the arena, and waited until the familiar ritual ran its course. Rehearsals for various ballets began in the evening, and according to some strange local custom, performances were scheduled to start at eleven at night. By that time the temperature had plummeted, and I was glad to have packed my winter clothes. Given the adverse working conditions Trinidad had to endure and the number of ballets in which she was dancing, I was surprised, and even somewhat concerned, at how calm Trini had remained. She never showed the slightest sign of anxiety, until the day before her first and only stage rehearsal for *Giselle.*

That afternoon we worked in the hotel's reception room, where the floor was so slippery that she could do nothing more than mark through the ballet. We had still not even touched one of the second-act solos, and had only pieced together a tentative ending back in London. With a tape of the score, we started from the beginning, as if cramming for a test. But Trini lost her way in the sequence of action. She was unable to follow through with each thought and movement while at the same time anticipating the next. This was especially difficult for Trini without Peter and the rest of the cast being present. She had to visualize each of the scenes, continually staying ahead as the storyteller, with only the music to guide her.

After an hour, she was on the brink of tears and about to come apart.

I stopped her, and asked, "What's wrong, Trini?"

"Is just the more you tell me now, Gelsey, the less I think I remember."

She was overwhelmed by the details. What was disturbing was seeing how much of the ballet had escaped her, even since leaving London less than a week before.

I gave her a hug, and told her, "But that shows how much you know! Now you can see all of those places you still have to work on. I want you to go and have a good rest. Don't worry. Try to get some sleep. We still have time."

We went at it again later that afternoon onstage.

I asked her to try her first solo in the second act, when the spirit of Giselle first confronts the Queen of the Wilis and feels her evil power. This sequence starts with a series of hops in arabesque, essentially turning backward around yourself. The steps are murder. One false start and you find yourself spinning out of control—which was exactly what happened to Trini. She looked like she had fallen off the planet, and I knew just how she felt.

She cried, "Oh, my God! Gelsey, what happened?"

Moving toward her, I said, "It'll be all right, Trini. I've done that too."

"What I do wrong?"

"You forgot to keep your upper body turning out while you went around. Remember? As you turn right, you're resisting to the left. Don't let your right side drop into your right leg."

The sun was still high enough in the sky to be a torment. After mastering these "horror hops," she moved on to a series of jumps covering the stage, first across the front, then diagonally upstage. The challenge for Trini here was to create the illusion of being under the power of Myrtha, the Wili Queen; Giselle must look as if she is being moved by unseen forces, at the same time resisting the evil spell. After seeing Trini's first attempt, I felt like both of us had failed.

"Trinidad, you're flapping around again! And you're going to crash into those Wilis over there."

"But I have no room," she pleaded.

"You do have room! You have to control the step."

We went back to basics, with her pushing against my chest to feel the resistance she needed; then I pushed her across the stage, telling her, "If you don't fight becoming a Wili, nothing happens in this ballet. Albrecht won't get to visit and there won't even be a second act!"

After demonstrating again, I said, "Now you do it your way and make up your mind which foot to start on and which wing you want to exit through at the end."

As she started off, I prodded, "Trini, faster on that run! Otherwise, you look like you're having a jolly old skip over to see jolly old Myrtha. . . ."

"Let me try again!" she insisted.

And so she did, fiercely determined, her pride on the line. The sudden improvement was remarkable.

"Good! That was really beautiful! Could you feel that?"

"Oh yes! My heart . . ."

"It has to be there every time, Trini."

The night of the dress rehearsal was one calamity after another, starting with a run-through early in the evening. The ballet master, placing the corps of Wilis in the second act, used up most of our precious time. All I could do was sit and wait at the front of the stage, fuming. "Can't have those Wilis knocking into each other," said my husband. Injuries had actually reduced their number along the way. With only minutes remaining, I found Peter at the back of the stage, and asked if he would mind going over the end with Trini. He was more than happy to rehearse, but she was nowhere to be seen.

"Peter, will you wait while I go find her?"

"Yes, I'll be right here," he promised. He was bundled in a bright red sweat shirt, trying to stay warm.

I found Trini in the tentlike dressing rooms that were hidden behind the stage. She was half dressed, and still busy sewing her toe shoes—a task which should have been completed long before. I rushed back out to Peter and worked on some steps with him, adding a few refinements with which he might help Trini in the last act. After running back and forth between them again, I finally managed to pull them together and rehearse the ending, which we had simplified so hope and love would be as clear as those bells that chimed with the arrival of dawn, breaking the Wilis' vengeful spell.

Giselle was to move slowly upstage to the cross, turning back to Albrecht, touching his upturned palms with her own, and leaving something with him in that moment of stillness, creating an illusion of eternity. But Trinidad seemed to have forgotten everything. The final dress rehearsal promised to be nothing less than a disaster.

Which it was, in a sense.

Trini was uncertain and hesitant, groping to find her way while the ballet passed her by. She had not had enough stage time, and suddenly found herself disoriented by props, lights, bodies, and costumes. Often falling behind the music, she appeared lethargic. Yet many of her mistakes were the kind she would not likely repeat—the kind that make a lasting impression. I could see her being jolted by so many tiny lapses, split seconds too late.

This was what she needed to experience, difficult as it may have been for her. Such is the purpose of stage rehearsals. She knew as well as anyone where she fell short; the holes were apparent enough. One ballet mistress, not long on sensitivity or insight, yelled out early in the first act, "Too shy! She's much too shy!" Fortunately, Trinidad didn't hear her. That sort of offhand comment would have been anything but helpful for a seventeen-year-old trying to get her bearings. The deeper problem was that neither Trini nor Peter convinced anyone their characters were in love. He might have been able to get by, dancing the role of the deceitful nobleman, but her feelings toward him had to be clarified—and we were running out of time.

The catastrophe was not without comic relief—a frog or toad found its way to center stage and delayed Myrtha, danced by a usually confident Janette Mulligan, on her first entrance. The creature might have been a subtle omen. The rehearsal dragged on until the wee hours of the morning—when a shouting match broke out between Peter and the conductor, Andrew Mogrelia. The latter worked wonders with a Czech orchestra, which had been flown in from Karlovy Vary; apparently, none of these musicians had ever played the Adam score.

But neither their accompaniment nor patience could be faulted. We had simply reached the hour when tempers were bound to flare.

Afterward, I met Trini at the front of the stage. The lights were going out around us. She was obviously distraught, and looked as if she were about to apologize to me. But I gave her no chance. "Trinidad, you did exactly what you had to do out there. Don't worry about the mistakes. The only thing you have to do now is tell us the story. We have to believe in your love for Albrecht no matter what! Even if you don't feel him loving you back, you just keep on giving him your heart. It doesn't matter if you forget this or that."

"Really?" She looked as if she were in shock.

"Trini, don't do this performance to please me. I know you love this story. Do it because of that! Nothing else matters. You can forget everything else I taught you. The steps will be there for you when you need them, and so will Giselle."

She flung her arms around my neck, and said, "I love you, Gelsey."

"And I love you. Now get some rest." She started across the stage, and I called after, "Oh, Trini. Try to remember to make those second-act exits faster . . . okay?"

She just laughed.

On the evening of her first performance, a gigantic full moon appeared above the trees, as if on divine cue. My husband and I visited the dressing room, not long before she was to make her entrance, and gave her a *merde,* a tiny gold heart. Trini was a quiet bundle of nerves—surrounded by open gifts and wrapping paper, cards and flowers from various well-wishers; everyone in the company seemed to be rooting for her. I looked down at her toe shoes, and asked, "Those aren't going to clunk out there?"

"No, they're pretty good . . . soft . . . I think."

A quick check told me they were still too hard. While she finished touching up her makeup, I knelt on the floor and spent five minutes whacking away with my hammer.

"Just for luck," I told her.

But she needed no luck, or perhaps made her own.

She was often radiant, at times even magical. I sat in the audience, cutting off the circulation in my husband's hand, becoming teary by the end of the mad scene. No doubt I was her harshest critic; and there were moments she missed; but I knew I was not watching the same little girl I had first seen back in London. When I saw her whip off that first fiendish solo in Act Two—at the speed of light and with total control—I thought if that were all she did all night, it would be enough. Moments later, she made one of her entrances from the wrong side of the stage, and yet managed to get away with it. She had drawn us into Giselle's inner world.

She drew in the rest of the cast as well; they seemed unusually spirited and locked into the action. Trini got the support she needed from Peter, whose passion appeared to become more and more tender. The central adagio in the second act had moments of such grace and beauty I could almost hear the audience gasp. She was one of their own, and at the end, she received the praise she deserved, from spectators whose hands, like mine, had to be suffering from frostbite.

Backstage, Trini seemed unsure whether she had been really good, or only fair. I offered as much assurance as I could with my embrace. Then we laughed about the silly mistakes.

I was especially pleased because she was becoming aware not only of what she had accomplished, but of what she had yet to fulfill. Her second performance was uneven, although there were a few improvements here and there. Yet nothing marred her joy, and I felt such immense happiness sharing it with her. As the company dined and celebrated in the hotel late on our last night, I told Greg, "The only question is whether or not she can bring what she's learned into other ballets."

"I imagine that once you start thinking as an actress, it must be pretty difficult to accept working any other way."

"It's not that simple," I said. "You have to be constantly encouraged to work like this. It's not something you learn in a month, or even a year."

Shortly after the company returned to London, critic Judith Cruickshank wrote in the *Times:*

> . . . to Sevillano's natural gifts has been added a comprehensive understanding of the role which is evident in every step and gesture.

Critic Jann Parry concurred, writing in the *Observer:*

> This was a Giselle refined to the essence, with none of
> the extravagance of a young dancer's portrayal.
> Schaufuss' faith that Trinidad would in the end benefit
> from Kirkland's rigorous and passionate analysis has
> paid off. What Gelsey has given her is a foundation on
> which she can build, an interpretation instead of an
> instinctive reaction. . . . there was nothing obvious to
> applaud and no histrionics in the mad scene; but many
> of us were in tears. . . .

My work was done. Giselle is a lifelong role—one of the few—
and Trini would either continue to grow with it, or not, depending on her own inner drive and the sort of direction she received. After dancing the role in London that July, with Matz
Skoog as her partner, Trinidad won another accolade in the
Times, with John Percival calling her performance "as true and
touching an interpretation of the role as I have seen from a
young newcomer in almost twenty years."

Peter was pleased with Trini's progress and with the kind of
experiences we had been through together—pleased enough to
invite me to return the following year to stage and dance
Tudor's *Leaves Are Fading.* I appreciated Peter's offer; but the
project came down to my commitment to performing, and I was
ready to seek a more ambitious alternative. My husband and I
traveled to Cork, Ireland, where I applied for the position of
Artistic Director of the Irish National Ballet.

With the visual delights of Granada still fresh in mind, I found
the city of Cork something of a letdown, with its grim commer-
cial buildings and dilapidated warehouses. Nothing seemed to
correspond to my romantic preconceptions of this country. As
Greg and I stood on a bridge that ran across the murky waters of
the river Lee, I asked myself if this were the same Ireland Dame
Ninette had known as a child. In spite of the drabness and my
misgivings, I went ahead with an interview arranged with the
company's board in a downtown hotel.

The selection committee was comprised of about a dozen
local businesspeople and prominent members of the commu-

nity. Accompanied by my husband, I faced them in a conference room and did my best to answer their questions and concerns. They seemed a bit surprised by the rather conservative
and traditional sort of direction that I had in mind. I told them,
among other things, that any company I directed would have to
be heavily weighted toward the classical repertoire, and that it
seemed to me, many of the large theatres were wasting enormous amounts of money on extravagant sets and costumes and
every sort of gimmick, rather than investing in the dancers.

"The appeal nowadays," I said, "is more and more to the eye,
less and less to the heart. In New York, glitz and slick marketing
have almost done away with quality on the stage . . . and
London's not far behind. But it's laughter and tears that move
audiences. All I can say is, put dancers onstage who know how to
dance. That's the one thing that I've learned to do, and the one
thing I have to teach."

A young businessman voiced the board's primary interest,
asking me, "But how can we expand our audience?"

I replied, "You might try giving the audience ballets that are
more than glorified aerobics classes. The theatre can still be a
place where great stories are told—and people walk out so
caught up, or so uplifted they tell their friends, 'You must see
that ballet . . . and those dancers!' It's that kind of excitement
that builds an audience."

With a flash of Irish wit, the same young man said, "So, you'd
be ask'n us to swim against the tide then?"

This inquisition seemed to go on forever, perhaps only an
hour in real time. When it was over, I watched a company class,
then toured more of Cork. The company was actually a tiny
troupe of dancers with extremely limited resources, though a
new theatre and ballet studios were being constructed in a
building that was under renovation. The overall situation appealed to me. I liked the idea of working in a completely out-of-
the-way sort of place, out of the limelight. Yet when I was subse-
quently offered the position, I decided to turn it down.

My husband challenged me. "They have a very capable administrator, and you wouldn't have the media looking over your
shoulder. You could try your hand. . . ."

"No," I told him. "I don't know why, but I have to finish this year on the stage. Maybe you're right. Maybe I secretly want to dance forever."

"Tell me another one."

"I have to finish what I set out to do. Then I want time to think. Is that asking so much?"

By the end of August, I was back in the studio, preparing to dance *The Sleeping Beauty* with the Royal Ballet.

I had about two months to pull myself together for two performances, November 13 and 19—once again, I would be working myself into condition at the same time I was rehearsing the ballet. Before getting underway, I spent one afternoon in a London hospital—where I was put to sleep for a few hours, and the company's surgeon injected a potent combination of cortisone and Xylocaine into my troublesome hip. The idea was to relieve that one source of chronic pain long enough for me to hold the endless balances in the famous Rose Adagio of the first act.

The medical procedure was at least an initial success. My right hip was numb enough for me to lift my right leg high into the air for the particular developpé step that I was going to need as Princess Aurora greeting each of four princely suitors on the fateful occasion of her sixteenth birthday. But I still lacked both the stamina and muscular control to sustain the shape of the character; and I was yet a long way from even discovering those qualities of movement I was going to need to embody that shape. How was this fairy-tale princess to take on flesh and blood?

That was both the terror and the lure.

One evening, after listening to me air some of my fears, Greg said, "I don't see why this role should be that much more difficult than Juliet. You're still building character through movement."

"But what actions are there to play? She pricks her finger, and sleeps for a hundred years. Then she wakes up . . . just in time to marry her prince. She seems so passive. We only see her when she dances. Who the hell is she?"

"You've had your own hundred-year sleep, and you're anything but passive. You have a story to tell. It might not be as rich as a Shakespeare play, but—"

"But you haven't even seen the steps," I said, cutting him off.

"Doesn't matter." He was scrambling toward the stacks of books we had accumulated during the past months and piled in a corner of the living room.

Ignoring me, he said, "There's a line from a Schiller play. It goes something like, 'There was more truth in the fairy tales of my childhood than in all that life has taught me. . . .' "

I was curled in an arm chair, watching him and wondering if he had taken leave of his senses. He was digging through books, turning the neat stacks into chaos. His frantic activity seemed absurd—as if he were becoming even more desperate than I was! He spluttered at me, "You chose this ballet, right? So you might as well start thinking about where it came from and what it means!"

And so we did, going through various librettos and early versions of the tale, including the Charles Perrault story upon which Marius Petipa and Ivan Vsevolozhsky based the libretto for the original production, first presented at the Maryinsky Theatre in St. Petersburg in 1890. Undoubtedly, the allegorical elements in the ballet, as tightly spun and intricately woven as in any of the published tales, owe much to the famous collaboration between Petipa and the composer, Tchaikovsky. However many actual Petipa steps survive, the action is wondrously evoked by the music. The struggle between good and evil—introduced in the Prologue and portrayed through the figures of the benign Lilac Fairy and the wicked, hunchbacked fairy, Carabosse—plays itself out only to set up the ultimate fate of Princess Aurora.

It was her christening, and the gifts and blessings she received from the good fairies, that provided me with the first clues to her character. I entered in my journal a few days later:

> Aurora becomes the leading voice for the next three acts. My characterization has to start in her infancy, in her crib, before I even make my first entrance! During the Prologue, she is blessed with every sort of natural gift: beauty and eloquence, grace and musicality, spirit

and poise. She will learn to dance and sing and play instruments. But the most precious gift is that symbolized by the lilac, the flower of wisdom, which can only be attained with self-knowledge. . . .

In Act One, on her sixteenth birthday, just when the Princess is blossoming and ready to have her first experience with love, Carabosse sneaks in with the dread spindle, as if to say, "Aurora will never know love! She's going to be trapped in adolescence forever. She's going to die . . . on the spot . . . and all of those lovely gifts she received are going to be useless!"

Aurora pricks her finger on the spindle, but the Lilac Fairy appears, and says, "I'm going to turn that evil wish into something good! The Princess will not die, but sleep . . . with the whole kingdom . . . and one day she will know true love."

The events are magical, but what is real in this story? What is human about her character? What is the beauty that sleeps within her? The spell is cast at the end of Act One—for a hundred years Aurora sleeps and dreams, and finally comes to understand everything that has happened to her. The Lilac Fairy conjures up a vision of sublime flirtation in Act Two. The spell is lifted by the kiss of Prince Florimund—the awakening brings about the wedding festivities for the court in Act Three.

With the hundred-year sleep, the period changes from the 17th to 18th century. Aurora is the dawn, symbol of birth, renewal, a new age. She has to master her own inner world before she can act in that outer world to fulfill her destiny. Her dancing must reveal each phase of maturity, from naive innocence to radiant womanhood and the most profound love. Her every step, gesture and movement has to flow from inner necessity.

Over the coming weeks, I would tell and retell the story, trying to find her inner voice, while asking myself how I was to dance this character so the allegory would come across for my modern audience. Aurora's gifts were those of the artist. Wasn't her coming of age more than a diverting spectacle and escapist fantasy for the court?

The ballet became for me a kind of window opening into previous centuries, during which the form of classical ballet had evolved—along with the rigid set of rules governing the positions and steps, and the precise way they were to be taught and executed. I went back to Petipa's more ancient predecessor, Jean Georges Noverre, the French choreographer once called "the Shakespeare of the Dance." Noverre was already arguing against the stultifying academic rules and the lack of content in ballet as early as 1760, when he published his *Letters on Dancing and Ballets*. His book set forth the dramatic ideals and principles of classical dance as I had come to know them. But could they be brought to bear on the unrelenting stylistic demands I was to confront in *The Sleeping Beauty?*

One afternoon Greg and I sat in a tiny room at the opera house and watched a video of Margot performing the role. When her image appeared on the screen, dancing the Grand Pas de Deux in the third act, Greg swiveled his chair around toward me and said, "What monarch, living or dead, could ever hold a candle to that kind of nobility?"

"Or what ballerina . . . ?" was all I could say.

For the better part of three decades—after opening the 1939 production in London, then vaulting with the company to a status of international renown a decade later on its first New York visit—Margot Fonteyn was identified with the role of Princess Aurora. *The Sleeping Beauty* set the classical standard for the Royal Ballet, even became its Bible. But I soon discovered something essential had been lost, or forgotten: the glorious lyricism which Margot and a few of her contemporaries brought to the role seemed to have become stilted, while the other characters had turned to wax.

It was as if only the steps remained—and a faith that they held the secret to style. Supposedly, if you danced them correctly, the story would tell itself, and your character would come to life. I had never worked this way and was in no position to start now —I had only two performances, and would be matched with a new partner, as Florimund was a role Anthony was no longer performing. He gave me a choice of men in the company, and I had decided on Stephen Jefferies, an experienced principal about my age. Stephen did not have the natural line or proportions of a classic prince, but I knew such limitations could be overcome if he were clever, and his spirit willing.

"What good theories do you have for us today?" Stephen asked before one of our rehearsals. For a second I thought he said "good fairies"—and told him so. I knew him well enough to be able to count on his jovial laughter as well as his effort in the partnering. A rapport was established quickly between us during the early going. Stephen often came to rehearsal after he had been working on another ballet, a retelling of Mary Shelley's Frankenstein tale. The modern choreography was taking a toll on his body—the lifts were causing the muscles in his shoulders and neck to tighten—so at times he appeared to be hunching in the most awkward fashion. I couldn't resist teasing him about it.

"Some prince you are! You look more like Frankenstein every day!"

Good-natured he was, as well as talented.

If Stephen started out as Frankenstein, I was surely his Bride. The two of us benefited a great deal from our work with Donald MacLeary, the repetiteur who kept us going through more than one crisis. Donald had been one of the greatest partners at the Royal Ballet, and he always gave us a stellar example in the studio, enabling me to help Stephen understand what I was going to need in the most troublesome passages.

I was less worried about us being mismatched than I was about me being unprepared. The physical routine was not ideal. I had to build strength as quickly as possible, and went back to company classes, except when the schedule allowed me to work with Oliver Symons. David Howard would not arrive from New York until the last couple of weeks in my rehearsal period; so there was no continuity to my conditioning regime. Rather than a rotation of teachers, what I really needed was consistent therapeutic work. Even had I been in top form, company classes left much to be desired as far as my body was concerned.

I often felt rushed and disjointed. The rapid pace and structure of exercises kept me from following through with the whole body; so my breath tended to be unrelated to the patterns of movement. My unusually long legs and short torso made matters more difficult for the simple reason that I had to travel further whenever bending through the knees—without enough time between pliés, for example, I would find myself straining just to hold on to arm positions and keep up with the tempo. Instead of feeling my muscles lengthen, and becoming energized, I was knotting up and growing fatigued. By the end of class, I was frequently ready for the morgue.

I went from the masseur, a former dancer in the company named Paul Benson . . . to the osteopath, Demetri Papoutsis . . . to a body-conditioning specialist, Dreas Reyneke, a former member of the Ballet Rambert. Each of the three men, in his own specialized way, kept my body from falling apart. Paul worked on my snarled muscles; Demetri aligned the skeleton; and Dreas devised a personalized training program to increase stamina and flexibility in the areas of the body that were most lacking. Only through these combined efforts was I able to survive from day to day.

I should have been in excellent classroom shape, even to attempt this ballet. But that was my folly—my choice, as my husband occasionally reminded me. I also should have had decent toe shoes for the pointe work in the ballet. Yet I had only nine pairs of shoes that actually fit, which I put aside, saving three pairs for dress rehearsal and three for each performance. In the meantime, I took class and rehearsed in toe shoes that belonged to other ballerinas. I had the feeling when I wore these shoes that the steps looked as if they were being danced by someone else. But that was merely a fantasy.

Only the frustration was real.

The ongoing irony was that I appeared to be fine on the outside, or so I was told, even when I felt a total disharmony on the inside. I expected one of those muscles somewhere in the body was going to snap, sooner or later, like a string tuned too high. I humored myself with the idea of retiring, and gradually came to believe it. But if this ballet were my last, I had to find a level of meaning in the story that would enable me to rise to an occasion like no other.

Petipa's steps are the simplest in the world—basic classroom steps, often repeated four times in the ballet, as when Aurora receives her four suitors. In class, you might be able to make four attempts to perfect each step, whereas onstage each rendering must be flawless and bound to the one preceding it in order to complete both the thought and the feeling that has to be conveyed. If you smudge even one of the steps, the meaning of the phrase blurs, like a garbled sentence. If you are uncertain about timing or accents in the phrase, the steps come off like words recited by rote, without conviction. How many dancers speak this language without having the slightest idea what they are saying?

One day I hobbled into the dressing room, carrying my bag of shoes and complaints, muttering, sounding perhaps like one of those strange street characters who issue dire warnings about the end of the world. I plopped down on a bench, acknowledging Monica as I started pulling off my leg warmers and shoes. She would play the role of Carabosse in the first of my performances.

"Hello, Gelsey," she said cheerfully. She was in a practice outfit, finishing up a snack. Monica must have had some time to kill between rehearsals. Seeing my swollen feet, she asked me, "Are your metatarsals up?"

"Up? I suppose so. What do you mean?"

"Can you do this?" Monica placed her bare foot in front of me, pressing on the floor so each of her metatarsal bones lifted conspicuously, running back from the toes, all the way along the top of her foot.

"Don't curl your toes under," she instructed me.

I tried. My right foot passed the test. But my left foot, the one I had fractured, was completely debilitated. The little toes felt like they were brain dead.

"No," said Monica, flexing her foot, "those metatarsals should be raised. They're not up . . . you see?"

I saw. The more I looked down at my naked foot, the more disheartened I became.

Monica was silent, as if concealing her surprise that I was so weak in such a crucial area. Those little muscles around the metatarsals in my left foot were going to have to absorb tremendous shock.

She demonstrated the exercise again and advised me how

many repetitions to do each morning. I confessed to her, "I'm not so sure I can get through this ballet . . . and make the steps tell the story . . . and it's such a beautiful story."

"It is beautiful. But, Gelsey, you really must concentrate on the steps. Think about doing them correctly, and worry about the story later."

"Right," I said, almost without thinking.

As I never made any separation between steps and story, I was amazed by those who were able to put them into different compartments, as if mind and body could somehow work apart from each other. Unless I had a reason to move, I would be totally paralyzed; Princess Aurora might never take her first step, and neither of us might ever make it onto the stage.

Yet the steps did offer certain valuable clues.

While still in the dressing room, I went over some of my notes and questions on Aurora's first-act entrance and the Rose Adagio.

> Aurora enters like a gentle stream of light. Is she skittish? Nervous? Why is she late? Where is she coming from? Does she know what to expect? Does she bewitch us with her outer beauty . . . or do we see something of her inner spirit? Is she conscious of her beauty? Is she an overly protected child due to fearful parents? Pampered? Spoiled? Should she try to assert herself in any way? Is she timid or shy with the suitors? Does she blush with all of the attention she receives? Does she attempt to surprise everyone, including herself?
>
> Is she self-centered? Is she amused by the suitors as they compete in paying compliments to her beauty? Must she marry one of them? When does she know none is for her? When does the emphasis change from them affecting her . . . to her affecting them? Is she polite on the first balances, just trying to please the suitors? Does she become more secure on the second round of balances, perhaps even demanding that they please her?
>
> This will be her first experience outside the protective sphere of her parents. Is she at all hesitant as her

father leads her to the suitors? Does she look to him for encouragement? Does he give it? When she gives the roses to her mother, what does she say? Are they a gift for Mother . . . or is she asking Mother to hold them for her while she continues to dance? Has she prepared this dance for the occasion?

In her solo, should the formal arms framing her face be an expression of joy as well as a gesture that she knows is beautiful to look at? What mimetic qualities are needed to clarify her age and innocence? Does she try to hold on to each moment, or should she be on her way to the next shimmering step? Have the good fairies been teaching her to dance?

Her confidence and joy must build throughout the act until she encounters Carabosse in disguise and takes the spindle. She's not yet able to distinguish good and evil. . . .

Realizing I was late for rehearsal, I hurried out of the dressing room, making a brief stop in the basement cafeteria to grab a cup of coffee. I found myself thrown back in time for an instant, passing Kenneth MacMillan and Mikhail Baryshnikov on the stairs. It was my first encounter with Misha since an ungraceful parting of ways almost three years before. Traveling in opposite directions, we exchanged faint smiles and hellos, all very civil and distant. I knew that Misha had somehow obtained an advance copy of my autobiography, and that he had already declined to be interviewed by "60 Minutes."

There was no reason for either of us to stop.

I didn't even ask myself at the time what he might be doing in London. The following year, under Misha's direction, Kenneth would mount a new production of *The Sleeping Beauty* for American Ballet Theatre.

Were they too thinking about this fairy tale?

Once inside the studio, I went to work straightaway with Gerd, who, in her capacity as the senior repetiteur, introduced me to the Royal Ballet's current staging, which was similar to the company's initial production. The version of the ballet that I danced at ABT had been staged by Mary Skeaping in 1976, and it too traced back to the Maryinsky Theatre's former ballet master and notator, Nicholas Sergeyev, who first introduced the ballet to the West.

It was strange to realize, as Gerd demonstrated Aurora's entrance, that I carried so much of the past in my muscles and reflexes. As that initial ABT staging had been done for Natasha and Misha, the steps, as I recalled them, reflected still another phase of Russian influence; naturally, the two of them had drawn on their own recollections of the ballet. They had learned it at the Kirov, where the choreography had certainly been revised over the years since the time that theatre was known as the Maryinsky. The burden now fell upon me to sift through all of the options for each particular step, with an eye to shaping each phrase, each moment.

What was the first step? In the modern Kirov production, Aurora entered with repeated grands jetés. This rather stunning leap derived from technical refinements in the classroom, attributed to Vaganova. The Royal Ballet entrance, possibly closer to Petipa's, called for a pas de chat—a smaller kind of jump, which seemed to make for a slightly different quality. But the ballerinas of Margot's generation had preceded that step with a more telling arabesque—as if to establish the character when Aurora first appeared, between a pair of upstage columns, behind which she was to enter. She simply paused there, surprised and delighted, and then proceeded into the first solo variation.

There were countless possibilities; however, that initial arabesque, framed by the colonnade, was no longer done. The set had changed; there was no room for such a movement. According to my friend, critic Judith Cruickshank, the same arabesque might have had a different purpose in Petipa's day—he was a very practical man, who knew well enough that he had to show off his ballerinas if they were ever to marry nobility or enter into some equally advantageous arrangement. Was he giving them the opportunity to be seen in an alluring pose, to appear ravishing for the imperial court?

Was Petipa matchmaking for his dancers, and at the same time, making a cunning statement about dynastic succession in his choreography? Historical speculations aside, I had a more practical problem to solve. These steps were going to have to fit me like my own skin. I would eventually make up a kind of mini-jeté, on the scale of the pas de chat, working with David Howard to achieve the buoyancy and sharpness I needed to bring it off. But the idea behind this opening passage had actually come from Gerd. She was the one who made me realize Princess Aurora was greeting those who had gathered for her birthday party. That got my wheels spinning.

Gerd told me that the style must change from act to act. But how and why? I must have driven her slightly mad, with the constant stream of questions and requests for her to demonstrate for me. Yet she did seem to enjoy the challenge. While she may have been reluctant to articulate her thoughts, Gerd possessed a wealth of knowledge, stored in her body. I asked her to repeat the entrance mime, and her voice trilled with exasperation. "Oh, look," she said, "it's very simple!"

Then she showed me.

When she stopped and I saw the color invading her cheeks, I tried to explain, "Now listen, Gerd. I'm very serious. I ask you to do the scenes over and over because they come so naturally to you and so unnaturally to me. I didn't grow up on mime or the classical repertory. Each time you move, you become a young girl. You make a lovely Aurora. But I'll never get that far unless I can figure out what you're doing."

A look of embarrassment and pride flashed into her face. "Watcha want me to do then?"

"Gerd, at the end of the solo, Aurora's arms are up and her eyes are gazing out . . . like she's taking in the beautiful light of this day. She must see something out there. But, then she turns and rushes back upstage to greet her parents. What makes her do that? How does she know . . ."

"You just turn 'round and run to them. You have very little time, Gelsey!"

"But if I'm facing out, wouldn't I have to hear them before I turn?"

"Well, yes, but you just . . . go!"

She showed me again, and I slowed her down until I was able to steal her "secret." What made the transition appear so fluid and spontaneous was visible only for a split second.

"There! You see! That lift in your upper body says you've

heard them, and you're so happy they're here! It's those little things no one remembers, Gerd, and they make all the difference. Now, let me try with the music. One more time. . . ."

I was sleeping less than before, getting up early simply to keep my journal going. In the quiet moments between opening my eyes and crawling out from under the covers, my thoughts were already speeding into the studio ahead of me. I had now and then indulged myself in imagining the performances were over, but that mental game was no longer possible. We were well into September, and time was passing much too swiftly, even as my past suddenly caught up with me, like an uninvited guest intruding into the present.

One morning just after class I was called to the phone in Iris Law's office and told that Patrick Bissell was on the line. At first I refused to accept the call; but he would not take no for an answer. Patrick was one of my former partners at ABT—the one who first introduced me to cocaine. The shock of hearing his voice almost made me drop the phone. He said he was in Washington, and that he had been up all night reading a copy of *Dancing on My Grave.* His voice sounded suspiciously nasal. He was obviously in a bad way, rambling, hardly giving me a chance to say anything.

"It was so much worse than you told it, Gelsey. I mean, I haven't even read a book since *Helter Skelter.* I'm no reader. All I know is that somehow you got the truth down, and . . . I love you, Gelsey. I just want you to know that. I'll always love you. . . ."

There were no romantic undertones in his words. Patrick was in his way making a desperate plea. He seemed like a child tugging at my sleeve, and saying, "Can't I come with you? Can't I come too?" He didn't want to be left behind, and yet he wasn't able to leave the dance world, or the drug world. I had tried to tell him there were no quick cures for addiction—it had taken me more than two years to reorganize my life and my art, to put the poison behind me and return to the stage. I had no doubt he was still in deep trouble.

The phone call was an extraordinary disruption. Patrick had

apparently agreed to be interviewed on "60 Minutes," and that was how he had come to have the copy of my book. Had he decided to clean up his act? Or was he maneuvering to turn the situation to some perverse advantage? The need for the drug could make him say or do anything, whether it was in his system at the moment or not. And yet, there was a person in agony behind the voice. Perhaps the threat of public exposure was somehow getting to him.

There was no way to know. I had seen his futile efforts to straighten himself out in the past, and remembered the awful time I had finding enlightened support for my own struggle. The best intentions of friends and professionals had not been enough. During the period of time I was under the influence, I was unable to distinguish manipulative agents and the like from those in the dance world who sincerely wanted, and even tried, to help me. Miraculously, I had fallen in love, and I had become outraged at the drug and its culture. And even so, I had to be carried off to safety, almost against my will. But who would do that for Patrick?

Several days later, Diane Sawyer arrived in London, along with her producer, Jan Legnitto. Greg and I met them for dinner at an Italian restaurant not far from our flat. I had hoped that by talking with Diane before doing the interview I might get over my case of nerves. The first thing she said after joining us was, "Your book pulverized me, Gelsey!" That threw me. I figured she might simply be trying to put me at ease in order to pulverize me with her questions in the interview—which was, after all, her job. She did seem quite earnest, as if she empathized with me in some mysterious way, as if she already knew me.

Slowly, over the course of our conversation—and much to my surprise—I found myself trusting her, or at least the sincerity of her interest. Not that I wasn't still intimidated and wary. Diane was gorgeous and intelligent, and she possessed that sort of glamorous image television seems to encourage us to believe in. I usually expect to be put off by such people, by the airs they are apt to put on, or the practiced congeniality they so often exhibit. But Diane turned out to be different.

We avoided the subject of ballet until she told me about her own childhood experiences with a dance class, and the minor trauma she recalled when, years ago, she and her sister had been asked to imitate an icicle and a snowflake. I got the impression Diane hadn't liked the casting. Her easy laughter almost allowed me to forget why she was here. I suggested we go into the studio so she might have another try at that exercise. She seemed to be game for anything. So was Jan, who had done some research; she later gave me a copy of an article from the *New England Medical Journal* that linked scoliosis and stress fractures in dancers to early dieting and delayed onset of menstruation.

It was only common sense. You starve yourself, and your bones warp and disintegrate. But if the modern aesthetic could have such an effect on the body, what was the impact on mind and spirit? Was there not some deeper reckoning to this curse? Such was the heart of the controversy as I came to see it, stripped of the drugs and scandal and personalities. Was I an exception who happened to go to unhealthy extremes? I was becoming a kind of case study because of the fame that had attached itself to me over the years.

The interview took place on a Sunday, in the crush bar at the Royal Opera House, under a steady glare of lights. The most trying moment came when Diane asked me to watch myself on a video monitor, interviewed by Merv Griffin in 1981. I suddenly had the feeling we were in a courtroom, and Diane was pointing to exhibit A, asking me if I recognized this person. What a horror! To see how wretched and stoned I had been back then; and to think that soon, another audience of millions would identify me with that unbearable image.

It was my own eyes that devastated me. I remembered how they had looked in 1977, when I was Clara, gazing out through a snow-streaked window at the end of *The Nutcracker*. A generation had seen the film, which seemed to me like the starting point in a tragic series of before-and-after shots, arranging themselves in my mind. How could those eyes, so full of light and hope, have lost their way in this world?

My words kept getting stuck between my tongue and brain.

We took a short break for lunch, but otherwise stopped only for the camera man to change his film. I no longer even knew my name when the cross-examination was over. Jan and Diane were somehow going to have to turn the six-hour interview and three decades of my life into fifteen minutes of air time. I couldn't imagine how they would make sense of the story. After shooting one of my rehearsals, they told me they had the footage they needed.

We said our good-byes, and they wished me well, with much warmth. I was relieved to be freed from distraction, yet sorry they had to go without seeing my performances. They were taking those bits and pieces of me with them to be edited into a graphic profile. What was done was done, I told myself, never to be done again. I had assumed that others from the ballet world would be interviewed as well. But nobody else would agree to talk with Diane. At the last minute, even Patrick backed out.

Another event was soon threatening to divert me from the ballet. My book was to be published in America during October. My husband and I received almost daily batches of reviews in the mail, and read them with immense curiosity. What an astonishing chorus of voices! They ran the gamut of opinion. We saved all of them, even those that sounded like obituaries. I had touched a nerve; but that was, at least in part, what I set out to do. The personal and artistic issues I raised were apparently too sensitive for a few critics to bear.

Yet I was delighted most of them were at least willing to acknowledge that some redemptive force must have come into my life. Was it really so mysterious that I should come to see my need to love as the one part of me that was worth protecting? Surely there was a selfish aspect to it, that I should need to be loved in return. Those needs had welled up inside until I had no choice but to find some way to disentangle myself from the drugs. What sort of courage did it take for me not to die? What sort of will did I possess that Patrick was unable to summon for himself?

Those questions would come back to haunt me, along with a card I received from Patrick's mother. I was still in the middle of rehearsals when it arrived.

Dear Gelsey,

    This is a note filled with gratitude and good wishes. I don't know how the book will be received. Whatever is said, I will not ever speak ill of you.
    You and my Patrick descended into Hell together. The book opened wounds for me that have never healed anyway. Your book freed me of any need for silence, and Patrick must now admit to his devils. Perhaps you have helped to save his life.
    I know now that you were probably high, but one night in New York you went out to find Patrick for me. I am still ashamed that I let such a little slip of a young woman go alone. There was good inside of you, Gelsey, that the drugs could not obliterate.

Patricia Bissell

Just over a year later, after spending five weeks at the Betty Ford Clinic, Patrick would overdose at his apartment in New Jersey. Perhaps he had gone straight during those weeks while still secretly looking forward to getting high again, or maybe he was finally making the effort to change his life—no one will ever really know. His body happened to be found December 29, 1987. My husband and I were dining with friends in New York.
    It was my birthday.

At the time I was rehearsing *The Sleeping Beauty*, of course, that excruciating tragedy was unforeseeable, although an ominous shadow had hung over Patrick for years. The furor touched off by my book took place at a distance, so my concentration and passion remained fixed on the ballet. While the "60 Minutes" broadcast and my memoirs suggested parallels between my story and the character of Giselle, I continued to measure myself against Aurora. This role forced me to reach inside and draw on resources I was no longer even sure I possessed.
    As the pressures mounted, the possibility of failure was never far away. One afternoon in the studio, I almost gave up on myself during the Rose Adagio. I had already done some work

on the balances with Aurora's suitors, those four amorous princes from the four corners of the world. I had been encouraging them to think about their characters, their nationalities and so forth. Something had to be happening between us if the passage were not to come off merely as a balancing act. Their steady focus would be as crucial as their support; and so I occasionally needled them about the meaning of the fairy tale—if only to keep them awake.

"Do I prick myself on the spindle?" I asked. "Or does the spindle prick me? What's the big idea behind the prick anyway?" That took us willy-nilly into the Freudian symbolism.

Freud was good for a joke, and I goaded them shamelessly with the blood and the curse, and all of those hidden levels of meaning—anything, at this point, was worth trying, as long as they kept their attention glued to me. The partners usually have nothing more exciting to think about here than whether or not the ballerina will take a fall. On impulse, I suggested Aurora might be most favorably inclined toward the French Prince, performed by Derek Deane. He was the one who would have to be there for me at the end of each round of balances. His partnering could either make or break me, depending on where and how he concentrated his strength.

By the end of this particular rehearsal, I was the one without any strength. My shoes were wearing through; I was dancing on a blister, a hangnail, and a set of metatarsals that were anything but "up." Anthony and Greg were watching from the side, unaware that my toes were screaming at me. Anthony, who was to play the role of Carabosse in my second performance, had to be asking himself if I would ever go the distance. As time ran out, I broke away from the others, as if I had already had my encounter with the spindle, and rushed to my husband, with tears spilling out.

"This goddamned body just won't make it!" I cried, wrapping my arms around him.

After venting some of my pent-up frustration, I managed to pull myself back together. Then I looked around for Anthony to explain this unseemly outburst.

But he had already gone. I found only a note waiting for me.

Dearest Gels,

I know you won't want to hear this, but Aurora is looking good. I did not come over to say anything as I could see you had collapsed into a heap with Greg, and I could lip read all of your protests and worries about the body from the head down!

Please don't lose heart—keep battling on for us, mere mortals. We would be satisfied with half of what you achieved today.

Much love,
Anthony

He couldn't help being a prince, no matter which role he was playing; and I realized again what a great piece of luck it was to have such a friend, and director.

There was no turning back now, though my body would keep trying to convince me otherwise.

In Aurora's third-act solo, I encountered a long diagonal of repeated steps that seemed to exist only to make a mockery of my effort. Years ago I was told—by someone whose identity has long since escaped memory—that I would have to go to Europe to study with a certain Russian teacher, if I were ever to learn how to dance this passage. Whoever this great authority was, she was said to be the only person in the Western world who actually knew the secret of the steps. Time had stripped the details from this piece of locker-room wisdom, except for one line that stayed with me: "It's something she does with her arms and wrists." As I had never made the journey to find out what the mysterious something was, I had no choice but to try to come up with the secret for myself.

Gerd showed me the diagonal as she remembered it. There were a series of sixteen small développés. While moving forward on pointe, the legs were folding and unfolding so the feet appeared to be threading a needle—at the same time, the upper body was to bend way over, and then gradually lift up while the hands made circles in the air. What the steps could possibly have to do with Aurora was beyond me.

The Prince had awakened her and the whole kingdom with his kiss. This solo was part of their wedding celebration.

"You need to make little circles," Gerd had informed me in one of our early rehearsals. "Relax your wrists and curve your elbows!"

That got me nowhere. I had to be the most spastic Princess to come along in years.

Technical corrections had not alleviated my awkwardness, and this time, Gerd's demonstrations had not provided me with a solution. What she did looked right on her, but wrong on me, as her arms were shorter than mine, and her body had softer, natural curves. When I attempted to copy her, I dropped over and quickly lost any sense of dignity or joy, both of which I could see were essential to the scene. I was falling into the trap of traps, thinking too much about that outward form.

One night, I set down the ideal I hoped to bring into the last act:

> Aurora is a woman who has managed to come to terms with her past. There was a time when she was unaware of the world and blissfully happy, when she first discovered her gifts . . . and later, a spell of adversity and sorrow. But now, in the present, she has another gift which allows her to envision and choose the path her life will take. She has weighed her actions and those of others, and can imagine her future. She is a beauty whose love enables her to see a glimmer of truth and shape her own destiny.

The following morning, while I was stretched out on the floor before leaving for rehearsal, the idea came to me—one of those flashes that arrived so suddenly it seemed to have been there all along—that Aurora might simply be recalling her tale to everyone and expressing her gratitude through that impossible string of steps. Almost as soon as the idea had dawned on me, I had second thoughts. Wasn't it too simple? Too obvious?

I was reluctant at first about bringing it up during the rehearsal; but fortunately, I was working with Donald MacLeary, with whom I never minded playing the fool. Donald usually shared my enthusiasm, and he even seemed to accept as a matter of course that I had to test each and every possibility before I would come up with one that suited me. I was comfortable confiding to him, especially in the delicate places where others might not have had the patience to follow through.

When we came to the diagonal, he told me, "Margot thought of this as a little Russian folk dance."

"Let me see," I said.

He was able to carry off the most remarkable imitation of Margot Fonteyn dancing the role, but this rendition was almost identical to what Gerd had done.

"I can see how that worked well on Margot, but I really don't think it's right for me, Donald. There's another version that I know, where Aurora breaks up that diagonal with two small attitudes. On each one, if you're absolutely still for a moment, it's as if a fairy were casting a spell with her wand. What I'd like to do here, if I can, is find a way to tell Aurora's story and indicate how she's going to share her gifts with all the kingdom. Let me show you."

"Right," he said. He quickly took a seat in front of me and called to the pianist, "Could we start from just before the diagonal."

I went through it again, trying for lightness and precision. I thought, as I finished, some improvement might be noticeable. But Donald said flatly, "I don't think I like that very much, Gelsey."

"Really . . . ?"

"Why don't you try it the other way," he suggested.

Donald was attached to that version of the steps, while I was reaching for an unshaped idea. We went back and forth a number of times until I finally asked him to help me without the music.

I began to sing as I started to move, making up the words as I went along, however out of tune I may have been. "When I was a little girl," I intoned softly, bending way over as if to take a child in my arms, "the good fairies blessed me . . . with music . . . and with dancing . . . and with beauty."

That line took me through about eight steps. I came back up

on the word "beauty"—with heart turning out, and arms rising as if to encircle the mind.

Drawing a breath, I went on through the next set of eight. "And while I slept, I grew . . . so now, these precious gifts can be given . . . to you . . . and to you . . . and to all!"

It was that breakthrough I had been looking for all along, and just as I finished, Donald's eyes told me he felt it as well. He smiled and said, "Good! Oh, yes! That works." The gestures were finally true—from my torso, through my arms and wrists, to my fingertips.

I had the voice I needed. Donald's encouragement spurred me on for the final grueling push—everything would have to be polished before opening night.

In the last weeks, I worked with David Howard on countless refinements. I also asked one of Donald's longtime partners to coach me. Originally from Lithuania, Svetlana Beriosova was one of the truly great Auroras of all time. She was teaching at the school, and she generously gave me the benefit of her experience with the role. Svetlana was rigorously classical; and once she stepped inside the studio, she seemed to be driven by that same sense of urgency and conviction that I sometimes recognized in myself.

We did lock horns over some of the finer points of style and interpretation; and there were a couple of times I thought I might not walk out alive. But this was a rare opportunity for me and for my partner, Stephen, to test ourselves. Svetlana gave us a key to the awakening that was sheer poetry. Between her and Donald, we had a continuous, vivid picture of the way an earlier generation had performed this ballet. The picture could not be reproduced, yet the spirit and sensibility behind it might be recaptured.

Musically, this meant not counting my way into oblivion. As teachers and ballet masters were relying more and more these days on counting music, that older, inspired lyricism was being replaced by a rather different approach, which I had struggled to avoid. The irony was that many former dancers from the company's golden years were teaching a younger generation to count and move on the beat, even though they would never have been caught dead dancing that way themselves. This was more than an expedient to save time in rehearsal. It was also a response to those modern scores in which rhythmic complexity forced a dancer to count, in order not to get lost.

There was one last vexing problem I thought I had solved with Gerd, and then, had to entirely rethink with Svetlana, for reasons of sentiment. I became aware early on that the beautiful steps Sir Fred had created for Aurora's second-act variation were not intended for my long legs, which were to sweep to the side in a phrase that was too short in musical time for me to sustain any grace. I felt like I would have to defy both the laws of physics and my own anatomy to squeeze myself into this piece of Ashton's choreography. I had managed to come up with another rendering, which Gerd had been helping me on for weeks. But I was going to have to throw it out.

Only days before the performance, Svetlana insisted that I include Sir Fred's solo, and made me realize I might hurt his feelings if I changed any of his steps. Well on my way to panic, I went back to Ashton's variation—even though Dame Ninette had seen the changes. Gerd was perplexed by my reversal. "After all of these weeks doing it one way, why suddenly go back now? You should stick to what you've been doing. You're just going to confuse yourself, Gelsey!"

I had to wonder whether Sir Fred would be more hurt by my not doing justice to his steps, or by my not dancing them at all. He was such a fragile, elflike man—the patriarch of the Royal Ballet, and its choreographic soul. The one who had guided Margot throughout her career. I had no choice but to do the best I could, to invest his steps with the same qualities I was trying to bring to the rest of the Vision Scene—to reveal what it was Aurora had discovered in her sleep that drew her perfect partner to her. I turned to David Howard, who helped me economize the motion of my legs and reduce some of the stress on the hips. Even so, those joints seemed almost hopeless.

I was sure I would come unhinged.

Autumn in London was beginning to feel more like winter every day—a damp chill was seeping into everybody's muscles. I almost came to believe Carabosse really had cast a spell, when an injury forced Derek, my lead prince in the Rose Adagio, to bow out at the last minute. There was no time to rehearse a replacement adequately, and there was only one person I knew who might be capable of stepping into this emergency. I convinced Anthony to let me ask Donald MacLeary. Donald did seem a bit flabbergasted at first. He was going to have to perform the role without even having the benefit of a stage rehearsal.

I suggested, with desperate humor, if he was able to ride those horses of his, he would surely have no trouble partnering me; after all, he knew my every movement, well enough to be as nervous as I was.

Between toe shoes and the death rattle of a cough, I was up most of the night before my first performance, as frantic as ever. The next morning, my husband once again helped me pack my canvas bag. Before racing out of the flat to jump into a cab and go to class, I advised him to bring along an oxygen tent when he came to the theatre. "For me, or for you?" he said, still able to laugh. What I had in mind was something that would cover the entire stage.

I spent the afternoon fighting through fatigue, trying to shake off the gloom that possessed me. It seemed everything had come down to a matter of luck and will. No matter how much I had prepared, I would never be ready, never be able to free myself from those worries ticking away in my brain. Had I threaded enough needles? Would my toe shoes melt? Would they make noise? They were still wet from being dyed. I took an hour to decide which shoe was my best bet to wear on my right foot for the balances in the Rose Adagio.

While making up, I gathered what force of spirit I could and sent out a few prayers, reminding myself again: *I've taken so much from so many and now I'm giving it back.* The door to my dressing room blew open, as if caught by a sudden draft. Then a hand holding a bouquet of roses appeared inside, followed by my husband. Before rushing back out, he left the flowers in the sink, and a kiss behind my ear.

Oliver had given me a short class; Danuta had done my hair; and Maureen had helped me into the costume. My muscles were already cold again. I spread a robe on the floor and did a few more stretches. My mother was in the audience, along with my brother, Christopher, and nephew, Stephane. Natasha had returned to London; she would be out there as well, and God only knew who else. Later, Gerd told me she had run into Rudolf Nureyev coming in the stage door. He had flown all the way from Marrakesh, and he wanted to know, immediately, if I were really going to do it. Gerd had ruffled, and sprung to my defense, saying with pride, "Of course she is!"—as if Rudi had asked the most absurd question in the world.

With minutes to go until curtain, I had the dresser take my tray of essentials ahead into the wings, and hurried through the door that led to the stage. I had to try those balances one more time—as unwise as this might have been just before I was to make my entrance. The Prologue was over; and the stage was crowded with dancers who were in the first act. I found Donald and the other three suitors—Guy Niblett, Phillip Broomhead, and Antony Dowson—near the front.

"Shall we just go through a few balances?" I asked them, trying to sound as nonchalant as possible.

What a comedy of terrors this was! Each prince, in turn, was to take my hand and then step briskly around me, turning and supporting me as I poised on the right leg. But each time I let go of a hand, I felt like I was releasing my lifeline. I was so tense, I kept going over backward, and when I tried to compensate, I swayed sideways and tilted forward. This Aurora wasn't able to stand on her own, let alone dance.

What had happened to those wonderful gifts?

I was about to have four one-armed suitors, as I held on to their hands and lurched about, steering them, with a hushed, hysterical edge in my voice. "Move right! No! No! That's too much. Back! Move back. Better. . . . But, I'm still way off, aren't I?" I let out a loud whisper, "Donald! Donald! Where are you? Quick!" He was suddenly standing right in front of me. "Look at this! I can't find my balance! What am I doing? What's wrong?"

There was Donald in his wig and costume, reaching out and taking my hand. "You aren't over your supporting leg, Gelsey. Raise your back leg a bit and now just breathe easy." I let go. He was perfectly still, looking at me with his soft brown eyes. He said, matter-of-factly, "Well, you are still going back, aren't you? You must stay right on top of that supporting leg."

"I know. But how? I can't feel the level of my body. I can't even feel the floor!"

With only seconds to go, Donald attempted to calm me, with a steady voice. "Better. Yes. That's much better." Yet not nearly enough. We continued with a few more steps until we heard the first notes coming from the orchestra pit and had to abandon the stage. I fled into the wings. How was this possible? After so much work, to find ourselves entirely at the mercy of chance! We wished each other *merde,* and murmured reassurances about everything turning out fine.

I pulled off my leggies and checked my ribbons, and then I waited, all the while listening for my musical cue and feeling disaster in my bones—where the hell was my character? Rushing about in the backstage area, I had scarcely enough time to touch up my face, then snip a few dangling threads from the costume.

Keep moving, I told myself.

I stood in the half light filtering out from the stage, and did some relevés, then some simple tendus battements. Then more stretches. Finally, I stopped moving and shut my eyes for a moment, taking slow breaths. I managed to conjure an image of Aurora in her chamber, being fussed over and loving every minute of it. Her shoes fit. She sparkled! Beckoned from a distance, she ran without hesitation—she raced toward the voices that called to her, until she reached the columns and peeked out between them.

I'm here! she cried in my inner ear. *Oh, joy! All of my dearest friends!*

And somehow, all of a sudden, there I was—running behind the columns, pausing for a split second, then dashing across a rickety floor and springing up into the air at center stage. It was the first in a long string of miracles. The princes were gallant, amazingly so, considering how I had terrorized them and myself. I could see each suitor hold his breath, as I let mine out, slowly, through each balance. And on the last one, after releasing Donald's hand, I lifted my arms overhead and held, until I sensed his eyes widen.

Aurora's confidence seemed to grow in spite of me. If it was Donald who provided the inspired support that got me through that first act, then it was surely Stephen who got me through the next two. Each time we came offstage, he was urging me on: "You see, it's not so hard . . . and we've just a bit more to go!" By the third act, my legs and lungs were gone, but the Grand Pas de Deux turned into everything either of us could have hoped for; there was a rare harmony, an ever-deepening joy—which was for me what made all of these weeks worthwhile.

When it was finally over, the house came down, along with the tears, and the daffodils showering on us from the balconies. After the last curtain call, an excited crowd, including Natasha and Rudolf, came back to greet me. It was more difficult keeping my balance in the midst of this bedlam than it was onstage. Rudi suggested I dance a few more of these in London, and then come to the Paris Opera. I declined the offer. The next performance was going to be my last. In the dressing room, I thanked friends and well-wishers; and after the coast cleared, Greg and I went on to dinner with Ivan Nagy, who was my very first partner in *The Sleeping Beauty* (at ABT) and lately the director of the Cincinatti Ballet. I was, as they say, walking on air, relieved just to feel a cold wind as we left the theatre. I thought, *I'm halfway home.*

I later found myself nettled by a minor technical detail that came up at dinner. Natasha had joined us, and pointed out that during a slow promenade in the Grand Pas de Deux my elbows had been too far forward and blocked my face. Unfortunately, she was unable to tell me how to fix those elbows without distorting the rest of my body and the overall shape of the character. For a Russian ballerina with Natasha's "dying swan arms," this sort of thing might not have been a problem; but my arms were not quite so pliant within the form.

So we discussed elbows for an hour over dessert.

Imagine!

Afterward, when Greg and I had settled into a taxi, on our way back to the flat at last, he said, "When I got up from my seat to leave the auditorium, there was one older fellow who had seen your Juliet. I overheard him saying, 'Well, she can do happy endings, too!' " This fellow must have missed those elbows.

Favorable notices from my British critics encouraged me to think the character had come across in spite of my technical concerns. John Percival's review for the London *Times* was titled, "Shades of Fonteyn," and identified that larger tradition I had tried to absorb; and Clement Crisp wrote in the *Financial Times:*

> The choreographic drama of the Rose adagio was presented with an exquisite lightness, each phrase lovingly savoured, poses easily held, the movement brushed in with extraordinary delicacy. We were watching both a young princess and a ballerina entirely mistress of her art. Miss Kirkland gave us, throughout the evening, a portrait of real cogency, as well as abiding technical delights. . . .
>
> The second act's vision was impalpably lyric, irresistible; the hushed quality of her dancing, sung to us, as it were, on a beautifully rounded pianissimo, was especially rewarding, but both the first and third acts were no less well-reasoned, and conceived as emotional and choreographic entities. . . .

I continued to think about refining the position of the arms; and in the days before my final performance, I went to work with Dreas Reyneke, whose expertise on body control led me to a solution: the secret of the elbows was really located in the back. By stretching and working muscles around my shoulder blades, I was able to win that flexibility I needed to lift and open my arms several inches further than I ever had, allowing me to express the feeling in that one moment in the last act that much more effectively.

It was like a note I had never hit before.

I was ecstatic, not so much because I was able to do it, but because I had learned how to do it. Aside from this little change, I took greater risks and mounted a more consistent attack in the second performance. I was saying good-bye to the stage and to the audience, or perhaps to this phase of my career. I saw no reason to try to explain what no one wanted to hear. The rumor had already hit the press. Gerd had been trying to dissuade me. "Are you sure, Gelsey?" she had asked.

I was sure.

"What will you do? Many of our girls have wanted to stop dancing. They try something else, but they all come back sooner or later, wanting to perform again."

Only my husband and mother accepted my decision. What better place was there for me to stop dancing than with this ballet and this company?

After the tumult of curtain calls, just as I was retreating through another crowd backstage, I saw Sir Fred himself coming toward me. He was accompanied by Iris Law, radiant and attentive at his side. At eighty-two, Sir Fred was rather frail; his hands were gnarled, and his breathing labored, yet that spirit of his was irrepressible. I was slightly overwhelmed when he approached and took hold of my arm. I could sense his elation, and felt him shaking like I was, as he kissed my cheek. He had choreographed a short piece for me years ago, to one of Chopin's etudes. That was the one time we had worked together. Unfortunately, it was during a period when I was unwittingly starving myself to avoid appearing in the movie *The Turning Point.*

I had hardly been at my best back then, and still felt a twinge of awkwardness, knowing he remembered.

He said immediately, "No one has done what you did with this ballet in years!" Without giving me a chance to respond, he went on, "Now, your tights . . . they are too light for Act One, perfect for Act Two and Act Three, but just a shade too light for Act One!"

All I could manage was a shocked nod. Sir Fred knew what he thought, and he was going to say exactly that—his tone was definite and enthusiastic. But why had he insisted that I change the color of my tights? Did he think I had another performance? His compliment bewildered me. I was expecting him to bring up his solo. He had to have some criticism there. I was sure he would say something.

When he didn't, I said, as lightly as possible, "Sir Fred, you know, I almost changed the steps in your Act Two solo. They are really difficult . . . with these legs and hips . . . especially that step from the corner, traveling back. I just—"

His laugh cut me off. "Oh, my dear! You could have changed the whole thing. I wouldn't have minded. Why you could've done anything you wanted, anything at all!"

I wished he could have seen how I intended to dance that passage, and regretted my not having had the nerve to ask for his advice beforehand.

He was still holding my arm, with both of his hands, "Now, Gelsey, what is this I hear about you retiring? I was told this was your last performance."

"It's true. I want to move on . . . to education. I think this generation can be helped in the studio, and that's really where I belong now—with these young dancers who are trying to learn. They do need some help, don't you think?"

"But how can they dance when all they've been taught is how to count!" He caught himself, and added firmly, "They need your example on the stage. You cannot stop dancing!"

"I don't believe that seeing me will help them very much at all, Sir Fred. They watch and they imitate, and they usually go nowhere that way. It takes so much more. . . ."

"You can teach them when you're my age, Gelsey. You must dance . . . you must continue!" He was not about to give up the argument. "You must!" he kept saying, until I promised to visit him and continue the discussion.

Of course, I was flattered Sir Fred thought so highly of my dancing—for God's sake, who wouldn't be?—and yet I was disconcerted. I knew, as every dancer knows, the body cannot go on forever; and I had already come to terms with myself in that regard. I was looking forward to returning to America, at least for a while, then finding a company or school where I might set out in a new direction. Sir Fred was insisting that I had an obligation to perform.

But did I actually have to perform in order to pursue my ideals in the theatre? Whatever drove me to dance all of those years had changed, along with my goals. I was no longer tied to the stage in the same way anymore. There were other paths for me to travel now, and I susp cted they would prove far more valuable in the long run. To others, I may well have seemed stubborn and selfish, but I was not going to give up my life as I had in the past; nor was I going to jeopardize my marriage. I could be quite fierce on that point.

That same night, Antho visited me in the dressing room and mentioned he was hoping I would dance with him in a revival of Sir Fred's 1958 production of *Ondine,* a beautiful ballet that had been Margot's favorite. The company was planning to bring it back in the near future. The role was that of a magical water sprite, one of those supernatural creatures which inhabit many of the nineteenth-century classics. Ondine was a marvelous challenge and a powerful temptation. I was upset I had to turn Anthony down; and for the next several days, I could think of little else but the disappointment I had seen in his face.

This was the end of the line, as unsettling as it had to be.

I found it impossible to say good-bye to anyone, and when asked about my departure, I simply promised to come by before leaving, the date always a week or two away. Yet there was still that promise I had made to Sir Fred. Much of the year, he lived in his country home outside London, but he also kept a flat near Harrods, where my husband and I visited him one evening a few days before our flight out.

He was as feisty as ever, an I was afraid he might start in on me where he left off. The th ee of us sat down in a small living room. A clutter of books on the floor surrounded his easy chair. I asked him, "Do you remember those days when you came to New York to work on *Turning Point?* I'm embarrassed to think how I used to tell you I was suffering from a potassium deficiency. I was so weak from not eating."

"Oh, yes," he said, recalling with a laugh, "I never knew what you were talking about. I always thought potassium was one of those strange herbal roots that grow in China. Had no idea at all!"

Sir Fred needed little encouragement to reminisce. He began with the first time he saw Anna Pavlova—when he was a teenager living in Lima, Peru. Pavlova had danced there during the second decade of the century, and he had been enamored. He said he was still able to see her vividly in his mind—her dancing had been the inspiration that led him to ballet.

Sir Fred worked his way forward in time with various stories and recollections, to London in the thirties, when he and Antony Tudor had crossed paths during the early days of British ballet. Sir Fred said, "I remember Antony working on the sets, always climbing up on ladders. That's where he began!"

After a couple of hours, Greg and I had been through the fascinating saga of Sir Fred's life. However, he was still going strong, as if he had only scratched the surface. He brought up his concern about the current state of the art with the simplest of observations: "You know, Margot used to ask anyone she heard counting in the studio to leave!" While expressing a passionate loyalty to the theatre, he also voiced some strong reservations about the way his ballets were danced nowadays. Sir Fred asked Greg to stand in as a partner, then demonstrated in the middle of the living room.

"There are so many moments they miss, you see. Nobody can do them!"

I knew he had been an extraordinary mime, and the years seemed not to have diminished his powers. He did a scene from his ballet *A Month in the Country,* and even with his infirmed hands, he was able to make each gesture speak. I was enthralled, just to watch him place one imaginary rose into the buttonhole of my husband's lapel. After slowly working his way through several of these lost moments, Sir Fred turned back toward me, and asked, "Do you know what Carabosse says now in the Prologue of *Sleeping Beauty?* She says, 'You . . . me . . . forgot.' " As he spoke, he mimed each word with meticulous care, then went on, "But she should be saying, 'You . . . forgot . . . meeee . . . !' "

He changed the quality and order of his gestures; his voice became quite loud and guttural—a frightening accusation. "You see," he explained, "without that . . . there is no clarity. We have to feel her evil. That terrible egg-go!"

It took me a moment to cut through his accent and realize he meant "ego." His point was not to correct Carabosse's "grammar," but to reveal the nature of the character by shifting emphasis to that boundless "me"—here was a being utterly incapable of love. The sweep of an arm into her breast said it all.

Sir Fred wove his own spell; and by the end of the night, I was the one who was falling under his enchantment. Regardless of our age difference, I shared most of his sentiments about the art. I asked, "Do any of the young choreographers come to you for advice?"

"No. They already think they know it all. I do sometimes watch their ballets. But I don't say anything. You can't even use the word 'grace' anymore. Why, no one knows what it means!"

"Has no one ever asked to work with you? I mean, to learn about choreography and—"

"Oh, I don't know what anyone could learn from me, Gelsey."

"Well, I would certainly love the opportunity to work with you. I think I might learn something."

A smile wrinkled across his face, as if he could see I had taken myself by surprise.

The idea of entering into such an apprenticeship, even for one ballet, seemed to justify the effort of pushing through a few more performances. And so, we sealed a pact. I agreed to dance in the upcoming revival of *Ondine* and act as Sir Fred's assistant, and he agreed to come into the studio for a few hours each day, until he needed to rest. He had done as much the year before, restaging his version of *Romeo and Juliet* for Festival Ballet. In deference to his age and health, he said he would need a car to bring him to and from the studio. My husband quickly jumped in and offered to do the driving.

We said good night several times, before finally making our way out the door.

When Greg and I left London that December, I wasn't sure whether my body would ever really allow me to come back again. But I knew I was going forward. My toe shoes were packed away in the same old bag. A year of doubts and dreams had been stored in my journal, placed inside another piece of luggage I carried with me. I was sorry to be leaving, and at the same time, thrilled to be going home again. During the long flight back to America, those contrary emotions kept me awake. There was no quelling the rush of anticipation.

My husband and I eventually resettled in Connecticut, and started working on these pages. I stayed in shape and tried to avoid the limelight as much as possible. It was troubling that I was no longer welcome at those theatres where I began my career, but the Royal Ballet continued to beckon, and I put in a brief stint of teaching for the Cincinnati Ballet. Greg and I were invited to the White House during the spring of 1987 to have tea with First Lady Nancy Reagan; and later in the year, I was honored with a Victory of the Spirit Award at the Kennedy Center, an event sponsored by the National Rehabilitation Hospital of Washington, D.C. Otherwise, for the most part, I kept out of sight. Blessed with more than a fair share of happiness, I was content, for the moment, to write and live quietly while the future unfolded.

The Fates somehow conspired against that wonderful plan to work with Sir Fred on *Ondine*. Tendinitis prevented me from dancing the next year; the ballet was mounted by a ballet master (Christopher Newton) from a film, and Sir Fred was delighted that it held up as well as it did. Greg and I returned to London for the opening, and saw him briefly at the final dress rehearsal, in the audience at the opera house. He said, with a familiar touch of mischief, "Gelsey, now when are you going to dance? I have one foot in the grave, and one foot in this theatre!"

I told him I hoped to be dancing soon.

He laughed, and said, "You'd better hurry!"

Some months later, Sir Fred died peacefully in his sleep. Between his passing and that of Antony Tudor only a year before, I felt more keenly than ever the fragility of everything I loved in ballet. No doubt their works would survive on the stage, but a tradition and a way of thinking about dance—which these two choreographers symbolized for me—seemed to be slipping away. It was as if that elusive shape I pursued had become outmoded, or perhaps irrelevant, given the needs of the times.

Among the keepsakes I brought back from London was a letter I had received from Mr. Tudor, whose words became all the more poignant, as I asked myself what lay ahead.

Dark, damp, dreary November
afternoon. God!

Dear Gelsey,

So the days come and go, and no one knows what's
happening. Just like the good olde days. You may learn
that although some ballet "ladies" acquire a reputation
for being temperamental and consequently unreliable,
this is also quite true sometimes of the male type of the
species.

I do hope you move on and teach. Centre-of-the-body
consciousness is a primary necessity that far outweighs
the mechanics of high kicks, etc, for one can embody an
ideal of humanity. But an unmalleable spine, with au-
tomated legs and flappy wrists can only produce the
non-genuine. Not that the non-genuine is always unde-
sirable. If it were, dancers surely wouldn't waste so
much time acquiring it. You would be nothing less than
a saint if you would give so much of your own energy to
their conversion. You are still youthful and very vital,
whereas some old choreographers are exactly that—old,
behind the times and perhaps not as vital as before.

Anyway, I'm happy you're there being looked after.

Love,
Antony T.

While I continued to give myself class every morning, my
spirit hung in a balance. Whenever Anthony Dowell called to
ask about my dancing Ondine, I tried on several hundred pairs
of toe shoes and attempted to summon the will to overcome my
body. But there was something missing for me now. I wondered
if this book could have any meaning beyond my own life, if my
career in the theatre would continue beyond these pages. "We
still don't know whether it's a tragedy or a comedy," said Greg,
as we began to organize our last chapter. The deadline had
already passed, and he was encouraging me to return to my
journal, which I had given up after *Sleeping Beauty*.

I needed one more miracle.

New York, December 21, 1989. I have come full circle, and no one is more astonished than I am. This morning, after an absence of five years, I returned to ABT, not to the theatre, but to the offices and studios on lower Broadway. What brought me back was an unexpected invitation from the new director, Jane Hermann, who now manages the company as it prepares to celebrate its Fiftieth Anniversary. I arrived early to give a press interview on the upcoming gala, and had the opportunity to watch class and visit old friends. I wandered around with my husband for hours, moving from studio to studio. In the middle of the afternoon, we sat in on a rehearsal of the Rose Adagio.

The Princess was being danced by a talented ballerina who was struggling with the role. I told her, "That's really beautiful, technically, but we need to see your heart." I soon found myself in the middle of the studio. I was in sneakers and blue jeans, demonstrating for her. "When you go over, it's as if you're taking a child in your arms. You have to fight like hell to keep those arms down and the level of your body up, no matter how awkward that may seem to you at first." She was all ears, and so, I kept after her, "This ballet is about love, right? What makes those gifts of yours magical?"

Soft winter light was coming in the windows behind her. She was a silhouette, and for a moment, I thought I might have been dreaming. I stood there and watched her, held fast by the grace I saw in her effort, and by my own joy. It seemed I had been in the studio forever, and had no intention of leaving.

I was keeping a promise to myself.